D0310070

RIVERBALL!

A rugby fairy tale

*For Clarty
and for the club*

RIVERBALL!

A rugby fairy tale

Simon Ravens

VSP

Published by Vision Sports Publishing in 2015

Vision Sports Publishing
19–23 High Street
Kingston upon Thames
Surrey
KT1 1LL

www.visionsp.co.uk

ISBN: 978-1-9095-3456-8

Printed and bound in the UK by Short Run Press, Exeter

FSC
www.fsc.org
MIX
Paper from
responsible sources
FSC® C014540

Contents

Chapter 1

*~ in which we fail to find any fairies, travel round
the world to discover the Dale, and see a sheep in the
clubhouse ~*

If I say that what you hold in your hands is a fairy tale, I should begin by making one thing clear: there are no fairies involved. No, the players of Wharfedale RUFC are not winged sprites, or any other kinds of mythological creatures. They are certainly not goliaths or titans – a fact that we on the touchline sometimes lament when we see yet another super-sized team thunder out onto the pitch, and wish that our pack didn't look like such a regular-fit beside them. But as often as not that regret doesn't last beyond the Dale's first steal at the breakdown and bolt for the line. The team are who they are. At least physically, the main players of this book are pretty regular types.

In what way, then, is this a fairy story? Quite simply, it's the story of a sporting team achieving something barely credible – not just for one game, or even for one season, but for decades. On the face of it, this 'barely credible' achievement may not sound particularly impressive: it involves no trips to Twickenham and only the rarest lifting of trophies.

Wharfedale's feat is to be the longest-surviving club in English Rugby Union's National League 1. To those not in the know, even that statement may be misleadingly grand, since in reality our league is, behind the Premiership and Championship, only the third tier of English rugby. But to scroll down a few of the clubs which have passed through the division's skylight or trapdoor (and frequently both in quick order)…

Birmingham & Solihull
Blackheath
Cambridge
Coventry
Doncaster
Fylde
Leeds
London Welsh

Manchester
Nottingham
Plymouth Albion
Richmond
Rotherham
Rosslyn Park
Worcester

… is to wonder what a club from a small village in the Yorkshire Dales is doing there. Not just doing, but evidently doing *quite well*, since at various stages, and to various degrees of floored disbelief amongst its supporters, 'the Dale' have recorded victories against all the teams in that list.[1]

Of course, in an age when one signatory on a well-upholstered chequebook can bring success to any club, regardless of its support, Wharfedale's achievement does not, in itself, indicate much. Yet the success of the Dale has emphatically not been bought, and this is where the real fairy tale of the club can be found. On and off the pitch at Wharfedale, wealth is conspicuous only by its absence. From the undulating pitch we play on, to the single small stand and the modest clubhouse beside it, visitors to The Avenue could be forgiven for thinking that this is just another village club. In truth, the powers that be at the Dale have always seemed as proud of their caution off the field as they are of the team's enterprise on it. It is, they stress, a community club.

Defining the community which Wharfedale RUFC represents is not easy. Sure, Wharfedale is clear enough to mark out geographically. A dale is a valley, and Wharfedale is the valley of the river Wharfe, running from the high country of the Yorkshire Dales for about fifty miles, first south and then east, eventually losing itself on the flat lands out beyond the A1. But not all of Wharfedale would claim kin with Wharfedale RUFC. The two largest towns in the dale, Ilkley and Otley, have significant clubs of their own, and are not really part of the Dale's parish. Further down the valley, where it platters out onto the Vale of York, the locals are about as likely to be followers of Wharfedale RUFC as are the sheep which graze the head of the dale. In fact, the club probably has a greater affinity with the sheep: they form the traditional economic staple of the area, and a particularly fetching one of their number is the model for the club's crest.[2]

---

1 This, be forewarned, is not the last unbelievable truth you will be confronted by in this book.
2 And one of them, famously, made a dramatic entrance into the clubhouse bar after a match. He (or she – I can't say I noticed which) was an unwilling guest of Rob Baldwin, then club captain. On behalf of his team Rob was, I suspect, responding to the usual opposition banter about the nature of our relationship with sheep: he dived outside, and returned a few minutes later with a wrigglingly reluctant fleece on his shoulders. *Author's note: no animals were harmed in the making of this footnote.*

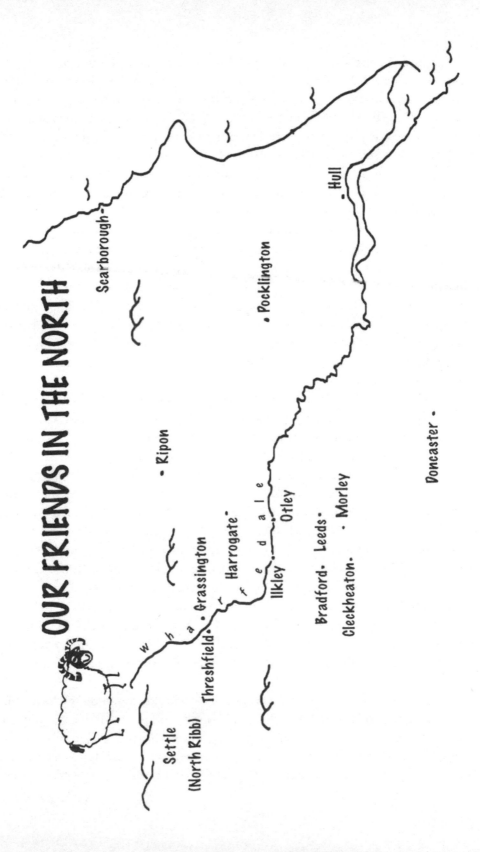

OUR FRIENDS IN THE NORTH

Scarborough-

Hull

Pocklington

Ripon

Grassington

Harrogate

w h a r f e d a l e

Otley

Ilkley

Bradford- Leeds-

Cleckheaton- · Morley

Doncaster -

Settle
(North Ribb)

Threshfield-

Actually, when it was founded by the local doctor in 1923, the club's original name was *Upper* Wharfedale, and this probably gives a better clue to the club's identity. In those days the players were mostly farmers from the top end of the dale, and to say that the team was a family affair in its infancy is an understatement. Back in the early days there were fewer than twenty playing members, which included seven sets of brothers – so regularly there were only eight surnames on the teamsheet. As early as 1935, though, the club minutes record that 'a keen discussion then took place on the advisability of playing members from outside the district' – and the door had been opened.

Nowadays the club is in Threshfield, a sister village to Grassington. Together, these villages and the surrounding area have a population of a few thousand. Still, the club does have a wider parish, even if its boundaries are vague. Increasingly, after the Second World War many of the players came from neighbouring dales. And as clubs elsewhere in Yorkshire have declined, and transport has improved, so Wharfedale has acted as a magnet for aspiring rugby talent from Leeds, Bradford and beyond. A few years ago, even a pair of Tongan cousins, one of whom had married a Wharfedale lass, were welcomed to the fold. As long as they buy into the values of the club, all are welcome.

So although the articles of its faith may be narrow, geographically the club's church is broad. For example, visitors to The Avenue are often taken aback to hear our PA announcer, Ian 'Adge' Douglass, give the pith in a rolling Somerset burr. Whilst I'm almost prepared to believe that some of the Dales farmers who stand alongside me are part of an indigenous species, the notion of a Wharfedale birthright is not a currency I really buy into. Actually I can't, since my own route to being part of the Wharfedale tribe, and the rugby faith, is a roundabout one.

Time to introduce the story-teller. Me. Like Adge, I was born down in the South West, and although I was brought up in Yorkshire, it was nowhere near Grassington. As for rugby, well, I was a sporting nut, but coming from a musical family meant that as a boy my evenings and weekends were taken up singing. I played rugby a bit at school, but after that I was only ever a spectator. And to be honest I was more a soccer man until after I finished at university, when I found myself working as a musician in New Zealand. Living two hundred yards from Athletic Park in Wellington inevitably realigned my sporting focus. From then on it was rugby or rugby.

When I came back to live in Wharfedale I toyed with watching my local club, Ilkley: it was a good outfit, but clubs are like shoes, and for me Ilkley was just not quite the right fit. Then I read, in the Yorkshire Post, that only a few miles up the valley, Wharefdale played in a much higher league and 'provide entertainment intentionally, by playing a delightful brand of 15-man rugby: forwards and backs always look to keep the ball alive in the tackle, like a rustic, bargain-basement version of Toulouse'. Never mind Toulouse, I thought, that sounds like the same mindset I knew in New Zealand. So one afternoon, at the end of the 2007-08 season, I drove up Wharfedale and stood in the Shed. Okay, this team wasn't Toulouse, let alone the All Blacks, but the idea was the same. It was certainly good enough for me. And what a place! It seemed almost comical that high-level sport could be played in such beautiful scenery. I went home and suggested to my wife, Caroline, that we bought season tickets.

From then on, home matches were inked into the diary. As the seasons passed, we increasingly began to pencil in away matches, too. Then, in 2014, a few events persuaded us really to invest ourselves in the Green Machine. Around the time of my fiftieth birthday I signed off on two long-term musical projects, a book and a recording. They had been all-consuming, and Caroline suggested that a sabbatical might be in order. Great! Which of our long-held plans should we pull out of the draw? Should we complete our round of the Scottish Munros, trek in to the north side of K2 on camels, or tandem down to the Med and back? At this point Caroline was told that she needed a new hip. So much for athletic endeavour. What project could we find that would get us out of the house, but not our limbs out of joint?

"Why don't we do all Dale's away fixtures too?" I suggested. "Just for a season. Think about it… lot's of the clubs are in nice places: we could take the dog and make a weekend of it. And now we've made a few friends on the touchline it could all be pretty sociable."

A few days later, Caroline came back with her verdict.

"Fine – I'm up for it. But that's only the weekends taken care of. I've been thinking that if you wrote about it, it might keep you quiet during the week as well."

Deal!

I'd never written a word of sports journalism, and when I listed them, my credentials as a rugby insider were not great. In no particular order, they were:

- My brother's first wife's mother's cousin was once an All Black selector
- The legendary All Black flanker Michael Jones once did circuit-training in the gym with a friend of mine
- Er, that's it…

Still, the more I thought of writing about Wharfedale, the more I liked the idea. Even without any notion of how the next season might pan out, I knew that the club's tale was too good not to tell. I also knew that left to their own devices, the Dales farming community at the heart of the club would never tell it. Make no mistake, they were delighted to have it told: when they found out what I was writing, these Dalesmen couldn't have been more generous in sharing their warmth and wit. But after a while I noticed that their stories were always about the achievements and escapades of others. About their personal contributions, *nada*. It just wasn't in their makeup to blow their own fanfares. Co-incidence or not, it stuck me that the public voices of the club were not Dalesmen at all: Adge was from down by the Court of Camelot; Gordon, the outspoken programme editor, hailed from the Kingdom of Fife, and the forbears of Ed Williams, who writes the match reports, were Sons of Glyndŵr.

Wharfedale's story, then, hadn't really barged its way into the media world. The closest that the club had made it to the national consciousness was when the chairman of rugby at Esher, broadcaster John Inverdale, wrote in the *Daily Telegraph* about his first visit to The Avenue:

> To be among a large crowd at a thrilling National League match at *Wharfedale Rugby Club with the sun beating down from a crystal blue sky, the Yorkshire Dales rocking and rolling into the distance and lambs gamboling in the fields, with a decent pint of beer in hand (optional) was to have found sporting nirvana.*

And if that sounded like rugby's own version of *Paradise Lost*, then I for one was nodding in agreement. Inevitably, being relatively removed from the world of sporting commerce means that any visit to The Avenue feels like a step back in time. Unlike many of the grounds we visit, at The Avenue you won't be blasted by music after every try (our faltering PA system just wouldn't cope). And I suppose the rugby which the Dale play has often been a bit yesteryear too. Somehow, our play has never been the feast of pick-and-drive, or the carnival of defensive alignments, that a lot of top teams seem to celebrate nowadays. Don't get me wrong, we play to win: in years when the Dale's strength lies up front, or in months when the dale's mud lies heavy below, sighting the ball can be quite an event. And in those circumstances, when we're awarded a scrum five metres out, we don't actually *want* to sight the ball. Years ago, it was for moments such as these that the cry of *RIVERBALL!* came about: amongst the pack it carried the code that the ball wouldn't be seeing the light of day until they were metaphorically down to the Wharfe – or literally over the try line. These days the pack can still play that game. Yet despite the wonders of *RIVERBALL!* for decades Wharfedale have had a reputation for playing as if they are, well, *playing*. And given half a chance, that's just what we do.

But however much the story of Wharfedale might sound like it belongs to a mythical era of woolen jumpers and soapy leather balls, the truth is that it's very much a present-day reality. It is actually a story of change. The club's remarkable life simply wouldn't flourish unless it perpetually recalibrated its heart and soul to tick with the hard-headed dictates of the modern game and the modern world. Yorkshiremen might have a reputation for head-in-the-sand obstinance, but up in Wharfedale we occasionally look at the scenery around us. There's a virtue to playing heads-up rugby off the field as well as on it.

That, in a nutshell, is us. The Dale. An unremarkable body with a quite unique character. Fairy people? – no. People in a fairy tale? – well, judge for yourself…

Chapter 2

~ in which we farewell a season, battle with an old foe called Otley, and celebrate! ~

It's not always like this. We're stood in shirtsleeves, soaking up the early evening spring sunshine, chatting away on the touchline with barely a care in the world. Shortly we'll cheer our team onto a pitch that's covered in grass and perfectly flat — always a talking point for a Dale supporter. Yes, we're away from home, but unusually we've travelled with the firm expectation of a win — and not just that, but a trophy if we do. Emphatically, it is *not* always like this.

You see, it's not a league match, but the final of the 2014 Yorkshire Cup. This is the last match of the 2013-14 season, and there's a very end-of-term feel to the whole thing. If we win, then there will be icing on the cake. But even if we lose, our efforts in the league over the last nine months mean that at least we'll still have a cake to eat next season. For the supporters, this evening feels like a reward for all that shivering and nail-whittling we've put ourselves through over the winter.

Most sports teams, in this day and age, view a cup competition as either an interesting diversion or an irritating distraction from the league they play in. That's certainly the way it is with the Yorkshire Cup, which in truth is a shadow of its former self. In this evening's match programme there is a list of former winners, and sifting through this is like taking part in an archeological dig through the history of rugby in the North of England.

Amongst the first winners, back in the 1870s, was Wakefield Trinity. Nowadays, rebranded as Wakefield Wildcats, they play Rugby League — the 13-man game which was conceived around 1895, when working class northern clubs opted out of the amateur Union game in favour of a professional set-up.[3] In fact a number of those early Yorkshire Cup winners — Halifax, Dewsbury, Batley and Castleford — are now very firmly Rugby League towns.

After these sides left Union in what many of us regard as the real Great Schism, for about ninety years the centre of Yorkshire Cup gravity moved about

---

3 This, it strikes me, is as good a place as any to say that this is a book about a Union team playing league rugby, not about a union of men playing Rugby League. Clear?

twenty miles further north. A small but significant shift. Headingley, Roundhay, Harrogate and Morley, which are suburbs and satellites of Leeds, are the list's chief recurring names. During those years, when leagues were a taboo in Rugby Union, the Cup really meant something. In terms of serious competition, it was *it*. But when a national league structure was introduced to the English Union game, the Yorkshire Cup quickly took a back seat. And when the Union game finally embraced professionalism in the mid 90s, money dictated a new set of imperatives to the top clubs. Holding aloft 't'owd pot' was not one of them.

Nowadays, Yorkshire clubs which play in the Premiership and Championship are not expected to field teams in the Yorkshire Cup. And even at our level, Wharfedale have managed to progress to the final largely on the back of our second team. However one-eyed we can be, we're not kidding ourselves that winning the Cup this evening will mean that we're the top side in Yorkshire.

Does this evening's final mean anything, then? Well as a matter of fact it does, at least to the seven hundred of us gathered on neutral territory in Bingley, because our opposition is Otley. Upper Wharfedale against Lower Wharfedale, if you like. Historically, the balance of power has been with Otley. For goodness sake, they first won this competition in 1889, nearly forty years before our club was even formed! That was the first of Otley's nine Yorkshire Cups – compared to our solitary triumph in 2010. A few years ago Otley flirted with the big-time, when a few fast men took the club for a ride up into the Championship. The old guard at Wharfedale muttered about the dangers of the wheels coming off, and Otley did indeed crash back down, first to National 1, then another level into National 2 North. And this is where they still sit, having finished their season closer to the bottom than the top of that league.

That is history. This is the present, in which Otley begin well, pushing us back towards our own line. But the Dale turn the ball over, and then do what we have been doing intermittently all season: a lightening break, a couple of quick passes, and our fly-half Tom Barrett is in under the Otley posts. Lightening? At this level of rugby? Well yes, that's probably not overstating it, because the initial break was made by a young lad called Taylor Prell, who only last week was lining up for England Under-18s. I'm not alone in thinking that he's the quickest thing we've seen in a Wharfedale shirt in recent years. Taylor might not be with us for long, but before he heads up into the rugby stratosphere we're going to enjoy him while we can. That's also how we feel about the man alongside Taylor in the back-line this evening – even if Dan Scarborough is heading in the other direction on the rugby ladder. Back in 2003 Dan made a solitary appearance for England and now, after a rugby career taking him around the world, he's back home, teaching locally, and playing for the Dale between times. On one side of our back line, then, it's very much a case of master and pupil. England past and England potential.

So we've only just kicked off, we're 7–0 up, and all is as it should be: in theory we can look forward to eighty minutes of romping, rampant rugby. Except we know we can't. This is Wharfedale, and although our ideas on how best to play the game might bear some resemblance to the All Blacks, the Part Greens' notion of how best to finish a game off certainly don't. The story of the match is one in which the Dale focus, show a few flashes of inspiration, and pull away, only for our concentration to slip, allowing Otley to claw back within reach. Too many times we've seen this scenario, and too many times we've been edged out at the death, for us to feel any confidence in the outcome.

Even as I'm watching, it strikes me that this display pretty much sums up the season we've just enjoyed and endured. As usual, last summer we'd all looked at the league fixture list and wondered quite when we could expect our first win. Most of last season's big guns were lying in wait before Christmas. And worse, we knew better than to expect the newly-promoted clubs to be a pushover: they often come with an upward spring in their step, and see our league as just another rung on the ladder. The prospects looked grim. But as so often happens, the team confounded our expectations. By mid-December, with eleven (11) victories to our name, including famous wins against Coventry and table-topping Doncaster, there was a fair bit of joshing in the Shed that we were being sucked into a promotion dogfight. We were only joking, though, and the team underlined that by losing at home the following week. And again straight after Christmas.

Then we looked at the table as a whole, and we didn't much like what we saw. Whereas in past seasons two or three teams had imploded on and off the field by Christmas, this time the bottom half of the league was very tightly bunched. With three clubs to go down, we still needed wins. Instead, what followed was an uninterrupted series of losses at The Avenue, most against the teams just below us. So it was with a mixture of relief and disbelief that we greeted sporadic, outrageous wins away from home. Despite these, the water kept rising around us, and it was only in mid-April (ironically on a day when Doncaster were very firmly pushing our noses under) that results elsewhere conspired to throw us a buoy guaranteeing our survival in National 1 for another year. We could breath again.

Our league season finished happily, then, but will this cup final? It looks far from certain. A stray pass here, a wayward kick there, and Otley are snaffling every tit-bit we're offering them. Yet in one respect they can't match us. A good few of their penalties and conversions sail wide of the posts: it's exactly the kind of kicking performance to be expected at this level – not bad, just not reliable. For us, pretty much every chance is taken by Tom Barrett. He even pops over a nonchalant drop goal when nothing much else seems on. All of which is a bitter-sweet experience for us, because we're watching Tom's last match for the Dale before he heads up into the Championship to play for Rotherham next season. Tonight, his points look like they could be the difference.

At half time, when the Dale are 24–10 up, I spot one of Tom Barrett's future team-mates in the clubhouse. This time last year it was Mark Tampin who was leaving us for Rotherham, but he's back here to cheer on his old team-mates. Even when players just briefly pass through the Wharfedale ranks, the experience seems to stay with them. On the Rotherham website I've noticed that Tamps ranks The Avenue as his favourite ground, and claims his best rugby moment to be 'staying up with Wharfedale' – a few simple words which, to those of us who witnessed the epic moment twelve months ago, evoke one heaven of a wonderful memory. More of that later.

We've another notable past player here this evening. This one, though, is also a future player. James Doherty. In the first half I've spotted him in a Wharfedale sweatshirt, standing in our technical area. He played for the Dale for four seasons when he was fresh out of Sedbergh School, eventually captaining the side. Since then he has climbed up the ladder as a full-time professional in the Championship. He always said that he would eventually come back to the Dale and here, at the ripe old age of twenty-seven, he is. Ready to go for the start of next season.

Still, we've forty minutes to go of the present campaign, and all our half-time smiles turn sour after the restart, when Otley run through a non-existent Dale defence to get back within one score. Game on. There's no doubt now about how much the match matters to each side. Our other winger is the relatively senior Prell – Josh. He's still only nineteen, but after a year of playing for the First XV Josh has acquired some street-wise savvy to go with his obvious potential. He needs it, too, when he gets clattered by the forearm of the Otley fly-half. The ref doesn't spot it, but it's right in front of us, and even though Josh keeps enough of his wits together to recycle the ball, there's an audible wince from the crowd close-by.

"Did you see who did that?" my friend and fellow-spectator Alec asks.

"I think it was their 10."

"Hmm. In which case Josh has just been done over by our fly-half for next season. Or so I hear…"

Actually, during breaks in play there's quite a bit of this grapevine gossip on the touchline. It's a nervy time of year for supporters, with aspiring players coming and going. We want our young lads to do as well as they can for themselves, but for ourselves we'd be happy for them not to do *quite* so well that they're lured elsewhere. Our management may be secure in the knowledge of players coming in, but on the sideline all we see are likely holes left by good players going out. If any of the other Otley players are hoping to join us next season, they'll have done themselves no harm in this match. They play some classy rugby of their own, and as we get towards injury time they're within a score – 34–29.

At this point, inevitably, nerves seemingly tingle down to the fingertips of every player on the pitch, and for five long minutes no-one is capable of doing anything decisive. Eventually, after a series of spills and knock-ons which in another context would be comical, the referee puts us out of our misery, blowing for full time. We cheer, then look at each other and try, quite unconvincingly, to appear that we weren't *really* worried.

Receiving trophies is not a skill the Dale have had to practise much, but our skipper, Chris Steel, does a good job of thanking the men in blazers, the crowd, and above all the opposition. Then the team gathers together for the obligatory poses. Dan Scarborough's young children are included (we're wondering whether this is his swan-song) and there's a fair bit of fooling around for the cameras. I suspect that 't'owd pot' has witnessed more respectful scenes, in the days when it was lifted by men wearing woolen jerseys, and whose moustaches hid any unguarded smiles.

And then it's over. The evening, and the season. In the last of the light, the team troupe off towards the clubhouse, and to their own way of marking the event. For them, doubtless there will be celebrations at the outcome, but maybe a tinge of something else too. After all, for the team wearing the green shirts this evening, with comings and goings in the months ahead, they know that this game marks a final outing. For us, as supporters, it's easier. In another two months it may be a rather different fifteen men who take the field, but we will be cheering on precisely the same XV.

Chapter 3

~ in which our mission is unveiled, we enter the Theatre of Bleats, and wait for the cows to move off the pitch ~

Back in 1923, when the local doctor decided to form a rugby club in Grassington, his intention could hardly have been more modest. It was simply to spread the word about a game he had loved during his youth. As a schoolboy at Epsom College, Kenneth Crosbie had captained the First XV, winning the school's cup for sporting achievement. Then came more serious matters. First medical training at Edinburgh University, and service in the First World War.[4] His own man at last, the young Dr Crosbie then found his first and last job – general practice in Grassington. There, in the village square on Saturday mornings, he noticed that some of the young farmers gathered together with rugby boots slung over their shoulders. He found out that they were heading off on the bus to Skipton, ten miles away, to play for the club there. He must have felt a pang. Always on call, and with a young wife, the doctor could never commit himself to that regular trip. But perhaps if he formed a club here, he could do something for everyone – these lads could be spared a journey, and others could find out what rugby was all about. Never mind all that, the doctor could get his boots out and play again himself! Other local worthies were persuaded to get behind the project – a local vicar donated the first ball – and they were away. Upper Wharfedale RUFC was born.

In many ways, the club's present aims are just as humble. But, for a club which has no great ambition to win even its own league, it comes as a shock to learn that in one respect Wharfedale has a stated aim to be simply the best. Here, in full, is the club's current mission statement:

To be the leading community rugby club in the Country.

Well, we have a reputation in Yorkshire for plain speaking, and I don't think you can get much plainer than that. Those old challenges on breakfast cereal

---

4 For non-existentialists, the history of Wharfedale RUFC has presumably never happened, since in 1916 the Epsom College journal reported Crosbie as having been killed in action. The following issue included a tale-between-legs erratum, assuring readers that Captain Crosbie was alive and 'enjoying the best of health'. What a relief: we exist.

packets *…in a slogan of less than twelve words, say why…* would be no bother for the Wharfedale committee. And in case you were thinking that every club below the top level probably has a similarly neat intent, think again. From a quick internet tour of clubs around our level, here are some mission statements. The pithiest I can find is …

> *To provide all members of our community with the opportunity to enjoy rugby union football, regardless of age, ability or background. In a fun, safe and friendly atmosphere.*

… with the most long-winded being …

> *Our aim at – Rugby Club is to create an environment where rugby can be played and enjoyed by all ages from 6 to sixty regardless of gender or ability… strive for excellence not only on the pitch but also through our coaching, volunteering, involvement with schools and reaching out to the local community… provide facilities and coaching of the highest standard to ensure that those playing and watching are… nurture our players and ensure excellent retention levels by developing a club that has good facilities, outstanding coaching and a fun social environment… being a 'real' rugby club for our players, former players, all members, families and spectators…[5]*

… which, since it states a variety of aims in duplicate and triplicate, I think could be more accurately described as Some Statements of Missions. In rugby terms, the prose-style of most clubs favours an expansive game – multiple-phases, varied points of attack and fancy switch-moves – in which I can't help but imagine that the ball ends up being left on the floor.

Of course, even if you can sum up your target in ten words, it doesn't mean you can ever tell if you've achieved it. There's no simple white line to aim for here, and no league table. No matter. In this case, the significance of the statement lies in its intent.

Normally, when we arrive at The Avenue on a Saturday, I'm aware of a palpable charge to the atmosphere. Out on the field there are forty men going through their warm-up routines, with the opposition bellowing numbers into the air and generally trying to pump themselves up in what can often be a fairly withering environment. In the clubhouse, too, there is a feeling of intent – and not just towards the bar: you don't need to play this game to exude

---

5 Please be grateful: these are only brief highlights from the full statement.

testosterone. Even the weather, as often as not, means business, and is throwing its weight around.

Arriving today, things could hardly be more different. The feeling is not one of intent, but indolence. The midsummer sun is warming the pitch, coaxing the grass up and out into those bare parts pummeled by a winter's scrummaging. In a disarmingly quiet clubhouse the windows are open, and a few people are wandering round in shorts and t-shirts. Instead of beer and testosterone, the only whiff this morning is one of new paint and creosote.

Yes, this is Rugbyforce Day. Not so much a day for the club in the community, as for the community in the club. Members who have time to spare are asked to come and help spruce up the place for the coming season. For the first time since we started watching the Dale, we've decided to join in.

Odd, isn't it, how involvement in a club can gradually take us over. For me, in the case of Wharfedale there was no announcement of an imminent invasion – I just found that parts of myself had gradually been annexed. I think it was half way through the second match I ever saw that I found myself shouting "*DAAALE!*" 'Hmm', I thought 'I don't *think* I asked my larynx to do that'. Soon I started to recognise the players not just as a team, but as individuals. And then there were the people we were standing with: after a while we nodded to each other, swapped notes, and eventually forgot ourselves so much as to exchange names.

Along with all this the club began to appropriate our time. With our season tickets came the understanding that a few hours every other weekend were handed over to the Dale. Even going to away matches – which sounds like a dramatic step – is in reality an incremental change. For us, Otley was actually closer to home than Threshfield, so that hardly felt 'away' at all. But how about Sedgley Park? North Manchester's only another half hour in the car, I pointed out to Caroline: off we went. And Fylde? Another hour. And Tynedale? A day. With each extra mile the Dale support thinned out, so that by the time we'd used up a whole weekend to visit Cinderford, we were part of a hard core – the kind of people who not just enjoyed the show, but were prepared to paint the scenery beforehand.

And that's precisely what we're now here to do on Rugbyforce Day. In truth, it's never a penance to head up Wharfedale on a free Saturday, especially when the weather is like this. Caroline and I are greeted, handed a roller and a tub of paint, and shown the opposition changing room. So this is the 'airing cupboard' one opposition player publicly complained about? My own knowledge of changing rooms comes from those fly-on-the-wall cameras in the capacious bowels of modern super-stadiums, and I have to admit that this little space doesn't quite match up to those. From the condition of the room before we start, I think it's fair to say that the place has not always been respected by guests. What, for instance, is the story behind that great hole on the *outside* of the changing room door? I wonder what red card and red mist brought that on? But around the country there are doubtless other stoved-in doors, and doubtless some of these bear the imprint of a Wharfedale boot. *No-one is saying we're angels.*

These days, Rugbyforce Day involves about fifty people in various tasks. It wasn't always so. The club's minutes from the early years paint a different picture:

> *Owing to the field being a meadow and still to be mown, it was proposed that two members should be nominated to call the necessary meeting when work i.e. marking out etc. could be continued.*

What did 'marking out' involve then? Not much, judging by the raw materials they needed:

> *Authorised to spend the necessary money on the following items: -*
> *I. Red and White Paint for painting the cross-bars.*
> *II. Broomsticks and flags for new touch flags.*
> *III. Any bladders which might be required.*
> *IV. Sawdust for marking out the touchlines.*

Back in the here and now, as the morning wears on, the summer hum of indolence gives way to a buzz. Busyness. From around the building we can hear clattering ladders and laughter. And from outside we can hear voices on the pitch. Even though it's six weeks until the new season kicks off, a fair few players have turned up to train. Word has it that potential new faces are being tried out. There are communities within communities, and it's very obvious that the team have their own. It can't always be smooth going, but by and large they seem to like each other's company. Actually, they must – to be here weeks before official training begins. At least they *can* practise through the summer. Back in 1935, as late as September the club records remind us that there were other users of the 'pitch' whose activities had to be considered:

> *Mr Crabtree was instructed to see Mr Harker with regards to the field, and after he had been to seen him he reported that Mr Harker was taking the cows out of the field in a few days, and that he was willing for us to have a practice on Saturday.*

Wharfedale might not have the best of playing surfaces, but it has progressed a good deal in the last eighty years. At least it must smell better.

When it's coffee time, we head outside to see what the players are up to, and to enjoy where we are. And where, exactly, is that? I've given the wider picture of where the club lives. Now let's zoom in a little closer on our home.

Although I've said that we play in Threshfield, the truth is that we don't really play *in* the village. You have to drive half a mile up a no-through-road – The Avenue – to find the ground. This is significant, because the pitch isn't surrounded by houses, but by open green. On three sides there are fields with real, live livestock in them.[6] The scene smiles. People might like to think of the North as dark-stoned and sombre, but this is limestone country. When the sun shines on the drystone walls they glint light white, and even when it rains they never go duller than wetted oyster-shells. In Upper Wharfedale the weather might try to persuade you otherwise, but there's nothing forbidding about the land itself.

During matches we stand opposite the clubhouse, in the Shed, partly because it's the natural home of renegades, but partly because of the view. Look up to the left, at one end of the pitch, beyond the posts, is the high horizon is of Threshfield Moor. It rolls away up the west side of the Dale, until eventually it bends its way over the significant comma of Kilnsey Crag. Keep moving your eyes right, and beyond the clubhouse, down at the other end of the pitch, the narrative of the horizon is taken up again. The trees of Grass Wood provide a few curlicues, after which the limestone walls lead the eye up towards the top of Grassington Moor. The club's motto is *Vis ex montibus venit*, and yes, our strength really does come from the hills. Even when the game is going against us on a darkening winter's afternoon, for the spectators at least there's always some kind of solace to be gained from looking up and beyond the immediate.

But on a summer's day, like this, it's difficult to imagine that grim times could ever visit us here. For all the visible effort, there's plenty of laughter coming from the players out on the pitch. Later, when they come back into the changing rooms, they're still in high spirits. I've popped out to clean a roller, and when I come back in Caroline's eyes are out on stalks.

"That was interesting… one of the lads just came in from the shower looking for his towel. I don't know who was more surprised – him seeing me up a ladder with a brush, or me seeing him down there like… *that*. He backed out covering

---

6 In times when every great sports venue has to have a sweepingly dramatic moniker – I'm thinking here of the *Theatre of Dreams*, or the *Stadium of Light* – I keep referring to The Avenue as the *Theatre of Bleats* in the hope that it will catch on. It hasn't. Yet.

himself up. Funny thing was, he popped his head straight back round the door, stuck his thumb up, and said, 'Thanks for painting the changing rooms, love.' Well brunged up lad, eh?"

This, you might be relieved to know, is a good deal more intimate than we normally get with the players. That's our choice. Unlike a Premiership football team, in which several layers of shiny staff and gleaming security doors hermetically seal the players from their adoring public, at the Dale we're welcome to mix with the team in the clubhouse after a game. To be precise, the committee says that we're welcome. As for the players, I'm not so sure. I've never played rugby at any serious level myself, but I have been a performer, and as a musician the team I play with are always tight. Nothing personal, but my choir have always been *us* and our audiences *them*. When I conduct a concert I'm always happy – very happy – to see well-wishers and friends afterwards. But later, when it comes to winding down with a drink or two, I'm far more comfortable with *us* than *them*. There are secrets from the field of play which we need to talk – and more importantly laugh – about. As long as we've delivered a result to the public, we have no wish to share with them the tricks we've used to get it. I assume that the Green Machine needs to play it the same way. So, whilst we'll always pass the time of day with a player if we see him in the car park, we've not tried to embed ourselves with the team. Of all the communities within the community, the players' is the most vital, and we've always been happy to respect that.

Later, when we're cleaning up our brushes, David the club chairman comes over to thank us, and to make sure we come round into the clubhouse for "a bite of something" before we go. Cautiously, I whisper to him that I'm trying to write a book about the club. David sounds positive. *A relief!* So who, I ask him, could I speak to about the club and its past.

"Well you could start with that man," he says, indicating someone a few feet away. "Chris Baker. My dad."

So *that's* who he is! A familiar figure to everyone at The Avenue. Once David has introduced us, it's clear that Chris's memories of others will give me ready access to the lore of the club. We wander through to the clubhouse together, and as we do so Chris has already started sharing what he knows.

As for David's 'bite', this could better be described as a pig between two bread vans. Looking around the clubhouse, there's certainly a good spread of the Wharfedale community here this morning. Sat at our table is one of the Under-10s and his dad, and dotted around the room are plenty, like Chris Baker, whose playing days are over. It couldn't be more relaxed, but not far below the surface is the intent of that mission statement – and the sense of the heart which gives the body life. We're disparate, then, but before we go David herds us outside for the statutory website photo and in a moment – *click!* – we're one.

Chapter 4

*~ in which we meet some old friends, bring back a past
captain, and meet a chimp with magical powers ~*

First things first. What on earth is a 'friendly'? I think it was the great All Black
Zinzan Brooke who, after his supposedly gentle introduction to the English
domestic game ended in a whirl of flying fists, admitted he didn't understand
what a friendly game was. And even if they pull their punches rather than throw
them, I suspect that most players would share Zinny's ignorance. Everyone who
takes to the field in one of these games is, at the very least, playing for his place
in a side. Never mind that, if he doesn't have an appetite for a proper game after
a three-month break, he never will have.

So if you come to a Wharfedale pre-season 'friendly' expecting to see smiles,
laughter and matey banter between the two sides, you will be disappointed. Out
there every player has his business face on. Look beyond the touchline, though,
and you see will something else. In particular, look at the viewing area nearest
to the committee room. Although their blazers and ties may be of different
colours, judging by their affability the officials of both clubs are as one: friends.
This show of unity would not be evident with every club we know, but whilst
we can't choose our relations in the league, we most certainly can choose our
friends in the game.

Why are we friends with Stourbridge, our first opponents of the year?
I think we just seem to be doing what we do for the same reasons. Shared
values, you might say. Until a couple of seasons ago we also shared the same
league, but then Stourbridge carelessly slipped down the ladder. Doubtless
they could have gambled and tried to avoid the drop that year, as many do,
by clutching for expensive talent to save them. Yet that's not the Stourbridge
way, any more than it's the Wharfedale way. Shared values. And lest you think
that these values cost us, well in the short term you're probably right, but we
never pay the long-term price that some gamblers do. In other words, whilst
Stourbridge went down, they didn't implode financially, and each season since
then they have been within a whisker of coming back up. They fancy their
chances this year, too, and it's not difficult to see why. In fact, on the evidence

of this match you could be forgiven for thinking that it's Stourbridge who play in a league above.

For us, most of the positives to be drawn from the match against Stourbridge are concluded with the referee blowing his whistle to start the match. Before that, there's a distinct lift and bounce around the place. Len Tiffany, one of the car park posse, has a big smile across his face. Mind you, he always does. 'Tiff' is the friendliest man in a very friendly club. For someone like me, nosy about what makes the club tick, Tiff is a gift. As long as it's not about his own contribution — "I've done nothing, *nothing*!" — he's always happy to answer my questions about the characters who make up the club. Tiff shakes my hand and we wish each other a Happy New Season.

Then I spot Dan Solomi getting out of his car. For a couple of years, until a serious injury last Christmas, Dan was our most emblematic player. Standing at only 5ft 9, Dan has to be the smallest open-side flanker at this level or above. Take away his mop of frizzy hair and he'd look small for a scrum-half. It's not just his height that makes 'Salami' look a misfit in the scrum. Whereas most forwards carry themselves around the park like grouchy gorillas, all chest and menace, Dan shambles around with the big fellas a bit like Tarzan's chimp, Cheetah. And like Cheetah, Dan looks as if he's there for comic effect, often with a bit of a grin on his face, as if he's been put up for this forward business as a bit of a lark. His most telling resemblance to Cheetah, though, is that when the dramatic moment presents itself, Dan is always first away, flying on ahead of the others. A few years ago Dan was named in the *Rugby Times*' National 1 Dream Team — voted there by the (doubtless exasperated) coaches of all the teams in our division.[7] So if Dan doesn't bully and bludgeon, how come he's regarded so highly? Put simply, he's made his supposed liability — size — his greatest asset. Not only can he get to, and more importantly *down* to, a ruck quicker than anyone else, he can get away just as speedily — along with the ball he's just filched. We've seen his dart under the tackles of the big men so many times that by now we should sense it coming. But like a firecracker going off, it's still a shock — to the opposition even more than to us. Last year was a bad one for Dan — one injury after another. But when I ask him, Dan grins and tells me he's back in training. A good sign.

We're still nodding to acquaintances and shaking hands with friends when — *pee-eep!* — the referee's whistle blows and off we go. Before things turn sour, we have one more brief positive to enjoy: the return of James Doherty. Ironically, the week after he shook hands on coming back to The Avenue, James was offered a Premiership contract: even if the realistic prospect was warming a bench,

---

7 That team never took the field, of course: otherwise, looking at the team list now, I see that Dan would have found himself packing down with such top primates as England international Joe Marler.

it must have been tempting. But no, remarkably, he said he wanted to come back to Wharfedale. Even more remarkably, he's straightaway going to resume the captaincy. True, both other likely candidates for that job are unavailable for this match, but it could still be a tricky job to carry off. Not a bit of it. From the get-go, you sense he has the esteem of his team. Within five minutes of his quickfire decision-making and sniping runs, we're in under the Stourbridge posts. At which point, a sign should light up in front of us: *beware the early score*. Since we're all blind to experience, for all I know that adage really does appear. Either way, we're about to relearn its truth the hard way.

The Dale players aren't salaried, which means that they're under no obligation to be here this afternoon. With the holiday (and cricket) seasons still in full swing, this means that only four of the fifteen that ended our last campaign are here to start this one. A lot of experience is missing, and it soon shows. We're callow out wide, and shallow in the tight. You can hear an audible sigh amongst the crowd as we pack down and Stourbridge walk us back up the pitch as if we've just handed them the new mower to try out. A worry. After all, in the first half we're heading down the slope, towards the river. When we're facing this way, at the first sign that our pack has got the upper hand, then the crowd shout out a reminder about where they are to head for: on these occasions, as Adge occasionally reminds us over the PA system, "Riverball is the call!" But there'll be no cries of "*RIVERBALL!*" today – not even ironic ones.

It's actually the Stour fans who are making all the noise. There are certainly plenty of them over by the clubhouse, and they're in the best of spirits. 'Making a weekend of it,' is how we euphemistically describe this boisterous bonhomie. And even if we envy them, we won't begrudge them. Who wouldn't be singing, in the summer sun, watching their team teach some supposed betters a thing or two?

As for the Dale supporters, we're gathered in little conclaves, only half-watching the match as we compare notes and whispers. Who's out and who's in? Apparently Darlington, one of the teams promoted to our division, has successfully baited two of our team with tasty offers. And that Otley fly-half who earned our respect in the Yorkshire Cup Final – he's been tempted north by the same chequebook. There's worse. Rob Baldwin, a talisman at the back of the scrum, is said to have a dodgy back. And our young flier on the wing, Taylor Prell, has already been hooked by local Championship side Yorkshire Carnegie, so now joins the ranks of 'dual registered' players: in other words, our fully-professional neighbours down at Headingley have first dibs on his services. All in all, it's doom and gloom. Ironically, as we write off our chances for the year, the team are busy trying to prove our pessimism false, working their way back into the match, so that in the final few minutes we're camped on the Stour line with an unlikely chance of winning. But when the final whistle goes and we've come up short, this little loss seems to be the least of our worries. When things kick off in earnest, will we have a team to speak of?

Will we? Seven days later, we're breathing a little easier. A couple of our lynchpins are back, and down the dale at Otley we're at our best. Actually it's Otley that dot down first – *beware the early score!* – after which the Dale run in ten unanswered tries. That's right, ten! As a contest it doesn't always hold our attention, but as luck would have it we're part of a typical late-August scene in Yorkshire. Ten feet behind us at the back of the terrace is Otley's cricket ground. They're involved in a top-of-the-league match with Bingley, and whilst innumerable substitutions are made in the rugby, we can turn around and enjoy the cricket. At one point, towards the end of our match, I nudge Caroline, and point at both scoreboards. One reads 29–3, and the other 64–5. Yes, Wharfedale really have run up a cricket score, and suddenly look like world-beaters.

There's no gloating from us, however. Otley's plight is there for all to see. At one end of the ground, the club has had to sell off part of their old training area, where a new housing development is going up. And at the other, red tape marks out the whole stand as being unsafe. For the ground at Cross Green the glory days, most famously in 1979 when Bill Beaumont's Northern Division beat the All Blacks here, are long gone. There's dereliction off the pitch, and as far as Otley's tackling duties are concerned, dereliction on it too. It is, for those who understand the word, friendly. As for what these friendly matches mean in the context of our season, only time will tell.

Chapter 5

~ in which we meet the captain who never captained, and
visit Hartpury – where someone gives our back-side a boot ~

For the first few years of its life, no-one much noticed the young Wharfedale club. Dr Crosbie had a team alright, but to play a game it needed opposition, and that wasn't easy to find. In those days established clubs had established fixture lists: year-in, year-out, the clubs went on the same merry round. It all worked well, unless you were a latecomer to the party scene. Wharfedale knocked on doors, but apart from a few local clubs in the same fix, few welcomed them in. The club was, literally, going nowhere. And then, in the early 1930s, it stalled. Dr Crosbie was now in his forties, and his playing days were drawing to a close. So the club's initial impetus had gone, when the Great Depression filtered down to Wharfedale. Now, few people had the time or money for a frippery such as rugby. The club was down to fewer than twenty playing members.

In 1932 a Special General Meeting was called. There was only one topic for debate: was it worth going on? As the story has been told to me, the vote was tied and about to go to the chairman's casting vote – which would have been to shut up shop – when in walked a local lad, George Harrison, who had been unavoidably held up in the Black Horse. George was then only seventeen – *naughty boy!* – although he had been playing for the team for three years.[8] In later years George would go on to hold immense sway with the club, but even then he must have been respected.

With fuel inside him George spoke briefly – and cast his crucial, deciding vote that the club should continue. The rest, you might say, is this story. If the way George's descendants tell this tale makes it sound all a bit unlikely – a bit too much like the final scene from a black and white movie – well, this is Wharfedale we're talking about. If there's one thing I have learnt about this

---

8 Even then, to take the field at fourteen George had to play under a pseudonym. This only became a problem on the occasion when his PE teacher from school turned up to referee. Normally the club grumbles if the referee ignores the evidence of his eyes, but not on this occasion.

club, it's that it will squeeze the last drop of drama out of every situation. So who knows? Whatever did happen in Church House that evening, it was certainly definitive. From that date on, the club steadily gained in health and strength. Only two years later they were beating Harrogate and Hull in the Yorkshire Cup, and starting to make waves in the district. By the AGM in the summer of 1938 the club could boast a proud record for the season: P 28, W 21, L 4, D 3.

Things were on the up. And then, of course, reality intervened. For seven years there was no rugby in Wharfedale, or anywhere else around. More in hope than expectation, in that final meeting before the club suspended operations, the club had elected a new captain, Billy Harker. In 1945, when the club met to play again, Billy had left the area, eventually seeing out his days down in London. He would come back whenever he could, and on one visit he looked up at the honours board of club captains. Where was his name? True, he'd never actually captained a match, but he had been elected club captain, hadn't he? Down came the board, out came the gold lettering, and there the name of Billy Harker now proudly stands: the captain who never captained.

I wonder what Dr Crosbie and the pre-war players would think if they could see us now. As the league season gets underway we're not playing a local club who have scratched together a second team to give us a game, but travelling two hundred miles to visit a team of rugby's high flyers. Amazement aside, I hope they would have more belief in the outcome of today's game than I do. I know I should be positive, partly because in the days running up to the game I've been reading Tali Sharot's book *The Optimism Bias*. Basically, it puts forward the case that for evolutionary reasons our species is wired to look on the bright side of things. As I read, I'm nodding in agreement with all that she says. In theory it all seems irrefutable, but in practice, right now I can't help but notice a flaw: I can find no grounds for optimism when I look forward to Wharfedale's season.

During the friendlies, all the talk in the club has been about a single goal: surviving in National 1 for another year, and so making it through to a

A LEAGUE OF NATION
National 1 Clubs 2014-15

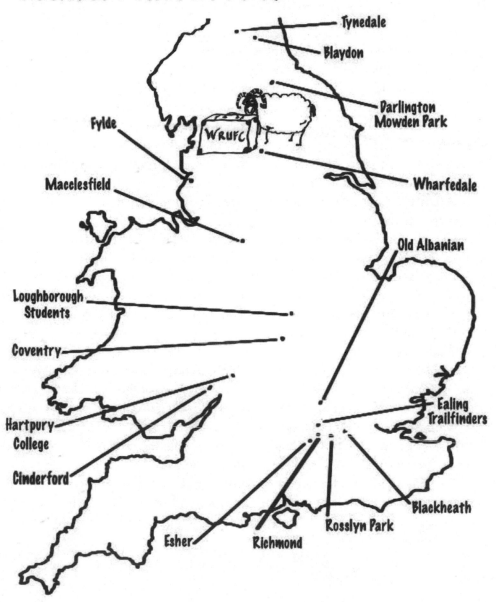

Tynedale

Blaydon

Darlington
Mowden Park

Fylde

WRUFC

Macclesfield

Wharfedale

Old Albanian

Loughborough
Students

Coventry

Ealing
Trailfinders

Hartpury
College

Cinderford

Blackheath

Esher

Richmond

Rosslyn Park

twentieth year in the league. To those involved back in 1996, making it to this level in the first place was a major achievement: the idea that we might be able to sustain the same level for at least two decades would have been beyond anyone's wildest dreams. And yet this is the tantalising prospect if we achieve our season's goal. That's a big 'if', and right now I'm not sure how we can achieve it.

I'm lost in these rather gloomy thoughts when Caroline asks me, as we drive through leafy Gloucestershire in the late-summer sun, what my prediction for the season is. Considering the glorious day, my response is plain and bleak: *relegation*.

My pessimistic reasoning is that our form after Christmas last season was dire, and it was only with a week to go that we avoided the drop. As it happened, it was the three newly-promoted clubs that were relegated, and a repeat of that scenario is unlikely since the new clubs in the division this year seem to be flushed with money and talent. Add to that the number of unknown faces in our new-look team, and I'm fearing the worst.

When Caroline asks me how I see our first league match going, again my answer is grim: *defeat*.

She asks for full workings to my answer, and I offer this: last week, whilst we were winning a game of tag rugby against Otley, our first league opponents, newboys Hartpury College, were taking a Championship side to the wire. If their pack could push Plymouth's around, will they even notice that we're there? And with their backs being England wanabees, we're likely to be chasing shadows for most of the afternoon.

So after two matches against clubs we think of as friends, we're down in the South West, to play against a club that we have little in common with. We have no 'history' with Hartpury College which, when we entered this league, didn't even have a team. Then, Hartpury was an agricultural college with about fifty students, set in an old country house estate. The house is now hidden amongst a spread of new campus buildings, and acres of pitches, which serve over three thousand students of land and sports. Some change.

The rugby side of Hartpury is impressive, and sees them in partnership with Premiership club Gloucester, as well as subsidised by the RFU. They certainly don't appear low on confidence. In today's match programme, Hartpury is how they present the National League 1 table.

6 September 2014

Position	Team	Played	Points
1	Hartpury College	0	0
2	Blackheath	0	0
3	Blaydon	0	0
4	Cinderford	0	0
5	Coventry	0	0
6	Darlington Mowden Park	0	0
7	Ealing Trailfinders	0	0
8	Esher	0	0
9	Fylde	0	0
10	Loughborough Students	0	0
11	Macclesfield	0	0
12	Old Albanian	0	0
13	Richmond	0	0
14	Rosslyn Park	0	0
15	Tynedale	0	0
16	**Wharfedale**	**0**	**0**

Well, we've no objection to being bottom at the moment. There's no arguing with the alphabet. But what are Hartpury doing at the top? Is their 'H' not so much silent as invisible? We've heard that they're mighty ambitious, and I can't help but wonder if this is where they see themselves at the end of the campaign.

All-in-all, Hartpury is a world away from Wharfedale. Whereas even our head coach is a school teacher who trains the players two evenings a week, Hartpury's pay-roll, I note from the programme, extends to a Strength and Conditioning Coach, and even a Performance Analyst. Even without the capital letters, we probably all fancy ourselves as performance analysts – if only we could get the coach to hear our words of wisdom! On the Dale side, someone who does have the coach's ear is Steve, a former player with a cute slant on what he sees. Walking behind the posts early on in today's match I witness a revealing mismatch of rugby cultures. There's Steve, squinnying closely at events in front of him, committing everything to his photographic memory. Then there's Hartpury's man on the ground, clipboard in hand, scribbling away. When a family of Hartpury supporters try to chat to their man he's polite, but makes it clear that he's not here to pass the time of day. The two analysts are stood virtually side-by-side, and during a break in play I notice Steve saying hello to his opposite number, and ask what kind of thing he's writing down. He's given the briefest glimpse of the clipboard. Later Steve tells me what he saw: "Tickboxes." Oh, didn't I say? Hartpury's man is former England captain Phil De Glanville: Steve is our coach's dad.

Hartpury have all these advantages, the accoutrements of the professional game, in spades. Hartpury's disadvantage is more difficult to put a finger on, but may outweigh all of the above. At least in comparison to Wharfedale, they don't have much of an 'us'. There are only about three hundred people here this afternoon, and plenty of those are shouting for the Dale. Numbers, though, don't tell the full story: I suspect that the fellow students, family and well-wishers who are here to support the home team have a fairly brief tenure as the *us* of Hartpury. They're pleasant and welcoming towards us as guests, but they look supremely relaxed about the whole thing. Although they raise a cheer when the team comes on, when the going starts to get tough and the team need a bit of backbone, the home support gives way.

The Dale following, by contrast, is always passionate, and like the team, punches above its weight. There are parents and girlfriends on our side too, but although they may start by donning a green scarf as a flag of convenience, it rarely ends up that way. They almost always catch the bug, since around them are people who have the club in their blood – to whom this all *matters*. Take Alec. He's a retired shopkeeper from further down the Dale, who has been following the team all his life. Our game certainly matters to Alec, but like a lot of Dalesman, he prefers not to let it show. Even his humour is masked – it reminds me of the pot-holes on the moors above Grassington, which the unwitting can pass by without even noticing.

All of us wearing green have a way to make our presence felt. There are the bangers, like my wife, who try to find a resonant metal advertising hoarding to clang. There are the haranguers, like Alec, who follow the action up and down the touchline and offer words of fortitude to anyone who will listen. And there are the hollerers, like me, who stay rooted to the spot and bellow. Hartpury are probably marking us down as a brutish northern tribe. Perhaps we are, even if we're only here to maraud points.

A clue to how things develop early on in the match might be found in the warm-up. Hartpury have banished the Dale team to a distant training pitch. None of us has seen that little snub before, and to judge from their comments as they trooped back into the changing rooms, I don't think our lads were impressed. Has it fired them up? It may well have, because against all expectations, from the off our forwards are all over Hartpury. In the opening exchanges we keep them pinned back in their own 22, where they give away a penalty. Then their scrum buckles, and in the ensuing collapse, their no. 8 tries to stamp his authority on the match. He does this literally, stamping his right boot down on his opposite number. This is plain crazy, because although play has moved away, he does this right under the eye of the touch judge. Now, let me just say that when I see our own 8, Rob Baldwin, shrugging his shoulders towards the officials with the air of an angel whose wings have just been ruffled, I know something very, *very* odd is going on. And it is. Red card! Hartpury will be a man down for the rest of the game.[9]

I have to say, this moment mutes not just the home crowd, but for a brief instant the visitors too. We're stunned. There we are, already up on the scoreboard, and with the prospect of playing the next seventy minutes against a depleted side, we're quickly having to rearrange the mental furniture of our expectations. Shift that pessimism out of the way, and make room for optimism! Almost all of us were resigned to a whipping: now we've been handed the whip. Probable victory. But we can't afford our silence to last long. Our support counts. From the penalty and lineout in the corner, we release the dam on our first "*RIVER!*" of the season, and on its current the Dale pack duly sail over the line.

"That's an impressive maul you've got," a friendly Hartpury supporter says to me. "And your vocal push is pretty dynamic too."

The conversion is kicked, we're 10–0 up, and that should be that. But Wharfedale being Wharfedale, the flow of the game then takes a winding course. As half time approaches we're ten points *down*. The ref is seeing only Wharfedale's sins, and we're being punished. Hartpury score two quick tries, and although we narrow the deficit with a penalty on the stroke of half time, we still troop off 13–20 down. The pessimism creeps back.

At the start of the second half, by contrast, the ref is seeing Hartpury's sins, and no longer ours. And we're capitalising. Another penalty kicked and we're back within four. Again we attack, again a Hartpury forward transgress, and now out comes the yellow card. It's up front that we now need to make things count, but that doesn't mean our backs have no role to play. When Hartpury have a scrum ten metres out from their line, one of our centres, Tom Davidson, leads the vocal charge, calling for the river. It's a cue to us on the touchline, too, which

---

9 This talk of '8's reminds me that, uniquely on the rugby field, the number has no positional name. Is it too late to put this right? Let's have a think. Well, he plays as the rear of a three, the other two being the open-side and blind-side flankers. 'Back-side flanker' would seem logical, not least because of what anatomical area this player becomes most intimate with at scrum time. But, of course, he doesn't play on a flank and, in any case, we abbreviate his colleagues to just 'open-side' and 'blind-side'. So 'back-side' would seem logical. Are we agreed? If so, you're now welcome to go and tell the 8 in your team that you think he's a great back-side, he's turning into a complete back-side, it's nice to have a big back-side in the team etc.

we take up. Together we're all reminding our eight where the metaphorical river lies, and that's where they head. Hartpury's pack is bundled backwards, and all they can do is scramble the ball into touch. We're just five metres out now. Catch, drive, try! Virtually from the restart we repeat the treatment with the same result – and with just over ten minutes to go we're 30–20 ahead.

With nothing to lose, the Hartpury backs now decide to run everything. It's early season, the sun has given way to an airless humidity, and Dale's part-timers are tiring. Hartpury go over to bring themselves within a score and then, in injury time, fling the ball wide to a grateful winger. Off he flies. On the touchline no-one can breathe. But the whistle goes, puncturing the air, and our lungs take in the oxygen that seems to suddenly wash through the atmosphere. Forward pass!

One final scrum for us, and one final call to arms. We secure the ball, kick it out, and we've won, 30–25. *Result!*

We're right by the Hartpury dugout at this moment, and as they gather their stuff to troop off, I see one of their replacements hurl his water-bottle to the ground.

"What is it with this bloody 'river' thing?" he asks no-one in particular.

To which I hear Alec answer, "Just wait for the return fixture lad – you might just find out then."

Chapter 6

*~ in which we rediscover our fortress, invite Darlington
inside, and meet an old young scrum-half ~*

This afternoon something happened which we haven't known at The
Avenue for the best part of a year. 281 days, to be precise. We registered a
home league win. Now, that fact might come as something of a shock in the
context of the tale so far, even though I've already mentioned the recent history
of our gruesome home run. Let's recap. Up to this point in the book we've won
a cup, thrashed our neighbours in a friendly, and made a successful raid down
to the South West. Despite that close reverse against Stourbridge, you could
be forgiven for thinking that Wharfedale's is a tale of battles won, and that our
home is a mighty fortress. If only.

Ironically, although on the touchline we've been bemoaning the number of
new faces in our team, today this probably counts in our favour. Only seven of
the starting line-up were regulars in that losing streak last season, so for at least
half of the team, there are no monkeys on their backs. It might also help that
today's opposition is not one of those teams that came last year and mugged us.

In fact, for the second week running we're facing newcomers to the division.
Like Hartpury, Darlington Mowden Park are fiscally flush. A few years ago,
a couple of eye-watering property deals left them as proud owners of a
25,000-seater stadium – the Northern Echo Arena. Elton John may be able to
fill it but not yet, we hear, the rugby club. Not remotely. And this, I'm afraid, is
where the jokes start.

"With a crowd of a thousand in there it must be like playing in the main
cavern of Gaping Gill," Adge says, welcoming the visitors over the tannoy
from the clubhouse balcony. "Let's face it, when we come up, we could bring
the entire population of Grassington, including the sheep, and the place still
wouldn't be… *wait for it!* …rammed."

Mowden have brought down a fair number of fans with them this afternoon,
and they receive Adge's gibes in the spirit in which they're winkingly sent.
A good sign. For our part, we're genuinely pleased to have another northern
club in our league: and no, there's nothing anti-southern in this sentiment. The

simple truth is that the club game in the North is in poor health, and needs every fillip it can get.

Whilst we wait for the teams to emerge, plenty is being said about last week's visit to Hartpury. Someone reports that the students sniped at our lads about how much Wharfedale paid their players per match. And as for our team having been shunted off the main pitch pre-match, I hear someone pipe up with a suggestion:

"Since they don't like sharing, when they come here, perhaps Hartpury should warm up on the field going down to the river."

"Mind you," Alec adds, "they'd have to share that with some real animals."

This quip is followed by no audible laughter, but by a barely perceptible chuckle. For the Shed, this counts as uproarious mirth. All this grumbling at Hartpury's expense is leavened by one piece of tacitly shared knowledge. *We won.*

The weather helps lighten our mood, too. We're still hanging on to this lovely Indian summer. It's calm and balmy, and although on the other side of the Dale the trees in Grass Wood are turning colour, there's nothing in the air to persuade them yet to drop their leaves. So, rather than huddling under the meagre roof of the Shed, as we often have to, we're spreading out and mingling. For Wharfedale this is a good crowd – seven hundred or more. Home and Away stand together, as rugby crowds tend to.[10] We shout for our side, and the visiting fans for theirs. Not for 'Darlington', I notice, but either for 'Mowden' or 'Park'. I'm always intrigued by how people in our league identify their club. For reasons which we'll come to in due course Blackheath, famously, go no further than shouting for 'Club'! Next week we'll be shouting for 'Dale' up at Tyne*dale*, but that's alright, since that dale's supporters will be rooting for 'Tyne'. I wonder what the these 'Park' fans will be shouting at Rosslyn Park. When I ask one of them why they seem to shout anything but 'Darlington', he gives me a funny look. Apparently there's another local club, called Darlington RFC, and there is what is sometimes euphemistically referred to as *feeling* between the two clubs. Fair enough. For us, 'Mowden' will do.

We stand together, then, but watch separate games. We each tend to see what we want to see – at least up to the point when the realities of the scoreboard interrupt. When the game starts it's evidently still early season, with plenty of errors. Knock-on? Forward pass? Offside? We have our own perspectives, and the referee has his: a penalty either way, and after quarter of an hour it's 3–3. Five minutes later, we're pressing on Mowden's line, and again the ref's arm goes out in our direction. Playing with an advantage, with the ball at the back of a ruck,

---

10 Unlike Association Football, in which *dis*association is the name of the game, in Rugby Football we happily associate.

this is decision time for the half-backs. With our returning star James Doherty out injured, this week we have a new scrum-half. Well, not exactly new – Philip Woodhead has been playing in a green shirt for more than fifteen years. He stands over the ball and instantly assesses his options. The penalty advantage is still there, but there's nothing much on. Rather than fire the ball back to the fly-half for an attempt – the usual routine – from about five metres out Woody dodges to one side and drops the three points himself. Woody. A great one for the unexpected. And how old is this old hand with the wise rugby brain? Thirty-five? Forty? Actually, he's only twenty-three. He came up through Wharfedale's minis, and made his debut for the Firsts when he was still at school. I remember it well. Not only was Woody small and slight, but he looked quite absurdly young when he first walked out on to the pitch. But Woody quickly showed every trick in the scrum-half book: bossing the pack, broken-field running, a tackle that could bring down any rampaging back-row with the most perfect timing, and a pass that's a thing of beauty.

Shortly after Woody's debut, I had a visiting New Zealand friend, Ewen, standing with me on the touchline. At the first scrum he pointed, shaking his head, and asked, "Just how old is that kid?" Well, I knew what he was thinking, and the kind of thing he wanted to hear: "Eleven. They tell us he's seventeen, but I don't believe them." Anyway, Ewen watched intently for about fifteen minutes, but said nothing. Then, with the air of a connoisseur, he pointed at Woody again and said, "That kid can *pass*." Praise indeed! Before long Woody was being noticed by men with clipboards, and still in his teens he was called up by Yorkshire and then England Counties. At scrum-half we're oversubscribed, then. As Steve says, with James Doherty back, "We've not just got one of the best scrum-halfs in the league, but with Woody as well, *two* of them."

At fly-half, it's a different story. To introduce the lad in the 10 jersey today, we have to briefly back-track to the founding of the club, and the family at its heart. Many clubs pride themselves on being close-knit, but when Wharfedale describes itself as a family club, it really means it. Names like Harker, Baker, Slater and Spencer echo down the club's history from generation to generation. Yet one family, above all, *is* Wharfedale. The club may have been formally founded by the local doctor, but amongst the movers and shakers he gathered around him was a Harrison. James Harrison had a butcher's shop in the village, and a finger in most pies. He was already in his thirties when the club was formed, and although he never played himself, James encouraged his two sons, George and John to play. Their names and characters – as captains, chairmen and presidents – we will come to again. For the moment, though, let us move on down the generations. Jimmy was one of John's sons, and Jimmy, a star player himself, duly had six children. The third was a girl, Jill, and it's her son Harry who is now making his debut for the Firsts. Amongst the Dale support there is nothing but goodwill towards the Harrison clan, and it's fair to say that the sentiment around is for Harry to succeed. He may well do in time, but today, sadly, he's just part of an unfamiliar and sputtering back line.

If we are to win against Mowden, it looks as if we'll be relying on the big men. As the half progresses they start to deliver. The first sign of this is the ref's yellow card, raised to one of Mowden's forwards after half an hour. Of course, when this happens, there's nothing tangible for us to celebrate. Although the 6–3 scoreline doesn't change immediately, we all know the mythical statistic — that on average a side down a man for ten minutes will concede seven points. So we all register a silent *ker-ching!* as we anticipate Mowden paying us for their indiscipline. But what's this? Before we know where we are there's a lapse in the Dale's security, and we've waved through their full-back to raid our own till. This heralds a period of unrestrained looting, with the rule of law struggling to keep up.

First, back up at their end, we find a predictable hole in their defensive wall and help ourselves to a try out wide. Then, with five minutes of the half to go, once more grimly defending their own line, Mowden transgress again. Another yellow card. Another *ker-ching!* A minute later, and again a likely try is stopped illegally. Again Yellow. Again *ker-ching!* We're losing count — not just of how many points we should be ahead, but how many men we're now up against. Never mind, because we keep cashing in, and at half-time oranges we troop in on top. I've no idea what our projected interim profit should be, but since we've been playing up the slope in the first half, 18–10 will do.

With the river beckoning us downhill in the second half, and the first few minutes of it against a depleted side, for once at half time the mood in the clubhouse is quite relaxed. A good barometer of how we feel is that I can't hear Adge taking to the PA from the balcony outside. When we're midway through any nervy struggle, Adge pipes up to remind us of our role in what follows. Not today. He draws the raffle, and that's all that's required.

It is, too. Darlington score first in the second half, with a penalty, and later add a try, but otherwise we have the nudge. There's nothing particularly scintillating in our play, but this is sometimes the way. At least up front we front up. From a penalty in Mowden's 22 we kick for touch — *confidence!* — and leave matters in the hands of our pack.

Now, our match reports are written by a committee man called Ed Williams, whose looks and surname tell of his Welsh pedigree. So does his writing which, I'm pleased to say, can never quite distance itself from the author's own passion.

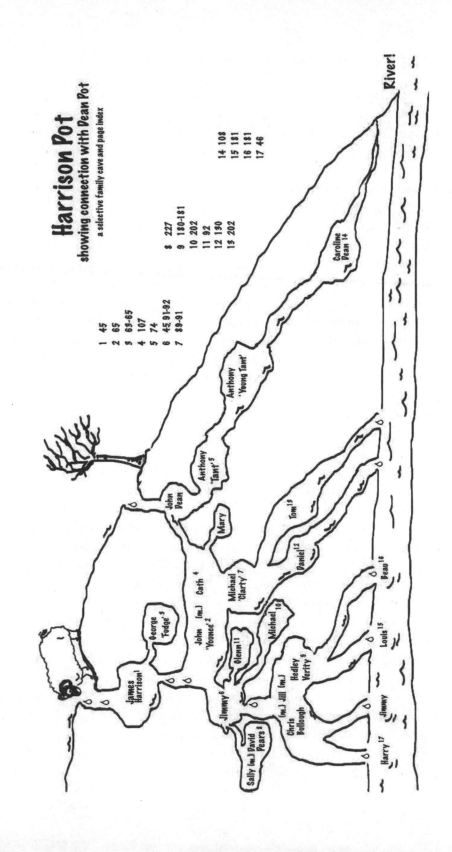

Harrison Pot

showing connection with Dean Pot

a selective family cave and page index

1 45
2 65
3 63-65
4 107
5 74
6 45,91-92
7 89-91
8 227
9 180-181
10 202
11 92
12 130
13 202
14 108
15 181
16 181
17 46

James Harrison[1]

George 'Fudge'[3]

John (m.) Cath[4]

John (m.) 'Younee'[2]

Jimmy[6]

Sally (m.) David Pears[8]

Glenn[11]

Michael 'Clarty'[7]

Michael[10]

Chris Bullough

(m.) Jill (m.) Hedley Verity[9]

Harry[17]

Jimmy

Louis[15]

Beau[16]

Daniel[12]

Tom[13]

Mary

John Dean

Anthony 'Tant'[5]

Anthony 'Young Tant'

Caroline Dean[14]

River!

Here's Ed on the crucial moment in the second half:

> *With cries of 'river' echoing around the ground they drove the full Darlington eight back with something approaching ease, and the inevitable penalty try, converted by Davidson, stretched the Greens' lead to 25–13.*

The referee evidently thinks that the penalty try should be punishment enough. But when, minutes later, the visitors' open-side stops another try illegally by kicking the ball out of a ruck, the referee shows him a second yellow, and then a red card – *ker-ching! ker-ching!* If the ref is trying to teach Mowden a lesson here, I'd have to say that they're slow learners. Moments later they collapse another scrum, and the ref runs round beneath the posts to award us a second penalty try. Under normal circumstances a penalty try is a bit anti-climactic: rather than that definitive, satisfying moment when we see a real player thunking a real ball down behind a real line, we're faced with nothing more tangible than the referee's opinion to concur with. This afternoon, though, this moment gets the biggest cheer of all, because it assures us of not just the win, but the winning bonus point for scoring at least four tries.

Happy days! A second league win – 32–18. I'm not counting my chickens, but even I have to admit that after two matches, nine points out of a possible ten is A Start. We don't need to wait for the other results to tell us that this is Good. There's one easy way I can tell that all the Green support feels this way. Often, before the ref has blown the final whistle, supporters will be drifting back to their cars. They might be driven away early by the weather, the looming result, the prospect of traffic going back down The Avenue, or as often as not all three. When things are bad, even those of us who feel the need to see the game through to the bitter end treat the final whistle as a starter's gun. Heads down, and we're off. Whatever the cause, there are many occasions when we have no wish to prolong this event we've all been looking forward to.

At the end of today's match, things couldn't be more different. By the time that the sides have cheered each other off the field, I notice that although the Mowden supporters have made their exits, few of our number are in a particular rush to go. For a good while we stand chatting to the coach's parents, Steve and Lynda. It's not really the time for picking over the bones of what we've just seen – it's more a matter of fixing travel plans for next weekend, whilst letting the adrenaline subside. You can sense this lovely easing going on all around the ground. On the pitch a few kids are running round with a ball, but that's the only activity to speak of. Across the pitch I can see Woody, who has come back up the tunnel to see his mates as he warms down with a few stretches. And in the opposite corner to the clubhouse, down at one end of the terrace we stand on, I can see three women grouped round a wine cooler, glasses in hand. Players' mums, perhaps, or committee wives? Just another small *we* in the larger *us*.

If all this sounds idyllic, then that's because it is. Loitering in the last of the September sun, I realise that this feels not like rugby, but cricket. And right on cue, as the cars move down The Avenue and the sound wanes around us, I hear a familiar but distant shout. There, only a few hundred yards away, on the cricket pitch across the river, the season is drawing to a close. Curious to see more, we take our dog, Sadie, for a walk in that direction, across the field that leads down to the river. With no rain to speak of for weeks, the Wharfe looks fairly listless, running over its limestone bed. We're closer to the cricket now, and from this distance can clearly see each shot and hear each appeal. There are only a handful of spectators over there, occasionally smattering their applause. I can't help but wonder what they've made of events on our side of the river this afternoon. In this bucolic setting, their own quiet game must have been dwarfed by the overpowering presence of ours, with its crowd of baying voices at a fever pitch of excitement. Above the river, amongst the empty spaces of the Dales, ours is an outlandish game.

Chapter 7

~ in which we travel to Tynedale to meet some kindred spirits, and meet the coach and his parents ~

In recent seasons there have been weeks, I admit it, when I can't bring myself to look at the league table. Normally it's when we've lost a game some time after Christmas, and I just know from other results that we're on the slippy-slippy slide. This last week, I've had no such problems. We're fourth. *Fourth!* Yes, I know, it's early days, but look where we are after we've beaten Mowden Park:

14 September 2014

1	Fylde	2	10
2	Ealing Trailfinders	2	10
3	Rosslyn Park	2	10
4	**Wharfedale**	**2**	**9**
5	Richmond	2	9
6	Tynedale	2	8
7	Esher	2	7
8	Hartpury College	2	5
9	Coventry	2	5
10	Blaydon	2	5
11	Loughborough Students	2	2
12	Blackheath	2	2
13	Darlington Mowden Park	2	1
14	Old Albanian	2	1
15	Cinderford	2	0
16	Macclesfield	2	0

It's not just looking at the league table that can swing the emotional barometer in the middle of the week. Looking at the fixture list, and imagining the next journey, can produce anything from a chuckle to a shudder. Give me a weekend in December, the prospect of...

Blackheath (A)

…and my shoulders slump as I contemplate dark hours parked on the M25, or wrestling through the Christmas shoppers at King's Cross. Arriving at Blackheath is a pleasure. But journeying there – *ugh!* No, give me mid-September, the promise of…

Tynedale (A)

…and I can't wait to get started. Now then, shall we head up past Kettlewell, over to Leyburn for coffee and then up? Or across to Ripon, then along the tops of rural Northumberland on the old Edinburgh road? Either way, the feeling is the same – *let's go!*

This year we go for the second option. On route, then, we can have lunch at the Manor House Inn, a pub on the moors just before the road dips down to the upper Tyne valley. We've arranged to meet Steve and Lynda there, and they bring the latest news from the training ground. For a start, there's more injury woe: our backline this afternoon will be makeshift.[11] What really threw Thursday's practice session into chaos was the visit of the drug testers. On Thursday evening the coaches were desperately trying to thread unfamiliar backs into a seamless line, with new holes always appearing as players were dragged off to provide samples. Does it come as a surprise that a village team like ours has to rub up against the dark underbelly of top-level sport? Perhaps, but however frustrating it might be, the truth is that we lie right on the shoreline between the dry ground of amateur rugby and the sometimes murky waters of the professional game. Like most law-abiding types, we're right behind the enforcers – until the moment they come and bother us.

So with these impediments on his mind, as we sit down to lunch on Saturday, Steve is a worried man. Then again, when it comes to sport, Steve strikes me as a born worrier. When it comes to work – juggling the duties of a Justice of the Peace with those of a builder – Steve's life seems a relative doddle: "I've spent all week working up on a roof. One slip and I'm probably dead. But this…today… this *matters*."

Steve played for various clubs in soccer, as well as in both rugby codes. Decent clubs, too, although if you believed what Steve says you would think that, whatever shirt he wore, he was always a complete imposter. "They played me in that team for a specific reason," he says about one club: "I was the only one that could start the boiler." I don't buy any of this for a moment, but there is no way I can ever get Steve to take his own sporting achievements seriously.

---

11 A word on injuries. I've noticed that every side, in every sport, believes itself to be uniquely blighted by injuries. We have that belief too, but I shall try not to offer too many medical bulletins.

About his son Jon, however, Steve is different. With Lynda, he saw Jon rise up through the ranks until at under-21 level he was playing for the North of England, alongside future internationals. Jon Feeley stood on the verge of rugby's big-time, until a serious injury sent him scuttling back to the bottom of the board. Still, he made his way back up to Championship level, playing for Leeds and Rotherham. He even wore Rugby League jerseys, training with Leeds Rhinos, and starring in Sevens for Bradford Bulls at Twickenham one year.[12] So Steve, as player and father, has invested a part of himself in countless clubs. But for him, and Lynda, Wharfedale stands apart. He's never known anything quite like it, and he's taken it to heart. Not everyone does. Some come, feel the heat, and step straight back. Others come and, as the old-timers say, they 'get it.' Well, Steve's a romantic, and he gets it.

Going to Tynedale, the journey is good, and so is the arrival. If we play 'friendlies' against the likes of Stourbridge and Otley, when we play Tynedale it's as close as rugby can ever come to a love-in. Here's the Wharfedale Twitter feed in the week running up to the game:

> This Saturday, First XV away against kindred spirits Tynedale. Two unbeaten teams. Should be a good clash.

And here's Tynedale's welcome to us in the match programme:

> *Wharfedale remain very much the closest club to us in location, background and attitudes and it always a pleasure to welcome back kindred spirits to Tynedale Park.*

Evidently we're even kindred spirits in the language we use to describe the kindred spirit of the other club. Why? Well, many clubs are rooted in their communities, but here we have a more specific match: *farming* communities. In the Tynedale programme I see that we have two farmers with names straight out of a Dickens novel: Dan Herdman for them, Dan Stockdale for us. Except this isn't fiction, it's fact, and for all I know those names are actually telling me what the ancestors of these men did.

So, our affinity stems from what we *do*: but it also extends to where we *are*. Both clubs are named after north-Pennine dales, and both lie beside rivers, across from which are small tourist-trap villages. In the case of Tynedale, the

---

12 Lynda tells me that since she was brought up as a Bradford fan, this was one of her proudest moments. The rub-side to this is that when I ask her what her worst experience of Jon's career was – expecting to hear about the injuries or the set-backs – Lynda hangs her head and says "having to hang out a Leeds Rhinos shirt on my own washing line."

village is Corbridge, and the ground has been described as 'the second-most-beautiful ground in the National Leagues'. At least, this is how Wharfedale describe Tynedale Park – albeit with a nudge and a wink. This is the one aspect of our relationship where Wharfedale claim – and Tynedale just about concede – bragging rights.

I suspect Tyne are happy to give us this because, let's face it, on the pitch they rarely give us anything. Over recent years our league positions have been similar, but in our head-to-heads, Tyne have the edge. Last year was one of those brass-plaque events when we came up to Corbridge and went home with the spoils. Although we've won both of our matches this season, few of us believe we'll be extending that happy run today. Our pessimism only deepens when we arrive to find our best uninjured back, Scott Jordan, sitting out the warm-up feeling dizzy. We can hardly believe it. The welcome is as warm as the weather, but the prospects for the game itself are going from bad to worse.

Right on cue, we see a potential pick-me-up: our second team, the Foresters, are up here to play Tynedale Seconds. The usual mix of aspiring youngsters and… who's that propping? Ah yes, forty-four year-young Neil Dickinson. Until a final cameo last season, for years Dicko played for the Firsts, although as a sheep-farmer he had to absent himself each year when lambing time came round. Just along from me on the touchline is another Dickinson – John, and I ask him about Neil. I assume they're related. Not so, he tells me. But John said that he gave Neil his introduction to rugby.

"When I stopped playing myself I used to run the Fourths. One day we were down at Skipton, and we were a couple of men short. Well, I always brought my kit along just in case, but then someone said to me, 'I've a mate here who's never played, but he fancies a go'. That was Dicko. Anyway, I arranged things so the two of us could play in the second row, just so I could keep an eye on him. In the tight stuff he was fine – he was a powerful lad – but at one stage someone made the mistake of passing him the ball: I remember him just standing there and asking, 'What do I do now?' He was a quick learner, mind."

Most of the Dale support has gathered down in the corner closest to the Foresters' match, and we're still looking at the Seconds when the Firsts take the field. As a result, rather than boinging out on to the field as the Greens do when they find their usual springboard of our cheers, they step out as if they're walking the plank. To any amateur psychologist, the dynamics of support are endlessly fascinating. Is it the place, or the people, that make the players feel at home? Today, Dale start out lacking the sense of either. Tyne kick off, and immediately the play is down the other end of the pitch from where we stand. Dale have come out without finding their support, and now we don't seem able to find them. It feels like 'them' and 'us'. The action is less than a hundred yards up the pitch, but it feels like a mile. Tyne are quickly up 3–0. It gets worse. Scott Jordan is giving it a go, but after one wobbly run he signals to the bench that he's not right. Five minutes in and we've now got a scrum-half at outside centre and a scrum-half at full-back. We've even got a scrum-half at scrum-half, although with a groin injury still mending, this afternoon Dohers might just be a scrum-quarter. Our back line, frankly, looks shaky. It's an accident waiting to happen, and on ten minutes it does: a flat pass from our fly-half goes straight into the clutch of Tyne's left wing, and we're 0–10 down.

It's difficult to see where our inspiration is going to come from. Then, just before half time, a charge from Rob Baldwin gets play downfield to where the Dale support is gathered. As if at the flick of a button, in this corner of a foreign field, suddenly they're playing as if they feel at home. It's no longer 'them' and 'us': now we're in this together. Some of the Foresters have showered and, pint glasses in hand, have come back out to cheer on the Firsts. We're raising our levels. Dale's river is starting to flow more strongly, and Tyne can't dam it. The ref awards us a penalty try, and in our excitement on the touchline a Dale supporter, standing beside me, suddenly finds himself toppling over the boundary fence. The plastic top rail has given way, and he's left bridged over the bottom rung, clutching what remains of his pint. By the time we've righted him, Alec claps him on the back to commiserate: "Sorry Jim, but you know the rules – that's four faults for knocking a rail off."

Altogether, our mood is lighter now. We head in only 7–10 down, on balance quite pleased to still be in it. That last five minutes felt like it came out of somewhere else – somewhere ninety miles south from here, to be precise. Home.

The problem is, although the Dale support is strong, we can't offer the team a shoulder all around the pitch. During the interval most of us have wandered up the touchline to the end we will be attacking. There's never much said about this – it's just a natural migration to where we hope the action is going to be. Yet as supporters we've now left our defences unmanned, and Tynedale find a way through.

We're soon 7–17 down, and from then on it's as if Tyne have erected a barricade on the half-way line. From the touchline we're still calling out, trying to hook the Dale up to where we know we can help, but it's like watching salmon trying to get up a weir – lots of effort, lots of endeavour, but you just can't see how it's ever going to happen. Each dart is flooded back to half way and beyond. But you know how it goes. Salmon *do* get up river in the end, and so, somehow, do the Greens. With ten minutes to go, our team is back in our corner and Chris Howick, who's come up through the minis to stake his claim in the Firsts this season, goes over. The support is up here by the Tynedale line, and so now is the team. With us. Tyne can't get out of their own half, but sadly for us, they don't need to. When they get a penalty on half way, a single well-aimed missile is enough to win them the game. Dale cross the line once more, but it's only enough to net us a solitary losing bonus point.

At this moment, the sides engage in that well-practised, well-choreographed bit of line-dancing, whereby the hosts make a tunnel for the opposition, the opposition makes a tunnel for the hosts, each cheer the other, and then the teams peel away back on to the field to form their arm-in-arm circles. The Huddle.

When they eventually walk off towards the clubhouse we're standing with Steve and Lynda. The coach sees his mum and dad there, and walks over to say hello. I've never spoken to Jon before, and I could think of better times for introductions. Jon shakes hands, but I can tell he is dwelling on the *what ifs* – *what if* we hadn't thrown that reckless flat pass that cost us the game? *What if* we hadn't hoofed so much attacking ball straight into the hands of the opposition? And *what if* we'd landed our two conversions? Basically, his cast members haven't quite delivered the lines he'd prepared them for. A silence with plenty of feeling.

"Hey," I try, "we're still going home with a point!" but John shrugs his shoulders and says nothing. He's not biting. Nor does he nibble at any of the other crumbs he's offered – that we've outscored them by three tries to two, that the pack went well, and so on. We leave Jon to deal with it as best he can. His dad doesn't look much happier about how things have gone, but perhaps he has a bit more experience of dealing with defeat. Steve announces that on the way up to Tynedale he saw a sign for a Saxon church, and they're going to go and investigate: "I think a bit of calm is in order."

Win or lose, four points or one, a trip to Tynedale usually has its consolations.

Chapter 8

~ in which a storm visits The Theatre of Bleats, Ealing descend on us along with a red mist, and we get blown off course ~

Whether it's *Call of Duty* or the *Antiques Roadshow*, interactive games are very much a thing of today. Being 'just a spectator', by comparison, is very yesterday. Only thing is, that doesn't seem to apply to rugby. Go to a state-of-the-art stadium like Twickenham, take your seat in Row R of Block Q23, and prepare yourself for a passive involvement in the modern game being played out down below. Sure, you can sing along with *Swing Low*, and shout 'Heave!' once in a while, but your contribution will influence events on the field about as much as a game of throwing-pebbles-from-a-beach-and-waiting-for-the-sea-level-to-rise. No, if you want to feel as if you're playing a part, go to yesterday's game, played at a trad venue like The Avenue. If you stand by the rail in the Shed on a Saturday afternoon, and share an opinion with a player, you might just get a reaction.

Lynda, standing beside me, has just had one – and from our captain, no less. He was reacting to some timely advice that Lynda had just shouted out.

"Keep your head Doherty!"

Well, since there's steam coming out of his ears, and he's just been haranguing the officials, she's got a point. He turns round towards us and for a split second glances towards Lynda. Does he recognise that it's the coach's mum? Unlikely. Or does he hear the voice of a teacher? Perhaps. Either way, he reacts like a boy who's just been brought to book. He shrugs his shoulders, and mutters something we don't catch. Basically, he knows that she's right. For the time being he gets on with the game. For the time being.

All this passion has crept up on us unawares. We've come up the Dale this late-September afternoon not exactly bearing the freight of expectation. We are, after all, playing the league leaders and favourites for the sole promotion spot – Ealing Trailfinders. Like Doncaster last year, Ealing have just been relegated from the Championship, but with money behind them they're planning on bouncing straight back up. The word is that they've actually strengthened their team since coming down. This is a team of hardened professionals, then, and we don't expect much from today's game. But hang on a moment… what was that mention of Doncaster? Weren't they in the same boat when they came up here last year? And what happened that day? A Famous Victory! So, whilst we might not have come expecting much, we're always hoping. Who knows?

In the first half we're playing down the slope, with a stiff breeze behind us. Gauging the value of these conditions is not an exact science, but the cognoscenti in the Shed think we need to be up by about fifteen points when we turn around.

Time for a word about the pitch at Wharfedale. To those who imagine that the rolling Dales miraculously lose all their innate character within the bounds of our touchline, think again. I imagine that teams turning up at The Avenue for the first time must feel like American parkland golfers rolling up to a Scottish links course: what will they make of all the swales and hollows, a devilish wind, and an uncompromising out-of-bounds? The Avenue really is like that. For a start, the slope isn't uniform. It undulates, so that even when playing uphill it's possible to be awarded a scrum on a tiny downslope and find that your pack suddenly look turbo-charged. Then there's the wind which, more often than not comes out of the west, blowing straight down the slope. To the unwary fly-half, though, the double-whammy of slope and wind can sing like a siren, luring him to kick. But even his most artful kicks can end up on the rocks, because the dead-ball area down towards the river is minimal. One extra gust of wind, or a bounce off a downslope, and the ball is boinging into the back fence, with the kicker left to face the murderous looks of his forwards.

This afternoon we've started by playing the conditions perfectly, pinning Ealing back in their own 22. Taylor Prell has been released by Yorkshire Carnegie to play, and before ten minutes are up he's showing his class, zipping through and around flailing defenders to score out wide. *Fantastic!*

Our pressure continues. Ealing are rattled. They keep infringing, and lose first one forward, then another, to the sin bin. From a ruck almost on the Ealing line we spin the ball out, and Tom Davidson cuts through to put the ball down under their posts. We've been playing for twenty-five minutes, we've just dotted down for the second time, and Ealing have barely been up into our half. *Fantaaaaaaastic!*

If I could go back in time and stop the clock at any one instant on 27th September 2014, it would be precisely then, right in the middle of that *Fantaaaaaaastic!* It wouldn't be five seconds earlier, when no score looked on.

And it certainly wouldn't be five seconds later when, having signaled a try, the referee is trundling over to check why the touch judge on our side is holding out his flag. Uh-oh! Beside the officials, Ealing's no. 8 is lying on the ground, and James Doherty is letting him know what he thinks of his acting skills. The ref runs off and makes his signal: no try! Instead, it's a penalty to Ealing. They clear their lines and the ball sails into touch right in front of us. Job done, their 8 jumps to his feet and trots off to join the lineout. It's at this point that Dohers loses it, giving the touch judge an opinion we can all hear.

"Their no. 8 needs a box of ******* tissues. He needs to ******* man up."

"James, James!" I want to tell him, "for a man with a degree in politics and philosophy, your current tirade is hardly philosophical, and it's certainly not politic." But I can save my breath, because Lynda is telling him much the same thing – and a bit more succinctly.

Sure enough, from this point on, the day starts to spoil. A couple of minutes later and our own 8 is lying on the floor in agony. Real agony, this time. Rob Baldwin doesn't feign injury. We know it's serious, and eventually he hobbles off supported by two physios.

I remember being at Athletic Park in Wellington on the day when the great Michael Jones snapped his cruciate ligament. The whole ground winced then, and as the grim prognosis became clear over the next few days, New Zealand went into a mild state of mourning. Well, we're a dale, not a nation, and with the best will in the world Rob isn't Michael Jones, but right now the feeling is similar. Sometimes you don't appreciate a player until he's gone. Four years ago Rob was offered the chance to go and play as a full-time professional at Leeds, and he took it. I can't say that he jumped at the chance, because 'Badger' had a long history with Wharfedale, and was club captain at the time. He also had a serious day job. Still, he couldn't resist, and with the caveat that he'd be back up with us whenever he could, off he went with the club's blessing. A year and a bit later he was back, with no regrets, and with a seriously improved technique and temperament. To be honest, before he left, Badger was a bit of a liability. If anyone was to be seen getting up from a ruck with a clumsily misplaced elbow or knee, chances are that it was our back-side (or no. 8, if you still insist). He amassed more than thirty yellow cards and three red ones before he left. That said, since he returned he's been, well, if not a changed man, certainly a tweeked one. The old combativity is still there, but now it's channeled into countless bison-like charges with the ball, and lion-like tackles without.

Even with this set-back, we're still 8–0 up when we head in at the break. Ealing head in too, but then straight back out. Their coach has them charging into the tackle bags during the break, clearly demanding a bit more mongrel from them in the second half. On the touchline I bump into Gordon, who does the programme. He isn't getting carried away at the prospect of defending an eight-point lead with the conditions against us: "Keeping them out's not going to be easy. I wouldn't be surprised if we end up seeing yellow ourselves in the second half."

Ealing duly take the fight straight to us, and within a matter of minutes they've drawn level. We're still scrapping, though, and the score stays unchanged until, with twenty minutes to go, there's a ruck over on the far side. It happens in a flash. From fifty yards away we can't see what the referee has seen, but he's in no doubt that he's seen something. In one movement he brings the whistle to his lips, and puts a hand in his pocket – and James Doherty has been shown the red card.

Down to fourteen men, we're facing defeat now, but it's not just the likely result that has suddenly curdled our mood. It's that we've just had the cosy blanket of self-righteousness pulled off. All supporters want to believe that they're following the Good Guys. And it's true that, so far this season, in the eyes of the officials we've sinned less than we've been sinned against. But if we needed a reality check, this is it. *No-one is saying we're angels.*

It gets worse a few minutes later when our winger, Scott Jordan, is shown yellow and we're down to thirteen. Inevitably, Ealing now power through us to the line. First Arthur Ellis, their flanker, who last year was turning out for the Ospreys, goes over: then Will Harries, a winger who only four years ago was lining up for Wales against the All Blacks, dives in at the corner. Class won't always win out, but today it will. An hour ago we were hollering and whooping, but we've been winded by everything we've seen in the second half, and no-one can summon much breath to cheer us home. So, as the last rites of our game are acted out, an afternoon which began with a low intensity for the spectators is ending that way. Dejection.

As often happens in these situations, our eyes stray from the pitch to the surroundings. Caroline points to the drystone wall at the far end of the pitch. A cow is looking over it, plaintively mooing as she stares out towards the play. We then notice why she's got her head up: behind her another beast is ardently humping away. A few others have spotted this action, and there's a bit of a teenage titter going around. In these circumstances, we take our entertainment where we find it. But as our noise fades out, the Ealing support fills the silence. One portly man in particular has well and truly found his voice. Or is it a ship's foghorn that he's found? Whatever it is, he's sounding it off now at regular intervals.

"*EEALIIOOOOOOOOOOOOOOOOOOOOOOOONG!*"

He's only a few yards from us, and eventually it gets too much for the young girl with him. It's his embarrassed daughter.

"Dad, please stop it – you sound like that cow!"

A few of us exchange glances, smirks, and the same thought: *well said!* In my case, however, a hypocrisy alarm is soon ringing. As someone who probably sounds like a bull seal trying to mate with a reluctant parakeet, this joke could just as easily be on me.

I'm certainly not having the last laugh when it comes to the final score of this match. 8–21. There's no denying it – Ealing have done a job on us this afternoon. All through the match we've heard them chipping away at our team verbally. We've seen them, too, laughing at our efforts, like the playground bully holding off an uppity little kid. They've done the job like old pros. They've got right under our skins, and lured us into a losing battle with the referee. There was only ever one winner there.

The bad feeling that has been there throughout the match shows no sign of abating as the final whistle blows. Right in front of us there's an all-inclusive scuffle on the touchline. When the ritual handshakes are offered, I notice that one of our players can't bring himself to accept the hand of his opposite number: and why would he when the Ealing lad is still mouthing off at him? Altogether, it's a bit sour. And very unusual. Rugby, we're told, is a game after which the players can always shake hands and share a beer. Always? If they do so after this, the beer will definitely be bitter.

We should be able to walk back down The Avenue with plenty of positives, ranging from the individual – how the young lad Matt van Sertima has developed in a month from a colt to a potential thoroughbred – to the corporate – how for half the match we held our own against professionals who are the best in the league. But no, that's not how it feels. We're likely to have lost one of our stars to injury, and another to suspension. It's more than that, though. From what we've seen, we've been poor sportsmen. We leave with a bad taste in our mouths.

Later, when we get home, we try to wash out the aftertaste by watching the end of the Ryder Cup foursomes on television. It works. The sporting spirit at Gleneagles is infectious. I can't help compare the niggle we've seen at the rugby with the evident camaraderie between the opposition golfers. They walk down the fairways chatting together, and it's all hugs and smiles on the final greens. Why the difference? Well, we're always told that it's easier for golfers because they play the course and not each other. We had that option today. If we had kept on course we could have done something memorable.

But no – we got blown off course into every water-hazard and sand-trap that Ealing put there for us. And as things stand, we're starting to look a bit bunkered.

Chapter 9

*~ in which we meet Younce and Fudge, read the runes of
an ancient church, send ourselves to Coventry, and play a
game of two halves ~*

Picture this. The year is about 1950, and an old cream-coloured Ford van is
tootling its way across Skirfare Bridge, under the shadow of Kilnsey Crag,
and down the winding lane back towards Grassington. Above the drystone walls
you can just make out, in green lettering, the words 'Harrison – Butchers'. It's
one of those lovely pastoral scenes, one that might be lifted straight from the
pages of a James Herriot book. Yet when that van stops, and the door opens, it's
going to give vent to a small volcano. Out will burst George 'Fudge' Harrison,
and you can be sure that some high-octane action will follow.[13]

There are many stories about Fudge, but a good many of them start with
that van pulling up – commonly with a squeal of brakes. George tended to run
late – often 'waylaid' in the Black Horse or the Foresters. When Chris Baker
describes George as being "fond of a drink," another old-timer within earshot
chips straight in with "and that's an understatement!" George had first played for
the team around 1930. Soon after that, remember, his had been the crucial voice
and vote which kept the club going. But George wasn't just talk. Along with his
elder brother, John, in the years leading up to the war he took an increasingly
active role in the club.

Chris, who first played for the club in 1949, remembers George as his first
captain. In one of Chris's first home games, the match had already been going
for five minutes when they saw George's van pull up. His morning deliveries
had detained him a while, and a liquid lunch a while longer. Moments later, kit
now on, out flew George, straight onto the pitch.

"Well," Chris says, "it was obvious that George had had a bit to drink already.
When the first scrum went down he packed down at 8, and when we got a
shove on and started to move forwards, I looked behind me and there was

---

13 Why 'Fudge'? George's niece Mary remembers: "Well, the van was vanilla coloured, and when we saw it pull
up we used to say, 'Ey up, here comes vanilla fudge!'"

George, face down in the mud. Not that he let it dent his confidence: when we were given a penalty a few minutes later George stepped up to take it himself. He ran up, swung his leg, missed the ball completely and went arse over tit!"

One Saturday, just after New Year, a game away to Selby was called off because of a frozen pitch. Chris and his mate Tom Slater were at a loose end, and at lunchtime made their way up to the Tennants Arms at Kilnsey: "I saw George's van pull up outside, and a few seconds later in he came. He'd been out delivering all morning, and was frozen. Anyway, he got himself a pint and went over to stand in front of the fire. The next thing – *woof!* – his overalls went up in flames. Well, what would you expect if you stood in front of a fire covered in animal fat? Anyway, we got him straight onto the floor, and rolled him up in a rug. I don't remember him complaining about the cold after that."

Of all the stories Chris tells about George, my favourite concerns an away trip to Richmond. Not the Richmond on Thames that we play nowadays, but the Richmond on Swale, two dales up:

"When we got to Richmond, George got off the bus and went into a butcher's shop run by a friend of his. Two minutes later, back he came, and told us that we would have to call in there again after the match. In the early fifties, meat was still on ration and even in the Dales meat was scarce, so whatever was going on was probably not quite kosher butchering, if you follow. Anyway, on the way back we stopped again at the butcher's. George shouted down the bus, 'Alright lads, make some room in the back, then come and give me a hand'. So we shuffled the kit round in the back of the bus, and a few of us went with George into the shop. In the back, there was a beautiful half-side of beef! Without further ado we carted it out to the bus, and off we trotted. Well, we drove back over the tops into Wharfedale with this great lump of meat wedged in the back of the bus, but when we got to Cray, George asked the driver to pull up outside the inn there. George hopped off and went into the pub. At that time it was run by a retired military man, Major Horner, I think he was called. Anyway, he was a pal of George. A minute later George was back on the bus, 'Right lads, lift it out, take it through the back and put it on the kitchen table'. Once we were in there, George asked the Major for a saw and a knife. 'Now then, how much do you want, Major?' he asked. It took quite a while for George to cut the joints but eventually – and after a pint, of course – we got back on the bus, and continued down to Kettlewell. Then it was the same routine at the King's Head there. And the same at the Tennants in Kilnsey. By the time we got back to Grassington he'd done a fair bit of business. By now it's half ten at night, and George's wife had already gone to bed. George stood at the bottom of the stairs and shouted up, ''Ey up Ann, these lads have done a good job for me today – can we cook 'em up a pork chop each?' She did too."

Eventually George's hard living caught up with him. Chris remembers going with Tom, beer bottles in hand, to visit him in Otley hospital when they were playing down the dale. George knew his number was just about up: "The box were ready, but they couldn't quite get the nails on the lid," he told them. So George died, in 1981, to be survived for another decade by his elder brother John – 'Younce'.[14]

Younce was a different kind of man. Where George always seemed to have a pint in his hand, Younce just had a pipe. Altogether a more benign character. For all that the club was his life, Younce was never the stereotypical rugby man. His daughter Mary thinks he was a feminist before his time. Once, when he was club president, during a player's birthday dinner in the clubhouse a stripper came in as part of the entertainment: John just picked up his plate and walked off to finish his meal out of sight. If Younce had a respect for women, it may be no coincidence that his own wife, Cath, was happy to become so involved in the club herself. After he passed on his formal responsibilities, Younce himself became the club's unassuming elder statesman. Not that he was one for preening. Younce dressed at the club as he dressed on his farm. When a carpet was first laid in part of the clubhouse, a newcomer to the club saw Younce walk onto it in his farm boots: "Hey! – you can't come in here dressed like that!" Younce said nothing, just retreated outside to take off his boots. Whilst he was out of earshot, some of the older members let the newcomer know who was who.

John died in 1992. There is an entry from the club minutes (which I suspect is as telling about the club, and about Dalesmen, as it is about Younce): 'It was suggested that a portrait of the club president John Harrison be put up in the club room. After discussion it was thought that a sketch would be more appropriate.' The sketch still hangs, hidden round the corner from the bar.

Time to digest some news. First the good. At an RFU hearing during the week James Doherty was cleared of foul play, and his red card was rescinded. Our home matches are videoed for the coaches to study, and I'm told by someone who saw the footage straight afterwards that Dohers did absolutely nothing:

---

14 Why 'Younce'? His son tells me: "When he was very young my Dad would go down to the shop and ask for 'a younce of baccy' for my granddad's pipe. So in the shop they would say, 'Here comes Younce' – that's how it started."

"So God knows what the referee thought he'd seen… or was persuaded to believe that he'd seen." It's a relief all round: for the player, to have his record restored; for us that he's free to play this weekend; and for all concerned to know that we *are* angels after all. *Ho-ho!*

Now the bad news. Rob Baldwin has torn ligaments in his knee, and is resigned to missing the rest of the season. This could be a disaster for the club – quite simply Rob has been our talisman of late – but how must it feel for the individual? How must it be for a serious sportsman, dealing with a lengthy spell on crutches? I can't imagine it. But far from feeling sorry for himself, Rob is quoted in this week's *Craven Herald* as saying that, 'Whatever happens I will be around the team, hobbling about and trying to help.' That's not Badger's agent or Wharfedale's PR office talking (they don't exist) – it's the man himself. Good: even if his team mates can't rely on his physical contribution, they will at least have access to Badger's spirit. If they can distil some of that, then perhaps all is not lost.

There's never a good time to lose a key player, but it's now early October and we have a run of matches ahead against the most prestigious clubs in our league. Blackheath and Rosslyn Park lie in wait, but first we have to travel to Coventry. And driving there, Caroline sees something she doesn't like.

"Uh-oh! Look – it's a sign for a Saxon church!"

I'm momentarily baffled: why should this be a problem?

"Remember driving past that Saxon church on the way up to Tynedale?" she says: "We lost that day. I bet it's a bad omen."

Welcome to the alternative world of the supporter. We might be cock-sure rationalists when it comes to trivia – the prospect of life after death, say – but faced with a really important issue, like divining the result of an away fixture in National 1, and if it's all the same to you we'll avoid walking under that ladder. Or driving past that old church. But, damm it! Now we *have* driven past that church, and perhaps our efforts today really are doomed. I'm left looking for any positives I can find.

"It may not be a completely bad sign," I eventually suggest. "At least we got a losing bonus point against Tynedale."

We had left the motorway, and were driving across rural Warwickshire, when Caroline saw the sign. Until then our moods had been surprisingly buoyant. You might have assumed that we would be pessimistic about our chances this afternoon, against a club with a great history such as Coventry. But remarkably, although they were once the pre-eminent club side in England, historically Wharfedale have had a winning record against Coventry. And never mind history, this season Cov have, like us, so far won two and lost two. So without being unduly optimistic, we at least set off with open minds about the outcome.

Then Caroline saw the sign for the church, and if my interpretation of runes is accurate, the best we can now envisage is a solitary point.

By half time it looks as if even a point is out of the question. Coventry have already run in six tries to our one, and the game is effectively over as a contest. It's as bad a forty minutes as we can remember. Still, to any of our number that are listening I still feel I should point out that we need "just" another three tries to get a bonus point. Lynda gives me a funny look. "Simon, I think getting three more touches of the ball would be something."

The daft thing is that when we arrived this afternoon, we wondered whether it might be Coventry, and not us, who would be short on motivation. The rumour going around the touchline is that within the next few days Wasps – *London* Wasps – are to announce their relocation to Coventry. That, surely, will test the backbone of the city's historic club. Coventry, let's not forget, is a club with serious pedigree. Never mind the legends of yesteryear – the likes of Fran Cotton and David Duckham (who I assume is over there in the main stand catching up with his old England mucker, and Wharfedale president, John Spencer) – even in rugby's professional era of snakes and ladders, plenty of internationals have found themselves on Coventry's square as they head up or down the board.

The clubs play their own version of snakes and ladders, of course, and since it's glory days Coventry has been heading steadily downwards, from the top level to ours. A few years ago, still with full-time players and ambition, they overplayed their hand and came dangerously close to falling out of the game altogether. Now they are operating more cautiously, but ironically it is Coventry losing the scent of the Premiership which has brought the London prospectors sniffing round.

We've been watching the first half from opposite the main stand. Not many Dale supporters have made the trip down, but those who have are divided into two groups. Over in the stand are the committee and club officials. They happen to be wearing blazers, but don't imagine that they form some kind of patrician elite: the Wharfedale blazers are not the stripy outfits associated with old school ties, but a plain dark green. The men inside them hold no particular caste or rank. All they carry with them is the history and tradition of their club: they're local men, and in various capacities have done serious time for Wharfedale. They're as close as Wharfedale come to an Establishment.

Over here on the standing side, our history with the club is shorter. Aside from the coach's mum and dad, Steve and Lynda, there are John and Rowena Burridge, here to watch their two teenage sons pack down in the back row. Then there are the parents of our young prop, Jake Armstrong. None of us lives within fifteen miles of Threshfield, and a few years ago none of us were even watching the team. If the blazers sitting under cover represent the old Establishment, it would be easy to think of us, standing out in all weathers in our coats, as the new anti-Establishment. But 'anti' wouldn't be at all right. Let's settle for non-Establishment.

All the Dale support is chewing the half-time cud of a 5–43 walloping. From here, down on the touchline, all we've seen so far is wave after wave of blue and white attacks, cavorting through our defence as if it's not there. Well, is it there? Difficult to tell from this angle. Perhaps Cov's sidesteps and switch moves really are unreadably brilliant. Steve, who has been watching the first half from his usual position behind the posts, wanders up to find us and quickly puts us right.

"That was a disgrace. When I see two defenders falling away either side of an attacker, I'm sorry, but there's only one word for that: *cowardice*." Strong stuff.

The first inkling we have that something might be in the air for the second half is when we see a few of our substitutes taking the field. A few? We start scanning around the field and count one, two, three, four…five new faces. Make that *all* of our substitutes. I'm imagining that Jon's half-time talk was, for want of a better word, pithy. I'm not party to what has been said, but I really don't need to be, because when a coach uses all of his available subs at once, for the team and us it carries with it the clearest implication: *don't think I wanted to stop there.*

The Dale have certainly received some kind of rap. They're back out on the field ahead of Coventry, and having used the first half as a bit of a light-contact warm-up, the men in green are now jumping up and down, clapping, and enjoining each other. Basically, they're now ready to start playing. Cov eventually saunter onto the pitch, in complete contrast, as if they are coming out for their warm-down. With their four-try bonus point already in the bag, however much their conscious minds tell them otherwise, sub-consciously they know that they have nothing further to gain from the match.

What happens next, then, is perhaps predictable. It's all Dale. Our pressure is relentless, and although we have to wait thirteen minutes before we cross the line, when we do, things then happen fast. Two minutes later Dohers flies through their midfield, offloads to Scott Jordan, and we're in beneath the posts again. Perhaps that bonus point might be ours after all. Sure enough, five minutes later Scott crosses for a fourth try to bring us up to 26–43, and we're yelping in disbelief. Whatever happens now, we won't be going home empty-handed. And we're just starting to wonder. Even with twenty minutes still left, victory seems impossible, but if we get to within seven points of their score, we'll be banking a second bonus point. At this moment, though, Coventry wake themselves up (or to be more precise, their disgruntled supporters wake them up). Their team must be a bit concerned, because when they're awarded a penalty, they gratefully take the three points to give themselves some breathing space on the scoreboard. Then, with the last play of the game, they cross for what one of their supporters refers to as a "consolation try."

And here we come to the oddest moment of the day. After the team cheers and handshakes, the Coventry players lope off a bit shame-facedly. Most of their supporters have made straight for the exit, and those remaining offer what sounds like, at best, one-and-a-half-handed applause. Hang on! Haven't Coventry just put more than fifty points on the board? Seven tries? A win and five points in the league? Maybe they have, but they have also committed an unforgiveable sin in the eyes of the paying fan: they've knocked off early.

That accounts for Coventry's exit. As for ours, we all make our way round the pitch to clap the team off. Genuine warmth, from the blazers and the coats together. Scott Jordan is a bit embarrassed, and apologises for the first half. The others look relieved that they've salvaged a bit of pride. And they all look appreciative of the support.

Ridiculous, isn't it? We've been thumped, and we're almost happy – because although in this afternoon's game we've been nearly thirty points in debit, in this evening's table we will be one further point in credit. Obviously on our way to the lesser teams we'll be sidestepping the Saxon churches, but if we do run into one on our way to the big clubs, and pick up the occasional point, perhaps not *all* will be lost.

Chapter 10

~ in which we find out about the Tin Man, Blackheath give us a lesson in history and in the present, and Biggles runs on ~

The Avenue may not be paved with yellow bricks, but wander up there when a match is in progress, and chances are that the first person you will clap eyes on is the tin man. That's Chris Baker. He's not difficult to spot – a tall man who gains at least six extra inches by wearing his Wharfedale beanie like an upturned ice-cream cone.[15] Now in his eighties, Chris played for Wharfedale teams across five decades, and was chairman after his body persuaded him to stop. These days, his chief formal duty is down by the entrance, operating the scoreboard – and at Wharfedale that still means 'doing the tins'. There's an electronic scoreboard at most grounds that we visit, but at The Avenue things are a bit more basic. When points are scored, we have to wait a moment whilst Chris shuffles through his pack of tin plates, and hangs up the relevant numbers. The board is in a corner down by the entrance to the ground, so if the action ends in a melee at the top of the pitch, occasionally I've seen Chris consult with those lower down in the Shed to see whether he needs to act. Altogether, modern communications have so far bypassed this little corner of Wharfedale.

The deliberation Chris shows in getting the score right is the essence of him. I don't think he will mind me saying that he is not as quick on his feet now as he must have been when he played, but he still has an imposing physical presence. And although his mind is sharp, I dare say that Chris's conversation has also slowed from the days when he travelled the world in the wool trade. Chris, then, is steady and incisive – exactly the kind of man who, over the years, Wharfedale have been grateful for on and off the pitch.

Back in 1949, when a seventeen year-old Chris first arrived in Grassington and climbed off the bus, he had no idea that there was even a rugby club here. It didn't take long to find out. The following day, the first shop his mother went into was George Harrison's, the butchers, down at the bottom of the street.

---

15 Conceivably Chris is here making an ironic reference to the funnel hat worn by the original Tin Man in the 1939 film of *The Wizard of Oz*.

"Rationing was still in place, so meat was hard to come by," Chris tells me, "and my mother played what cards she had. Well, when the butcher heard her say that she'd 'two growing lads to feed', my mother said his ears pricked up: 'Do they play rugby?' he asked. I think he was more interested in that than in how many sausages he could spare. My brother and I had played a bit at school in Bradford, so when he heard this Mr Harrison just said, 'We've a match this Saturday. Tell the boys to turn up, and we'll take it from there.' And that was that."

Having already left school, within months Chris had taken a job thirty miles away back in Bradford, where he lodged during the week. But his immersion into the Wharfedale team was rapid and total. Since his father had just been appointed Rector of Linton, the small village just down the dale from Grassington, Chris now had family up in Wharfedale, and each weekend caught the bus or cycled back to be with his new pals.[16] Later, when he was asked to play for one of the Bradford clubs – which in those days were a step or two above Wharfedale – he told them he wasn't interested.

"We weren't the only youngsters that got hooked in and stayed. There were boys from Skipton and Burnsall who would catch the bus up after school on a Saturday morning. George Harrison would see who turned up, and off we went. Then, Skipton had a much better club than us, but they would only field the youngsters when their regulars couldn't play. Wharfedale has always stuck by the youngsters a bit more, so over time the youngsters have stood by Wharfedale. And we were very dependent on the farming community. In lambing time it got a bit thin. And quite a few had problems with milking. If we were playing away at Hull, say, they had to find someone to milk for them. Not easy."

One of the faint absurdities of Chris's current role down by the scoreboard is that he has to sport a fluorescent yellow jacket. It's not exactly the hard shoulder of the motorway down there, and there is no chance of him being hit by anything with more substance than a falling leaf from one of The Avenue's trees. As far as insurance and liability are concerned, rules is rules. But Chris's glowing garb gives him the appearance of a health-and-safety pedant which, when he tells me about the club's earliest building work, is ironic to say the least.

"In the fifties we still had no clubhouse. We played in a field off the lane out to Grass Wood, and we used The Foresters at the top of the village as a sort of headquarters. We used to change in an upstairs kitchen, and after the match we had to wash in an old stone bath across the yard at the back. Some of the bigger teams from Leeds and Bradford made a few comments, so we asked Arthur,

---

16 To those who don't know the type of terrain involved, it's what the modern peloton would euphemistically refer to as 'lumpy': i.e., quietly murderous. Factor in the type of bike involved, and this ride is a prospect in itself. With a flaying eighty minutes on the rugby field to follow, it would have been a significant biathlon.

the landlord, if we could build a bath upstairs. Well, that was fine by him, but nobody thought about how much weight was involved. The bath took up about half the room. Not heavy in itself, but fill it with water, then put a dozen blokes in it…. it's a miracle it didn't bring the whole place down." Somehow I don't think it would get the green light nowadays.

"Using a pub as our changing rooms had its advantages, though. We'd get back from matches late in the afternoon, and in those days the pub would be closed then. The landlord would probably be asleep upstairs, too, but we had an arrangement – and I'd head round behind the bar and pull pints myself." The free house of our dreams.

"Still, a lot of the better clubs around were a bit sniffy about coming to play us. Well, since we played in a cow field, in one way they were right to be sniffy. But for them, everything was a bit down-market. Even walking out from The Foresters to the pitch was the best part of a mile. Anyway, we realised we needed better facilities, and for that we needed to raise some money. For years, in the third week in February, the club had a big event. The team put on a pantomime in the town hall. We had to rehearse for that – dance routines and God knows what. We had those rehearsals in The Foresters, so you can imagine what they were like. The performance was on the Thursday. The following night there was a whist drive, and on the Saturday night a dance. All in the Town Hall. We got big crowds, too.

"The players had to pay a subscription, and there was insurance we were supposed to pay. That was half a crown – quite a bit in those days. I remember one player, Norman Kayley. Now, Norman was the type who would never buy a drink if he could get someone else to buy him one – and he never paid his half-crown insurance. Anyway, in one match down at Ilkley, Norman broke a leg, and as we carried him off the pitch on a stretcher, he said to me through gritted teeth, 'Chris, if you put your hand in my back pocket you'll find my half crown.'"

That fixture against Ilkley, Chris recalls, was played on an evening mid-week.

"Back then, before leagues, bigger clubs like Ilkley already had an established fixture list, and wouldn't be able to find space in it for a little rural club with no pedigree. And you can imagine what all those clubs called us when they did play against us – I think 'sheep shaggers' came up more than once."

It would have been easy for Wharfedale to accept this lowly station. Yet for some reason they were not prepared to do that. It might sound like a riddle, but one of the secrets to Wharfedale's success is that the club has never been afraid of losing. What counts is the test. Win or lose, they will be better for the experience. This was as true sixty years ago as it is today. Then, if the big club just down the valley would not give the Dale a proper game, fine, perhaps a big club a hundred miles away might give us one.

So the travels began – to Lancashire, the North East, and Cumbria. And with the travels, almost imperceptibly, came success. It wasn't that Wharfedale suddenly won every game. Far from it: the minutes from the fifties often record that in terms of wins and losses we were becoming *less* successful, not more. But the losses were against better quality opposition, and whatever the results suggested, year on year Wharfedale were getting better. The one context in which the Dale did get to play the better Yorkshire sides was in the county's Shield competition. In this, the side were on their mettle. They felt that they had a point to prove, and Chris remembers how these competitive matches led to a radical change for the club.

"We'd never trained at all, but in 1957, when we got to the latter stages of the Shield, someone suggested we should get ourselves in better shape. We used the school gym. The headmaster was a keep-fit man, and had us lugging medicine balls around – that kind of thing. Nothing very sophisticated, but it seemed to work."[17] It did. Away to Cleckheaton, Chris scored the solitary try which took Wharfedale to the final of the Shield. Although Dale's style was all about to change, at this time the ball can't have seen too much air – at least not to judge from the refrain of a ballad which was sung on the bus to the final against Moortown:

> *Won't you get that ball out Wharfedale*
> *Won't you get that ball out now!*
> *Won't you get that ball out Wharfedale*
> *Every once a little while.*

Well, a final is no time to tinker with your tactics, so Dale stuck to the tried-and-tested, and the result was... a scoreless draw. Still, in the replay Chris's brother Richard kicked two drop goals, and Wharfedale had its first silverware. All those ugly, distant losses were suddenly worth it. Courtesy of our shimmies north and east, we had gained parity with our close neighbours.

And we were still climbing. From the sixties through to the nineties, with Chris increasingly active off the pitch, Wharfedale kept on improving until, in 1995, the club reached the dizzy heights of English rugby's third tier. Since then we have, effectively, sat on the same step. Not that it has ever felt like a static staircase. Between the aspirations and abasements of the professional era, it feels

---

17 At least by 1957 the team's training recognised that hands might have some role to play in rugby. Back in 1934, during the club's first cup run, the *Craven Herald* reported that 'Their only special preparation for the matches is an evening run over the wild moorlands in which Grassington nestles.' Tant Dean, who played in that pre-war team, remembered that 'The first instinct of a forward receiving the ball at a lineout was to drop it and start a dribble.'

as if Wharfedale has somehow perched itself between up and down escalators. This reality is not lost on Chris, because there's one other piece of signage he is still responsible for. At the end of The Avenue is a board advertising the details of our next game. For this, the visitors are actually given name recognition.

"Exeter, Worcester, Nottingham… I've made all the signs up, and I never throw them away. You never know when you'll be needing them again. I was looking at the Championship table in yesterday's paper, and I see that Plymouth are stuck at the bottom." Chris pauses. "Hmm… P l y m o u t h   A l b i o n," he says, almost spelling it out. "That sign took some making up. I'm glad I didn't throw it away. It looks as if I might need it again next year."

Speaking of big names, we now come up against one of the biggest – certainly in terms of rugby lore. Blackheath F.C. When you entertain Blackheath, you entertain history. Just as an entrée, and as our own contribution to the historical feast that Blackheath carry with them, let me offer this: Wharfedale against Blackheath is the longest-running rivalry in National 1 rugby. Now for us that's a piece of history worth chewing on, but as a claim to fame for Blackheath, it's not even the dust in the bottom of the peanut bowl. After all, this is the oldest 'open' rugby club in the world. Now, I know what you're thinking: surely they must have been *equal* oldest –mustn't there have been another club for them to play against? Aha! Thing is, their first match was against the old boys of Blackheath School – a 'closed' club, open only to former pupils. So, with two Blackheath teams playing each other, how could their supporters distinguish themselves when they called out? Simple – they shouted for '*SCHOOL!*' or '*CLUB!*' And 'Club', more than 150 years on, is what Blackheath supporters still call out from the touchline. That's Blackheath's nickname accounted for.

Now what about the 'F.C.' after their name? By contrast, we are are 'Wharfedale R.U.F.C' – the 'U.' making it clear that we play Union and not League. We're used to meeting clubs formed before the Great Schism of 1905 – they understandably termed themselves 'R.F.C.' But Blackheath 'F.C'? Yes, that's right, they existed before there was even a clear split between *rugby* football and *association* football. If they'd been formed a couple of years earlier, you feel, Blackheath would have a cameo role in Genesis.[18]

---

18 If Club didn't have enough of its history based in fact, it could always draw on its history in fiction. Not only was 'Biggles' based on an actual Blackheath player, but Sherlock Holmes has his Dr Watson playing for Club.

Personally, I think there's one character in Blackheath's past which really rubber-stamps them as an authentic piece of sporting history. Although his life reads like pure fiction, C.B. Fry happens to have been a real person. Even leaving aside Fry's remarkable public life (he was a delegate at the League of Nations, was a Liberal parliamentary candidate, was approached about taking the throne of Albania, and lunched with Hitler) his achievements in themselves constitute a history of early sport: at cricket, Fry was captain of Sussex and England; as an athlete, he was holder of the world long-jump record; at football, he played full-back for England and was an FA Cup finalist with Southampton; and (in his copious spare time) playing rugby? Well, who else could he have played for but Blackheath?

But here we are in the present, in which Blackheath hold less of a mystique. At least when we have played them at home, more often than not we have won. On route to The Avenue we take Sadie for a walk up on Malham Moor. Another gorgeous autumnal day on the roof of the Dales, with views over to Malham and down to Pendle. It's mid-October, but the Indian summer we've enjoyed still seems reluctant to leave. In that air and light it's impossible not to feel buoyant, and when Caroline asks for my prediction about the match, for once I am optimistic.

"If Adge takes the microphone, I reckon we'll win. Blackheath are only one place above us in the table, they lost at home last week, and I think if our crowd gets pumped up, we'll get on a roll and they'll crumble."

We drive down to The Avenue, are handed our programmes, and straightway I'm faced with an unexpected collision between present and past. In this case, the past is mine. There, on the Blackheath team sheet, is the name Alex Gallagher. Interesting. Didn't John Gallagher, the first Englishman to win the Rugby World Cup, end his playing days in a Blackheath shirt? I ask the Blackheath physio and she confirms that indeed, Alex is son of...

"Do you know John?" she asks

"Er, it's a long story, but no, not really I suppose."

Long story. Here's the guts of it. Back in the mid-eighties, and within a few months of each other, Gallagher and I landed in New Zealand as young men disillusioned with opportunities in the Old Country. From the top of the Millward Stand I used to watch him, first playing for Wellington, and then the All Blacks. In different ways we were both finding our feet in this new place, and although we never met, I think I identified with him more strongly than I have with any other sportsman. So, in answer to the physio's question, no I don't know John Gallagher. At least, no more than I know my own shadow.

Having had the snowstorm of personal memories well and truly shaken, I'm still watching the flakes settle when Adge (a good sign – it *is* Adge) welcomes the crowd. Having flattered the opposition and their followers, he duly warms up the home support to give the team a rousing welcome as they run out. That, sadly, is our loudest cheer of the afternoon.

The relationship between crowd support and team performance is always a chicken-and-egg affair. We do understand that the more we give out, the more we will receive back from the team. But we need *something* for us to pin our first meaningful cheer onto. We can't just cheer enthusiastically when the opposition is barging us around and refusing to let us have a play with the ball – which is precisely what Blackheath do from the off. Within the first ten minutes the Club pack have trundled straight through us twice, and we're 0–12 down. We have hardly made a sound, but we're desperate to have our say. So come on Dale! Just give us something – *anything* – and we'll do our bit. Nothing. As it is, all we can hear is a solitary Blackheath supporter behind the posts, bellowing, "*COMEONYEEEECLUUUUUUUUUUUUUUUUB!*" It's only a matter of minutes before we concede again. 0–21.

In these circumstances, sometimes even a single tackle can act as a suitable ignition, firing up the support and the team. After half an hour that's eventually what we get. The willing centre Matt van Sertima crunches his opposition number back in the tackle, and the ball spills out backwards. It's right in front of us in the Shed, and we roar. First to pick the loose ball up, though, is Club's right wing, and he flies straight through the hole which our centre's tackle has left. This afternoon we're trying out our third fly-half of the season, and although no-one is pointing the finger at him specifically, there's no denying that our midfield is… well, *isn't*. There we are, then, a minute after our supposedly catalytic cheer, another converted try against us, and we're 0–26. By half time, make that 0–33. When the players leave the field, a winded silence comes over the crowd. 0. Nil.

This is dire. This is shocking. This could be our worst ever afternoon at The Avenue.

Adge picks up the microphone again, but there's an odd pause between his sentences, as if he's having to remind himself about the unreal reality of what he's seeing. Normally, he attains the zenith of his peroration with a voluble crescendo, but today his words stumble over the pitch to us as if they've got stuck in the mud.[19]

For the Shed, in the second half we suffer the ultimate humiliation – not from the opposition players, but from the linesman on our side. A nice man (and I

---

19 If, to older readers, this sentence carries an echo of Leonard Sachs (the man who used to compere *The Good Old Days*) then it may just reflect the tongue-in-cheek fruitiness of Adge's rhetoric. To younger readers: have a look on YouTube.

say this not because Gordon, in the programme, is encouraging us to get on the right side of the officials, but because the linesman just appears to be genuinely *nice*). Anyway, after Club have scored twice more at the start of the second half to lead 0–45, this official starts trying to help us. Don't get me wrong, he's not bending decisions our way. It's much worse. He's suggesting with a smile that our side could do with some support.

"Come on," he turns round to say during a break in play: "Get behind your lads! Raise the volume a bit – they'll play better if you do!"

This, let's remember, is the Shed he's bantering with – the 'intimidating bear-pit' that, in the past, has frequently deafened opposition teams into submission.

"Trust me," I answer back, "we know our lines, we're just waiting for our cue."

But duly chastised, we try to shout for just about anything. That said, we're not exactly hunting as a pack. It's all individual efforts, and the support is slow in arriving. Solo voices are thrown into the air, but they all sound a bit small-man-in-a-box. Jake Armstrong breaks over the gain line – "*WAHAY!*" We've won a lineout – "*COME ON THE DALE!*" An attacking scrum for us on half way, and where should head? – "*RIVER!*" The official quickly looks round and gives me a funny look.

"River? What's that all about," he asks.

Thankfully play takes over, so I don't have to explain, which I'm glad about, because today the river looks a mighty long way away.

As it happens, with their win and winning bonus point safely in the bag, Blackheath start getting ready to go home, and we salvage some measure of respectability with two forwards, Simon Willet and Chris Howick, going over for tries. At one stage, Lynda even jokes that we're "drawing the second half. And come to think of it, we won the second half last week. Perhaps we should draw up our own league table based on second halves." Not so fast. Blackheath summon up one more try of their own at the death. We've been hammered. Hammered. 12–55.

The really depressing thing about this is that Blackheath were not that special. They were perfectly proficient but (as their league position suggests) not much more than that. They passed the ball well (which is historically appropriate since – surprise, surprise – they invented this aspect of the game) they ran strongly, and basically they knew where to stand. Perhaps they had brought a sleeve-full of tricks with them, but if so, they weren't called upon to show them. What has happened to the Dale team, that this time last year was riding high in the table? Let's have a check…

Crikey! Of the Wharfedale side which started against Coventry on this weekend last year – and won, by the way – only four players were in the run-on fifteen this afternoon. So, if we're wondering why we're not the same team, the answer is simple: we're *not* the same team. And this new team really is new. Half of them, it seems, are fairly new into long trousers: at last week's game, Gordon's programme informs us, our average age was just twenty-three.

And Gordon has another revealing statistic up his sleeve. In our first and second teams last week, no fewer than fifteen siblings took the field. This, of course, is precisely the kind of statistic of which, under normal circumstances, Wharfedale are hugely proud, since it really does underline how much of a family club we are. Yet these don't feel like normal circumstances. How abnormal they are can be revealed by one last statistic. When Rob Baldwin snapped his cruciate ligament, less than a month ago, we were 8-0 up against the league leaders. Without his physical and mental command, since then our points tally looks like this – F:38; A:126. With stats like that, we can only be heading in one direction.

As the crowd dwindle away, we stay talking to Steve and Lynda for a while. I ask Steve a question: "How many of our players do you think would get in their team?"

"Hmm. Perhaps Doherty. That's it." Steve thinks a bit longer, and adds, "We've a fair number that might get into their team in a few years time, but not yet."

It's true. At the level of rugby which Blackheath play we've a number of players who have a future. What we need are players who have a present. And a presence.

Chapter 11

~ in which we meet a mythical figure, wake from a dream to find ourselves at Rosslyn Park, the home of prince, and unearth a new Badger ~

When I started writing this book, I was intrigued to find the force behind the club's success. It must, I first thought, lie in the strong voices and vigorous characters whose presence impresses itself on anyone visiting The Avenue. After a while, it dawned on me that there was another human force at work. This one was hidden. It hid behind names. These names were always talked of with warmth and respect, but as for attaching the names to real people, I was clueless. Who *were* they? Of all the names mentioned, none recurred more often than that of Tom Slater. And no body was less visible. Even Chris Baker, who had first played with Tom over sixty years ago and was best man at his wedding, could never find him for me in the clubhouse. Chris assured me that Tom came to every home game, "But nowadays he tends to keep himself to himself". An enigma. Who *was* he?

Eventually, at half time during a game, Chris tapped me on the shoulder and said, "Come on – I'll introduce you to Tom." We wandered along to the other end of the Shed and there, at the back, was Tom. Yes, he had heard about my book. And yes, he would be happy to chat to me. "That's where Barbara and I live," he said, turning round and pointing to a house fifty yards away, "Come round for coffee on Monday if you like."

So Tom was able to tell me how he first came to the club as a sixteen-year old, after the war. Although he came from farming stock, higher up the dale, in Tom's working life he became Grassington's 'Man from the Pru'.

"Within a year of me getting involved, George Harrison had spotted that I knew which way up to hold a pen, and I was made club secretary. I did that until 1981. Family aside, all that time the club completely took over my life. Barbara's too, with her work on the Ladies' committee. But when I stopped, as far as being involved in the running of the club was concerned, I said, 'That's me finished – I've done my thirty years'." The way Tom recalls his sign-off, he might have been clocking out from a morning's volunteering work in a charity shop. And then he shows me the evidence of his labours.

"I've brought these down from the attic," he says, pointing to three plastic crates in the corner of the room. "They're all the minutes, letters, match reports and things – they go back to 1932. The club has never had anywhere to put them, so I've kept them in my attic. If they're any use to you…"

Any use? They're gold dust! The photographs and press cuttings are interesting enough, but the real steal are the minutes. There, in Tom's hand, is the plotline of a club progressing from the unwanted understudy of the local rugby scene, to the edge of the national stage. And throughout, I read the legend: *T. Slater to investigate, T. Slater to write,* or *T. Slater to act.* A silent force.

Nowadays Tom is one of the select band of the club's life members. Yet he's no grandstander – literally or metaphorically. In fact, he rarely even makes it over to that side of the ground. His garden backs onto the minis pitch behind the Shed, where on Sunday mornings he can see his grandson, also Tom, haring around in the Under-10s. I've already been told about this lad: a while ago someone who coaches the minis said to me: "Young Tom's the future – terrific ball skills!"

As well as the view, Tom's garden has a gate which opens into the club grounds behind the Shed, and this reminds me of how the old president of the MCC, Sir Gubby Allen, spent his last years in a flat with a door leading direct into the Lords Pavilion.[20] There, though, the comparison between the men stops. Tom is no patrician grandee who views his own playing time through a wonky, misted monocle. When I ask him about the Yorkshire Shield-winning team of 1957, apart from his memory of breaking an arm in the scoreless first match against Moortown, and being taken to hospital in an ambulance "with square wheels," Tom's telling remark is about the quality of the team: "We must have been comparatively good at the time, but to be honest if you put us up against the present team we wouldn't have a hope. You'd probably have to go down to about the level of our current Thirds to find the standard we played at back then."

Tom may try to downplay the merits of that team, but the club won't buy it. It knows that their achievement laid the foundation for all that followed, and every ten years – albeit with a diminishing band to toast – the club still holds a celebration dinner for the Shield winners.

Back in the day of toothy 0–0 draws against local opposition, Tom Slater could never have dreamed of this. On a balmy October afternoon in West London, the electronic scoreboard really is shining out an unbelievable scoreline:

ROSSLYN PARK 0-99 VISITORS

And it's true – from the moment the Green Machine stepped out on to the field, every lineout has been plucked clean from the air, rucks have been instantly cleared, all the passes have gone to hand, and our backs have been running freely and unopposed. But all good things have to come to an end, and eventually the warm-up is over, the players troop off, and the joker who had been playing with the scoreboard sets all the values back to zero.

Where were we? Ah yes, reality. And that, today, takes the formidable form of Rosslyn Park, who lie joint second in the table, and in many people's eyes will form the most serious challenge to Ealing's supremacy this season. On the forum of *rolling-maul.com* there's a predictions page – where followers of clubs in our division place their bets about the forthcoming weekend's fixtures. Of 54 posts this week, no-one has Dale down for a win, and we're marked down for a solitary losing bonus point by only one forecaster.[21] Everyone – *everyone* – has Rosslyn Park down for taking the maximum five points. I make that an aggregate score of 270–1. Certainly not 0–99. Dream on.

So here we are down at The Rock – Park's ground in Roehampton, just a few miles from Twickenham. This is our first visit to the capital during the league campaign. It won't be our last, either, because here in West London we're in rugby's historic – and National 1's current – heartland. Within about twenty miles of Rosslyn Park there are no fewer than six clubs in our league. To get here we've already driven through Ealing and Richmond, and if the South Circular existed outside the realm of the mapmakers' imaginations, a continuation of this route would land us in Blackheath.

Like Club, Rosslyn Park are another 'F.C.' – with a similar history of misty myth.[22] These days The Rock is crumbling. I think it's fair to say that it's more shale than granite. For better or worse the process of bulldozing away the past is already underway. New floodlights are already up, and plans are

---

21 This poster's moniker is 'Skipton Gardener', so he may not be the most neutral of pundits.
22 Park, for instance, were the first English club to play an international fixture, back in 1892. Past players include disparate greats such as the Russian Prince Alexander Obolensky, and the Wigan Rugby League legend Martin Offiah. Then there's Andy Ripley, an England great who, in his battle against cancer, achieved an almost saintly aura. At the other end of the celestial ladder, and certainly the most 'interesting' character ever to pull on a Park jersey, was a man synonymous with hell-raising – the actor Oliver Reed. Until recently, Reed's legacy lived on here, in the form of the ground's floodlighting, which he personally financed.

well-advanced for modern stands and an artificial pitch. First and foremost, though, Rosslyn Park have gained permission to build big digital advertising boards facing the idle traffic outside the ground: judging by the sparse attendance today, that will be a significant revenue stream. Anyway, let's hope that the character of the place doesn't get cleared away with the rubble, because as things stand it's wonderful. In fact, in some ways it all feels similar to The Theatre of Bleats. True, we're in the middle of a city of thirteen million, not a village of two thousand, and the ambient sound here is not of sheep, but of planes whistling down into Heathrow, but these are cosmetic differences. Rosslyn Park is what the Dale's old guard would recognise as a 'proper' rugby club. The welcome on the gate, and in the clubhouse, could not be bettered.

We've arrived in time to walk Sadie round the ground, and to find the best viewing spot. Opposite the main stand Rosslyn Park has its own version of our Shed, and this looks like the place for us. It's curious, though. Although it's roofed, and has three long benches, there is virtually no rise from pitch level to the back of the stand. In other words, if you're sat on the rear bench, visibility must be restricted to the back of the advertising hordings and the top half of the players. And that assumes there's no-one in front. If there are people on the first two benches, I imagine that the view would be like that from the back of a gallery at The Open: heads, shoulders, and only the occasional airborne ball. My suspicion is that nobody ever sits here.

And yet, as kick-off approaches, I look behind me to see that a fair few people have taken up residence on the back bench. There are only about five hundred here, so it's not as if it's the only place left. I'm baffled. Then the wine bottles and glasses start to come out. And go on coming out. Happy days! Just about everyone who sits down has brought something to the party. This being West London, it's quality stuff, too. It seems that they're a regular little tasting group, and I suspect that they're under the roof on the back row for a reason: after all, no-one wants to have his bottle of Haut-Médoc 2003 inadvertently wiped out by a clearing kick into the stand. His floodlights may have gone, but evidently the spirit of Oliver Reed lives on!

There is something fabulously incongruous about seeing Wharfedale run out in a place like this, amongst the chic apartment blocks of Roehampton. On one side of the ground the traffic is snaking its way round the South Circular, and above there are the low-flying A380s. The buzz of the big city is audible and palpable. When I arrive at a ground like this I always think that there must be some mistake: surely this isn't the place to find our team? Yet here they come, trotting out with all the appearance of normality. What can we do but play our part in the act, by making them feel at home? We cheer, bang the hoardings, and generally behave like well-meaning barbarians for the next eighty minutes.

There is no one way to watch a game of rugby. When I first stood in the Shed and watched Wharfedale play, in the early spring of 2008, I stood amongst spectators. I really couldn't have called them (and on that first occasion it was 'them') a crowd. They clapped when the team came on, and occasionally burbled their satisfaction at a try or dissatisfaction at a dropped pass, but as far as noise went, that was about it. In short, they reminded me of a cricket crowd. Well, at The Avenue that has changed over recent years. Here at The Rock, however, I feel as if I'm back amongst spectators. Frankly, the tasting club behind expect their side not just to win, but to pile on the points and win big. The players do too. When, after a few minutes in which Wharfedale have more than held their own, Park are awarded an easy penalty, they kick for touch and the chance of a try. Evidently they're here not just to collect four points for the win, but five for the win and four-try bonus point.

Sadly for us, Park's confidence is not misjudged. We're stood down at the western end of the stand, from where we see a constant stream of planes dropping over the horizon, and Park players dropping over our try-line. As the interval approaches, they duly score their fourth try. But even though Park's play has been dynamic, with flashing counter-attacks from deep, each try has been greeted by no more than applause from the home support. From those stood up outside the clubhouse I can hear some voices raised, but down on the benches they could be watching a steady opening partnership rattle up a few boundaries. I wonder what Park would be doing to us if their support was truly ignited: as Wharfedale know better than most, when the players and the crowd spark off each other's energy, the result can be nuclear.

Yet first you have to find your crowd. You might think that, with a population of millions, at least that part should be easy, but there any number of people touting the leisure ticket in London. Rosslyn Park are only holding the tiniest corner of the ticket, which accounts for their average crowd being less than Wharfedale's. In Threshfield on a Saturday afternoon the ticket may be a small one, but at least it's all ours.

From a Dale perspective, the less said about the first period the better. Then, on the stroke of half time, Wharfedale kick to the corner, win a lineout, and force their way over. At oranges, then, we're 7–28 down. Are we despondent? Not really, because the Greens are playing with heart and soul. And there's something else wafting around, too. *Déjà vu.* Although no-one is tempting fate, I can't be the only one remembering what happened at Coventry. Well, the script doesn't go quite the same way, because when the players come back out Park rip through our defences twice more: 7–42.

But at this point, the pendulum swings. Chris Steel, last year's captain, makes his return from injury, and immediately starts to make a nuisance of himself in the loose. Experience. There's nothing pretty about Dale's play from here on in, but we've spotted that if Park have an Achilles heal, it is defending the rolling maul. Josh Burridge has been given the back-side's jersey, and is controlling things like an old hand. With ten minutes to go, we may have still only displayed one scoring move – but at least by now we've displayed it three times! So the four-try bonus point is within our grasp – never mind that it's 19–42. Oops! Make that 19–49, as our all-out attack leads to another Park try from an intercept. No matter. Up the field we go again, until with the clock showing 79 minutes our pack is once again motoring towards the Park line. "*RIVERRRRR!*" Caroline, Lynda and I are offering every decibel of support that we can, attracting some fairly odd looks from the home support. There are children around, and they look a little frightened. Yet we're on a roll, and the way Dale's pack is heading, our cloud could just be given a silver lining. "*GO ON!*" This time Park stop our progress, but illegally. Penalty! Yellow card! We now pack down against seven. The nudge is with us. Penalty, but… nothing more than that. Scrum again. Penalty, and… "*YES!*" – the ref runs over beneath the posts to give us the penalty try, and that precious point to take home. We're ecstatic, and the Rosslyn Park supporters, to give them credit, are very generous. "Well done, you deserved it," one gentleman says to me, as if we'd actually won.

Let's get this straight. We've been mullered. We may (yet again) have 'won the second half', but that kind of victory fools nobody but fools. We know that we've come second by a distance. And yet we've got a precious little point to add to our pile. To those who believe that 'winning is everything', rugby's losing bonus point system must be anathema. Perhaps it is, but our relegation rivals will have exactly the same carrot dangled in front of them when they come to the big clubs. As it is, we've fought until the end, and it's difficult for me not to applaud a points system which rewards that mentality.

As we did at Coventry, we make our way round to clap the players off. And here we witness the best moment of the day. As the Burridge boys are greeted by their parents, Dad starts singing 'Happy Birthday' to Josh. Before we know where we are, half the crowd in front of the clubhouse are trolling away. I see Rob Baldwin, here in civvies as a supporter, joining in. And how old is Josh, the senior member of our current back row? Twenty. With Badger no longer on the pitch, we were needing someone to grow into the role. And quick. It looks like we've found our man.

Chapter 12

*~ in which we come face to face with Clarty, welcome
Loughborough, and Adge works his magic ~*

This is getting serious. I don't mean our league position – now fifth from bottom – which is almost always a cause of concern, but my own position in the club. When I had the idea of writing this book, I imagined myself standing back from the fray, reporting hostilities from a safe and objective distance. I knew all the stories about embedded reporters becoming mere ventriloquists for one side or other in a campaign, and I wanted none of that. And then – *fool!* – I mentioned to the programme editor, Gordon, that between times I was a writer. I quickly tried to cover my tracks – it was only a bit of music journalism, and a pseudo-academic tome – but no matter, my card was duly marked: *wordsmith*. Before I could blink, Gordon was asking me how I felt about preparing the programme for a match in November, when he had to be away. How did I feel? Well, I might have had some ethical issues about how it affected this book, but between you and me, I was chuffed!

Thing is, Wharfedale has not only the best venue in National 1, but also, I reckon, the best programme. Ours is certainly not one of those bland affairs in which the perkiest titbit on offer is that the home blind-side's favourite food is his mum's roast chicken. No. What Gordon brings to the table is, above all, spicy. Every fortnight his programme carries a witty little warning 'that this organ may contain opinions' – alongside a caveat that these opinions don't necessarily reflect those of the club.

All of which explains why, an hour before we play Loughborough, I'm wandering up and down the touchline of the Foresters' pitch, trying to find someone I've never met before. Gordon had suggested that I speak to Michael Harrison, our chairman of rugby, about something I want to write on. Who should I look for? Well, I assumed that 'Mr Wharfedale' would be one of the Blazers, but I needed a bit more of a clue than that. For no good reason, a few days before the match I had asked a neighbour of ours – one of those convenient types who just happens to know everyone who is anyone – if he knew him.

"Michael? – yes I know 'Clarty' well. Lovely man. Clever, too. Farmer."

"Right. But what does he look like?"

"Shortish, dark hair, and… you know what a gurning competition is, don't you?"

Well, none of the committee are exactly male models – they're rugby men, let's remember – but from what I can call to mind of the House of Funny Mirrors also known as The Clubhouse, I think I know who I'm looking for.[23]

There I am, then, a few days later, wandering up the touchline until – ah yes! – I've found my man. I confidently tap him on the arm.

"Michael… Michael Harrison?"

"Me? *Me*, Michael Harrison? Ha! Me, Clarty? No!"

"Oh I see. Sorry about that, but you know who I'm looking for, though?" I ask. "Give me a clue – what does he look like?"

"Clarty? He's an ugly bugger! I can't see him around, but he'll be up the touchline somewhere… by the way, why did you think I was him?"

I couldn't possibly say.

And that's not the end of it. By the time I've tapped half the committee on their shoulders and, evidently, slandered their good looks, I'm wondering what prehensile creature our chairman of rugby could possibly be. When I do eventually find him, it's true that he's unlikely to win any beauty contests, but aside from the (non-designer) stubble, he's not that different in appearance to the others. Except for one thing. No blazer. Clarty really does look like a farmer. All that's missing is a belt made of baler twine. But looks can be deceptive. I want to know about an on-going plan to restructure the lower leagues, and since Michael chairs the northern branch of the National Clubs Association, he's the natural person to ask: I quickly feel like a barrister being given a complex brief.

"Don't worry if you can't remember it all," he finishes up, with a bit of a grin, "just send me what you want to write and I'll check it through. I won't let you embarrass yourself in print."

And with that he's off, head down, to his next task. So *that* was Clarty. I've heard plenty about him. He comes from the third generation of Harrisons to be the club's lifeblood. Clarty was the younger of Younce's sons. As a youngster, alongside John Spencer, he played in the new Wharfedale Colts side which Arthur Morgan had set up. He was dynamite. Like Spencer, he played for England Schoolboys, and then captained Leeds University. After that, though, Clarty was never lured to more glamorous clubs. He only ever played club rugby for Wharfedale, first turning out for the First XV when he was just fifteen.[24] The

---

23 My wife points out that the new Deputy Programme Editor – balding, and with a beak like a raven – fits in nicely.
24 This was in 1959, when that kind of thing happened.

night before his debut Joe Stockdale, the then president, came round to the Harrison farm with an athlete's elixir for the youngster: a pint of milk, raw eggs and Guinness. Mind you, Clarty tells me later, "I refused to drink it – it were bloody disgustin'."

Since he was a fly-half, and played on into his forties, not surprisingly Clarty became the club's leading points scorer. All this, remarkably, was achieved with half a finger missing from one hand – courtesy of an encounter with a straw-chopping machine when he was just two. As time went on he was captain, coach, and committee man. Actually, it's probably futile to try and divide up Clarty's contribution into neatly boxed roles. From what people tell me, the simple truth is that Clarty *is* the club.

When I asked Len Tiffany what made the club tick, he just said: "Clarty. He's a brain like a computer – even when he's out on the farm with his sheep he just never stops thinking about the club, working out the next move!" But after he's said this Tiff pauses, because he's aware that although Clarty may be a one-club man, Wharfedale is not a one-man club. There must be something more to why the club is what it is: "These Dales farmers, they're used to adversity, and more than that, to overcoming adversity." And then Tiff pauses again. His first answer was too narrow, and his next too wide. His final answer sounds like a meditation on something he doesn't quite understand, but probably gets it about right: "Harrison, Harrison… there must be something in that blood!"

There must. We've already met Younce and Fudge, and here we have another remarkable pair of Harrison brothers. Clarty, you see, had an elder brother, Jimmy, and Jimmy broke the family mould. He left the area. As a youngster he had played in the '57 Shield-winning side, but to do this he had to return from his studies at Cambridge. There, he played for the university but missed the Varsity match – and so was never awarded his Blue. Then he went to teach in the Midlands, where he played for Coventry. Where Clarty was direct as a player, Jimmy was elegant: "He was a run-at-all-costs man," his brother remembers. Eventually Jimmy came back home, and briefly played down the dale at Otley: he wanted to represent Yorkshire, and there was a feeling then that only by representing one of the bigger clubs in the county could a player get noticed. Jimmy, however, remained Green at heart. His last teaching post was at Ermysted's School in Skipton, where he became deputy headmaster. Whilst there, he returned to a Wharfedale side he had first played for as a schoolboy. By the time Jimmy hung up his boots in 1979 he had played more than four hundred games for the club.

Yet Jimmy's real legacy at The Avenue is the junior section of the club. It was one of the first in the North when Jimmy set it up, and nowadays this bustling Sunday-morning mayhem feels as if it could spill over the sides of the Dale. Young players were Jimmy's legacy. Sadly, he died in 1983, before he could see his own son, Glenn, achieve the Cambridge Blue he never quite managed himself.

Back in the here and now, we've moved across from the Foresters pitch to wait for the main event. About which, there are two imponderables. One is the opposition, Loughborough Students. Like Hartpury, Loughborough boast a team with major prospects in the game. A lot of them have played at international level in their age-group, or are dual registered with one of the big Midlands clubs. The downside of this, for Loughborough, is that they don't really have a settled side. Week-by-week their line-up can change drastically: having lost their first five fixtures this season, last week they trounced Blaydon by six tries to one. About Luffbra, then, all bets are off.

But the real imponderable is *us* – the supporters. In our last outing at The Avenue we didn't even bleat: we lost our voice completely. Was that just because our team gave us nothing to shout for? Or was it because, warned in the programme about being disrespectful of officialdom, some of our loudest voices suddenly became self-conscious? Either way, we can't afford to repeat that performance.

In any sporting encounter, the minutes leading up to the kick-off are crucial. The coach's verbal skill, geeing-up the players to start with maximum intensity, goes without saying. It also goes without listening – at least on our part. I've no idea what Jon is saying to the players inside, but if it's half as impressive as how Adge is stoking the crowd outside, Loughborough will have no chance.

Adge is on the balcony, right above me, as he starts his words of welcome, and I'm able to study a masterclass in public oratory. In the course of a season Adge will work his way through the whole gamut of rhetorical devices. Although I haven't seen many men in flowing white robes at The Avenue, any passing Ancient Greek would spot the common species, like alliteration and analogy, and on occasion would witness rarer birds, such as epanalepsis and epizeuxis, taking wing.[25] Today it is the rhetorical question which is taken out of its cage. After amplifying Loughborough's credentials (a little lulling flattery for our guests and their supporters) and enumerating our own deficiencies, Adge has

---

25 These two terms meaning, respectively, 'banging on about something,' and 'banging on and on about something.'

posed an unspoken question: *what can be done?* The question he ends up voicing, however, is subtly different: *what can we do?* At this point he leaves a pause for us all to ponder what, in truth, is the only possible answer: *we can support!* Now the tide of his rhetoric has turned, and we are soon flooded by waves and waves of ways and means in which we can lift the team. As Adge signs off with a final exhortation flung into the Dales air, what questions do we harbour about the final outcome? *None.* Within about three minutes Adge has taken us from a smiling welcome, to despair at the reality of what might await, to the certain knowledge of what we can do, and what then *will* await.[26]

When the team runs out a minute later, they are greeted with a huge roar of support. In the warm-up Loughborough had looked significantly larger than us, but either they have shrunk, or we have grown, in the last few minutes, because from the off we're all over them. Even up the hill and into quite a wind, we're first to cross the line. The roar intensifies. And it's not just a roar. There's a great clanging sound off the hoardings, a significant part of which is emanating from just in front of me – courtesy of the coach's mum and my wife. And here I spy a rare chink in the Dale support. A few yards up the touchline from us I'm aware that an elderly gentleman, suavely dressed, is giving the bangers a truly withering stare. On their behalf I stare back. Two minutes later there's another roar, another clang, and another frosty stare. This, unmistakably, is disapproval. Is he planning to carry on with his silent objection for eighty minutes? We're in Yorkshire, for crying out loud, where our reputation is for plain speaking! I wander up to the gentleman and, with a smile on my face, ask a benign question.

"Are we alright up here."

Small pause. "Er, fine thanks."

Another pause. "Good." I wander back.

And that's it. That's the extent of this dispute in the Shed. But it does set me thinking. I had spoken to him because I was entirely sure of my ground. In other words, we've just been asked to make as much supportive noise as we can, and we're doing just that. As long as we're within the RFU's Code of Conduct (and we are) then if the scoreboard acts as a bangometer, turning over in our favour as the decibels ramp up, then that is all the justification needed. Tiff certainly thinks it helps. "Oh, it's you who bang the hoardings is it?" he said to Caroline when he discovered where the noise was coming from. "Great – that's worth a point or two!" As far as I'm concerned, and with respect to the gentleman stood

---

26 For all Adge's rhetorical strategies, perhaps his finest quip was the Freudian slip to end all Freudian slips. For the time and effort he had invested over the years, Adge was publicly thanking the President of the *Cock o' the North* Colts tournament (an unfortunate title, bearing in mind what was to follow). To startled looks from those gathered in front of the clubhouse, Adge observed how the President, "was still putting it in there, taking great pleasure from what these young lads have to offer."

a few yards to my left, this has nothing to do with personal sensibilities.

A game at The Avenue provides a pretty good pie-slice of the Dales community. It's a rural area, so there isn't much of a racial mix, but all classes and ages are represented, and that means it's a perfect goldfish bowl to observe how our character is on the move. The English (and yes, that actually includes Yorkshiremen) are traditionally thought of as reserved: we don't complain in restaurants, but nor do we hug the chef. Isn't that how we've always been? Well no, it isn't. It can come as a shock to realise that our stiff-upper-lip stereotype is only recent. Before the Victorian era, the English had a reputation for being effusive and unreserved. So, as far as the past is concerned, English reserve is a myth. How about the present, though? Perhaps our reserved behaviour is actually dissolving back to its unreserved state. Younger people seem to have much less of a problem in telling others what they think, or even how they feel: I wonder whether the younger people in front of us – the team – would prefer us to restrain or release our feelings? I suspect it's the latter. When I come to write it, the match day programme might just be a place to try and ask a few questions.

My thoughts are interrupted by a Loughborough try. And another. Aided by wind and slope, the general consent is that this afternoon Loughborough should have about a ten point advantage in the first half. At half time, then, when we're only three points down on the board, the Dale support is far from gloomy. We think we're still on course. Still, just to be on the safe side Adge takes to the tannoy again, just to remind us of the part we can play.

In fact, we've underestimated how much the conditions will favour us in the second half. Within three minutes of the restart we're ahead, and by the hour-mark we've got the four-try bonus point. And there's another to follow after that, so that with ten minutes to go we have the almost-forgotten luxury of an unassailable lead. Steve has felt sure enough to join us, abandoning his sentry point behind the posts: for about the first time during a match that I can remember, he's even lost his vexed, nervous look.

So this is it. This is what we come here – hoping – for. The low sun is canting its colours over an autumnal Grass Wood, the team are rolling on towards victory and, crucially, we know that we've played our part.

When the referee blows his final whistle we've won 38–20. A last roar and the game is over. Not the glow, though. We walk round to the bar with a lifted feeling – one of those rare moments in life when success, friendship and beauty coincide, and you would quite like the clock to just stop a while.

I had almost forgotten what the clubhouse feels like when the matches are over on a day like this. That's right, *matches*. In addition to the main event, the

Foresters have beaten Loughborough Seconds, and our Thirds have beaten Selby. That makes about sixty very happy campers, and that's before we've even got round to the spectators. It's busy in the bar, yes, but there's nothing particularly boisterous about the atmosphere. For all the fabled relationship between rugby and drinking, it's easy to forget that straight after a match, the majority of players will feel utterly spent. Later on, well, that's a different matter, but right now, no-one is on the charge.

Jon Feeley comes over to join us and, for the first time in a while, I'm not chewing my tongue in an effort to find anything acceptable to say to him. Actually, there's no need to say anything – just a thumbs up and a nod. Five points closer to survival.

Chapter 13

~ in which we travel to Old Albania to find out what an alickadoo can do, and to wish that he sometimes didn't ~

When you're brought on as a sub, and thrown a pass, there are two basic options: play it safe, or take a gamble. If there's nothing on, then fine, take option one. But if you see an opportunity, what will you do? Anonymously shift the ball on, or have a dart and risk it? It's a dilemma, and now that I've been passed the ball of doing the programme for our next home match, it's one I recognise. The safe option is to go down the route of flattering platitudes – to welcome the opposition, thank the officials, thank the sponsors, and offer some general words of flannel about the last match and the season so far. Yawn. Readers of the Wharfedale programme expect a bit more of an angled run than that. Perhaps I can head off in a slightly different direction. There's a risk that I will find myself isolated, and look a bit of a fool, but nothing ventured, nothing gained.

So what's the opening I've spotted? It's this. On the field the club is represented by a group of men with an average age of just over twenty. Off the field, in the committee room, the club is represented by men with an average age of, well, let's just say plenty over twenty. There's a gap here, and I don't think there needs to be. I'm not kidding myself that I can speak with the voice of youth – the voice of the team – but perhaps I can get them to speak for themselves. It would be good to hear what they have to say, and how they feel about the club. That, of course, is assuming that they *do* have feelings for the club. Perhaps, in an age of dual-registration and regular club changes, they have no great loyalty to the Dale. If so, I could end up getting nowhere. Still, I've seen what I think is a gap, and my instinct is to run into it.

Right. Where do I start? The coach is the obvious first target. A couple of days after the Loughborough match I email Jon, and tentatively ask him how he would feel about writing something. I'm cautious, because the only person I've mentioned my idea to has warned me that the team and those around it really won't be interested. "They'll be too busy," I'm told, and since they all work as well as play, I could understand that.

Still, it's half term, which may just mean that as a teacher Jon has a bit more time on his hands. I'm pleasantly surprised, ten minutes after clicking 'send', when I get a reply saying that yes, Jon would be *delighted* to write something. And I'm pretty much floored, the following day, when his piece arrives. Far from trotting out the usual sporting clichés, Jon launches into a passionate proclamation of his pride in coaching Wharfedale. Best of all, from my point of view, in recalling the last home match against Loughborough, Jon leaves no-one in any doubt about how the team view the noise of the crowd:

> *On such days, the atmosphere at The Avenue is unrivalled. It makes a difference. The roar is not just a noise, it is an indication of the passion we share for this club and how we are all emotional stakeholders in it. Suddenly the opposition do not face fifteen men, they face the whole of Wharfedale. It lifts the spirit and physical resolve of the players. In fact, it makes the difference.*

So much for English reserve! Some of the old guard in the Shed might raise their eyebrows at the directness of what Jon says, but when they read this they will hardly be in a position to question his loyalty to the cause. Do they? Perhaps. A bit. Thing is, Jon was not one of those who was born with Green blood in his veins. He was brought up in Bradford, and then spent his playing career at Leeds, Wakefield, Sedgley Park and Rotherham. At the end of his career Jon did eventually come to Wharfedale, theoretically as a player and backs coach, but by then a persistent injury was tapping its watch in his direction, suggesting that as a player, his time might be up. The Dale crowd, then, never saw Jon in a green shirt. They've never *cheered* for him, and I can't help but feel that he's suffered for that. It's not, I sense, that anyone one is against him. They just don't know him.

Soon, I think, the crowd will know the coach a little better. How about the captain's thoughts? I'm encouraged now, so jot down a few questions for James Doherty. The gist of them is that I want to find out not what James's favourite film, food and computer games are, but what makes him tick. I email him some centre and left-field questions. The first thing I ask James is why he was so clear in his mind that he wanted to come back to Wharfedale. And this, a couple of days later, is his succinct reply:

> As for what drew me back, it wasn't the standard of rugby, because we could play in chip shop league 5 and I would still play here. It's the bond people have here. It's intangible; you can't bottle and sell it. It is incredibly special.

Again, I'm struck by how much one of the generation at the Dale's coalface is shot-through with the unique vein of Wharfedale. To me, that's really all that counts. On the field and off, they may express themselves in a different way to the older members, but as long as the same spirit is there, I think we should all be content.

I'm getting ahead of myself here, though. We have an away match to deal with before my match programme. And trust me, I really *would* like to get ahead of myself and fly over the away game with Old Albanian. A sour afternoon, both on the pitch and off. Still, reality is reality, and we need to deal with it. Ready?

As with most grim experiences, this one begins with that most treacherous of all sirens: hope. Even more hazardously in this case, hope singing to us and sounding suspiciously like expectation. Old Albanian have yet to win this season. So, for once we've driven southwards without reservation. And now that we've arrived, and the match has started, our optimism has only increased. We haven't actually scored, but our pack has rolled theirs back twenty yards, driven over them in the first scrum, and won a penalty. We're right down in the corner, and rather than kick from out wide into a stiff breeze, we go for the lineout and drive. Right in front of us, we can clearly see that already the heads of the opposition players have dropped. Two of them are even involved in a rather tetchy dispute behind the posts: it looks as if at least some of them are already resigned to a long and fruitless afternoon's work. As for us, that first try on the march to victory is surely only moments away.

But no, as things turn out, that penalty is our high-water mark in the whole game. The Albanian pack decline to engage with our maul, leaving us offside. From the penalty, the wind sails Albanian's clearing kick into touch, back in our half. And hold on, what's this? One of our flankers is hobbling off. Our back row is already threadbare, and now we've lost one of them. Make that two, because five minutes later the other Wharfedale flanker is off injured. Now two thirds of our back row is playing out of position, and at a level which they could hardly have dreamt of at the start of the season. Josh Burridge, who at no. 8 is left trying to guide the substitutes through, is only a fortnight out of his teens. Behind him, Dohers at scrum-half is trying to organise an equally callow midfield. By degrees, the opposition begin to realise that they're not playing world-beaters. Their heads start to rise.

Now that we can see their faces, we can ask who these Old Albanians are. The first thing to say is that they are neither old nor are they Albanian.

Once upon a time they were old Albanians of a sort, when this was the club of St Albans School old boys. Nowadays, probably stronger than Albanian's relationship with a school, and more significant, is its link with another club. Saracens. Even walking through the car park this afternoon, there was no escaping the elephant in the room, since a number of cars are daubed with the Saracens logo. Yes, the club which topped the Premiership table last season use the lavish facilities here — seventy acres of pitches, and one of those gleaming clubhouses which feels as if it's only one mouse-click away from an architect's computer screen — as its training base. They have a vested interest in the success of Old Albanian, then, and a number of the Saracens squad are dual-registered to play for both clubs. A modern reality. Sometimes a blessing and sometimes a curse.

Over on the other side of the pitch, men are setting up a Guy Fawkes' Night firework display for later this evening, so for the match we have stayed by the clubhouse and bar. A mistake, as things turn out after the break. We've gone in at 7–7, and with the benefit of the breeze in the second half, we're still hopeful (if no longer expectant) that we will win. Sadly for us, during the break the home team have evidently been persuaded that this is a match they *can* and *should* win. More to the point, they've evidently been told *how*, because when Old Albanian come out for the second half, they target the breakdown and our midfield, and they're away. If they need any further encouragement, the wind in their faces soon dies to nothing. They run in try after try after try after try. We, in contrast, remain scoreless for the whole of the second half.

So from a Dale perspective things turn ugly on the pitch, and soon they turn ugly off it. As Albanian find their feet, their supporters find their voices. During the first half they have been quiet, drowned out by our healthy support, but as they recognise a probable victory they find a very positive spirit. We, on the other hand, find a very negative one. We? In truth, it's only a small minority of the Dale support that take a nose-dive. To our right is a small group of middle-aged Dale supporters. Alickadoos.[27] They have a dress-code of fashionable tweedy jackets, club ties, and denim jeans. I think the look is supposed to be that of the rural sophisticate. Looks, evidently, can be deceptive. They don't like what they're seeing in front of them, and start to offer some fairly unsophisticated observations. Actually, it's only one member of that minority who really sours things. But as they say, it takes only one bad apple to spoil the barrel, and I

---

27 Where does this word come from? Legend, or at least Wiktionary, attributes the term to an old Irish player, who remarked to a team mate reading a book "You and your bloody Ali Khadu": this, I should point out, would be more believable if there was actually a book or author called 'Ali Khadu'. Another origin Wiktionary suggests dates from amateur days, when hard-pressed club helpers, asked for more balls, players, games etc., replied "it's all I can do": eh? — I mean, how much do you have to drink to make that phrase sound like 'alickadoo'?

bet that if afterwards you had asked Old Albanian about the visitors on their touchline, we would all have got a collective thumbs-down. In particular, their right wing can't have been too impressed. During a break in play when his side already have victory in the bag, this player is standing in front of us down on the touchline.

"Oy you!" one of the alickadoos calls out towards the winger. Pause. "Why're you wearing pink boots?"

To which, impressively, the young lad answers back as he points down at his feet. "What, these? I just found them in the physio's room. They look good on me, don't you think?" He's having a laugh, but the lout on the touchline is having none of that. In everything he says there are big befuddled pauses, as his thoughts swim around, trying to clamber out through his mouth in some kind of order.

"Pink boots're for ponces," he shouts. Pause. "Are you a *ponce* or *WHAT*?" He's yelling now, so half the stand behind can hear what he has to say. "You *ARE* aren't you? You're a *PONCE!*"

Before the winger can offer an answer – I'm now thinking that "maybe in your dreams" would have been good – the play has moved off.

Standing on the touchline and looking out, what strikes me at the time is how many of our own team are wearing coloured boots. Hmm. The lout is only a few yards away, and I can't resist shouting a question back down the touchline to him.

"How about our full-back's pink boots? Is Taylor Prell a ponce, then?"

"Good point!" one of his pals answers me, still sober enough to feel a bit embarrassed. "Hey," asks the loud-mouth, trying to laugh the thing off, "is Taylor Prell a ponce too?"

Pause. "Aye, probably."

The more sober alickadoo smiles at us, points at his loud-mouthed friend and makes a drinking gesture. *Never!*

Alickadoos, like dual-registered players, can be a blessing or a curse. Last year, in the match before Christmas, a group of Dale supporters travelled on the train down to London dressed as a gaggle of Santa Clauses. They drank their way down south, drank their way across London, and eventually arrived at Blackheath for more of the same as they watched us pull off a notable win. The Club supporters thought they were a hoot, and even if the Santas were incapable of getting back across town in time for their booked journey home, and had to buy new tickets (ouch!) for the last sled back to Yorkshire, their bonhomie won the day. But hold on! Isn't the key word there 'won'? We *won* that day at Blackheath, and it's easy to look like winners when you are, well, winners. You find out much more about the character of people when they are losing. And that's emphatically what we're doing here at Old Albanian.

Anyway, I've no wish to start a slanging match with anyone – what's the point when at least one of us won't remember it tomorrow morning? Albeit with a significant nudge from my wife, we edge away up the touchline. I now find myself next to a lady I've never met, and during a break in play I'm trying to apologise to her about some of our supporters, but she cuts me off.

"You needn't apologise to me." She gestures to her husband, next to her, and says "I'm afraid we're with Wharfedale too."

"Oh right. Parents?" I ask.

"Yes." They're giving nothing away.

"Of…? I ask.

"We don't like to say really until we see how he's done but, err, it's the captain."

"Well I've not met him, but he's done well for me already this week – I did a piece with him for the next programme."

"So you're Simon, then? He told us about the interview – he liked doing it."

I'm still standing beside Steve and Maria Doherty when the whistle blows. We've been thumped: 7–31. Not even a bonus point, and this against the lowliest opposition we've yet played. Without doubt the low point of the season so far. After the cheers and handshakes, James sees his mum and dad, comes over, and leans his head over the railing. For a moment I think he's going to be sick. Not the best time, then, for his mum to introduce him to someone. She does though, and he's good enough to offer me a hand and a sort-of smile. We even share a few words. Then his head drops again. Silence. I can't help it, but I feel I've got to say something.

"I'm sorry…" I start, but can't think of anything to add. As soon as the words come out I realise that I'm not getting any better at consoling losers. What exactly am I apologising for?

James looks up at me, puzzled: "It's not exactly *your* fault, is it?"

Perhaps I will eventually learn that sometimes silence has its place. And today of all days… well, I'd like to just draw a line.

If only I could draw a line. But a few days after our visit to Old Albanian, a letter is published in the *Craven Herald* which biliously brings back the bad taste of last weekend. The correspondent is a rugby fan, who by chance came across the alickadoos returning home last Saturday.

> *Rugby's hooligans?*
> *After a great day at Twickenham, I travelled back to Skipton on the train from Kings Cross.*
>
> *I sat in a coach with half a dozen men in their fifties, some wearing Wharfedale Rugby Club ties. As they continued to drink and swear through the whole three-hour journey they delighted in offending the unfortunate men, women and children in the coach with their foul language, breaking wind and sexually explicit and grotesque songs.*
>
> *The train was full with nowhere to move to. A brave older lady eventually told them what she thought of their appalling behaviour, but this made no difference to them and they clearly enjoyed the offence they were causing. I was sickened by their behaviour.*
>
> *Does Wharfedale know it has members who behave like football hooligans?*

There we are. *No-one is saying we were angels* – and here's some fairly damning evidence. Apparently, what we had seen on the touchline at St. Albans was only half the story. For the powers that be at the club, I assume that this letter will be pretty devastating. Wharfedale, remember, aims to be the best community rugby club in the country, and here it is being shamed in its most public local forum.

There are Marxist sociologists who tell us that rugby's 'good behaviour' only represents a corrupt deal between the bourgeois and the Establishment (let's face it, we do call the referee 'sir') and that soccer's unruliness is a glorious expression of the proletariat's dissatisfaction with authority. Others will point out that a rugby crowd's aggressive impulses are satisfied by watching a full-blooded contact sport, whereas the soccer fan is frustrated by watching what is, at least in theory, virtually a non-contact sport. Whatever the truth of the matter, the fact is that to rugby people criticism doesn't get much more devastating than by comparing them to 'football hooligans'. This, then, is surely bad.

Not so fast. Perhaps surprisingly, once I've got over the shock of reading it, I'm actually quite pleased about the letter in the *Herald*. Don't get me wrong: I'd much prefer that there was no cause for complaint. But I'd seen these men at the game, and if I cared to think about it, how did I imagine things had developed afterwards? Did I really think that having got things out of their system at the match, the alickadoos would climb into the quiet coach on the train, open their books and slowly sober up with a coffee and a sandwich? In the real world that was never going to happen. So, if the letter is revealing a reality, then on balance I'm pleased to read it. After all, a blemish can't be dealt with until it has been spotted. And now that it has been, what will the club do? A clue lies in the club records, from 1973:

> *Concern was expressed at the behaviour of one of the members, and it was agreed that conditions would were to be laid down to this member: leaving the clubhouse not later than 8pm on Saturday nights, and not to serve behind any bar. The conduct of this member to be reviewed at next meeting.*

In other words, bad conduct was not tolerated by the club then, and it won't be now.[28]

Every rugby club must occasionally find itself policing the fine line between revels and riots. In Wharfedale's case, the club's position at the heart of the community means that its off-field activities have always been visible. In the early years the club's social life had been family orientated: the annual pantomime, or a guess-the-weight-of-the-sheep competition at the Christmas party. After the war, though, things changed. Now the youngsters wanted to do their own thing. We didn't have Elvis, but we did have the Ray Howson Combo, and the result was the same in Threshfield as in Memphis: hips swayed. To start with, the dances were on Friday nights, until the minutes record 'a general feeling among the players that the timing of the dances was not in the best interests of the club, with games to play the following day.' The day was shifted, but the issues surrounding the dances were not so easily dealt with. Before long, the club received a letter from a member who was, 'very worried about the behaviour of young people at the Beat Dances, which are nothing more than a 'sex orgy'. The Rugby Club's name could become a dirty word.' Needless to say, where there were winsome deer, there were also frisky stags, and they were willing to lock horns. The minutes are darkly suggestive about quite what was going on.

> *4 December 1973: Item: Mr Rigby be reimbursed for the cost of his spectacles, which were damaged while keeping order at the last beat dance.*

> *5 February 1974: Ray Howson Combo booked for the next Beat Dance. Behaviour at dances again came in for long discussion.*

---

28 I was right. I found out much later that the club did deal with it. Firmly. I didn't see the alickadoos again.

7 May 1974: Sgt. Gains addressed the meeting about last week's incident at the Beat Dance.

The club took control of its clubhouse, but outside the doors it wasn't — *isn't* — so easy. On one level, Wharfedale have my sympathy. They have a problem that most other rugby clubs don't have. There is no football club within forty miles of The Avenue — at least not one that travels the country and so unwittingly allows its worst fans to behave as if they're invisible to their own community. Every locality has its larrikins, but most offer them a choice of venue. For sporting maladroits in the southern Yorkshire Dales it's WRUFC or nothing. Ours in a broad church, it seems, open to all. In this sense, I have to admit with a sigh that Wharfedale really is a community club.

Chapter 14

~ in which we find a special tree, welcome Blaydon and Mr Salami, and find ourselves happily talking nonsense ~

Behind the Wharfedale clubhouse, in the middle of the car park, stands a horse-chestnut tree. Cath's tree. Most visitors to The Avenue will never notice it, but then, neither would they have noticed what Cath did. Not directly, anyway. But they most certainly would have noticed if she *hadn't* done what she did.

Cath was Younce's wife. She was also unofficial team secretary, although that doesn't even hint at her real involvement. Clarty's wife, Christine, tells me her mother-in-law "did everything for the club. *Everything*. Cath posted notifications out to the players – who was in what team for Saturday – and if a player couldn't make it, he had to ring and give backword. But there weren't so many backwords – because that meant speaking to Cath, and the players were genuinely frightened of doing that. Cath was a gentle character – until that phone rang."

When I ask Chris Baker about these phone calls he withers at the memory: "You'd ring up and tell her that your wife was due to give birth on Saturday, and there would be a pause at the other end of the line: 'well, can't you come on afterwards?' she'd say." An exaggeration, I'm sure, but from the lack of levity in Chris's voice as he remembers those calls, not *much* of an exaggeration. If Cath did end up buying someone's excuse, she then had to re-jig the teams and make sure people knew.

Then, come match day, there was the small matter of feeding the teams. At least here Cath was only one of a number. The Ladies' committee doesn't exist any more, but a generation ago it acted as a great counter to what the men were doing on the pitch. Jane Stockdale, the current hooker's grandma, remembers their work together in the clubhouse with nothing but pleasure: "Hard work, but great fun!"

Then there were the parties. Jane shows me a black and white photo, from the Sixties, of at least forty children gaggled around a smiling Santa Claus. She points out her son, Richard, in the front row. My eyes nearly pop out when I see this photo: I've sometimes looked at the current players' children in the clubhouse and thought of it as a healthy little crèche, but it's nothing like this. "Quite something, isn't it? Well, that was the club's children then," Jane says. "At one Bonfire Night party someone came in to tell me that a rocket had just landed on Richard's head. I was busy cooking, and I just thought 'Oh well, another parent will deal with it'. And of course, someone did. It's true, we really were a family."

Looking back on the old division of effort – the men showing off out on stage, the women grinding away behind the scenes – the simple response is just to scoff: simple, but simplistic. Things were different then. And, of course, things were about to change. Inside the club, playing numbers just became too large, and the catering was put in the hands of professionals. And outside, in society, a far more significant change was underway. The tide of gender equality was turning, and increasingly women wanted some action.

Now, if you asked Dale folk to list the players who have learnt their rugby at The Avenue and gone on to represent England, I suspect that most would come up with a very singular list: John Spencer. Actually, John has company.

Caroline Dean was only fifteen when she pulled on a Wharfedale shirt, as a member of Wharfedale Ladies. There were only about twenty playing members, and Caroline says they were all local. In that respect, then, the women's team was remarkably similar to the first men's team. Here's the difference, however. Back in 1923, few youngsters left the area. In the mid-nineties a lot did. Caroline Dean did, for one. Though still playing for Wharfedale, by seventeen she was also playing for Yorkshire, where she was spotted by an England selector. They wanted her to go down the elite route, and that meant the road down to Leeds. So Caroline left Wharfedale for Leeds Carnegie, and within a year was making her debut – and scoring – for England. Cruelly, that was her penultimate cap. Just before the 1998 World Cup she suffered a horrific knee injury, which seven operations have never quite put right.

Caroline went on to teach PE down in Leeds, and for years could barely even bring herself to watch a game of rugby. "To be honest," she tells me, "I was just angry inside when I saw someone in my position." As for the women's team at Wharfedale, when others left the area it dwindled and then went into abeyance. This is one of the few stories with Wharfedale that doesn't seem to have a positive ending. But hold the back page! Although Caroline still works down in Leeds, last year she moved back to Threshfield. Her links to the village are strong (her family still have the farm across the lane from Clarty's) and so are her links to the club (her male forbears all played for the team). Caroline still loves sport, and she loves working with young people. Perhaps the Wharfedale women's team is dormant, then, and not extinct. I hope so, anyway, because the greater the role played by women in the club, the healthier we all are. If the men–only antics down at Old Albanian reminded us of one thing, it's that when a club loses touch with half of its community, it loses touch with the whole of it.

Remember that ghastly home match a few weeks ago, against Blackheath? The one where the team forgot to play and we forgot to shout? I'm reminded of it this week when I'm writing the programme, one part of which is to introduce the officials. This section needs nothing too portentous – maybe a few words of flattering familiarity with a referee who comes to The Avenue regularly, or perhaps a witty welcome to a touch judge making his debut here. Not bribery, exactly, but let's put it this way: we don't want them badly disposed towards us, do we? But in doing my research, I realise that one of the linesmen, Dave Edmunds, was also officiating when we played Blackheath. There's a fifty percent chance, then, that Mr Edmunds is the man who, during the second half of that game, turned round to the Shed and encouraged us to get behind our team. Well was he? I'll email him to find out.

> Hi Dave,
> Can I ask... when you were running the line at The Avenue last month in the Blackheath game, were you opposite the clubhouse in the second half? If so, you may be the one I'm referring to in the following bit of my programme for the Blaydon match:
> 'Having been rightly reminded, by the regular editor of this tome, that our vocal duties as supporters are to shout for our team and not against the officials, in the match against Blackheath last month we seemed to undergo an identity crisis and forget how to do either. We were virtually silent – so much so that far from instructing the officials on how to their jobs, in the second half, we in the Shed suffered the crushing embarrassment of having an official tell us how to do ours. It's true. During a break in play the Assistant Referee turned round and suggested that "you should get behind your lads – they'll play better if you do" etc. etc. Oh, the ignominy! Here was the Shed, the 'bear-pit', being given rudimentary vocal tuition!'
> So Dave, was that you?
> Thanks,
> Simon

And the answer:

> Thanks Simon,
> Yep that was me, at least give me the credit of mentioning me by name!
> Best,
> Dave

No problem. I insert his name into my text, at the same time amending one fantastic typo: according to the team sheet Clarty has sent me, our tight-head prop will be Ja*ne* Armstrong.

When Saturday comes, I realise that this is going to be a day to test the strength of the Wharfedale support. For a start, bizarrely timed to coincide with virtually every club rugby match in the country, there's the small matter of England playing the All Blacks, live on television. That should knock a bar or two off the gate for our game: thanks for that, Twickers. Then there is a Saturday morning of November rain straight out of the Old Testament: thanks for that, Baal.

It looks like this might be a day to test the strength of the Wharfedale team, too. Earlier in the week I have heard that neither of the flankers, injured last week, is back in the frame for selection. And then I hear that Luke Stevenson, the latest on our conveyor belt of fly-halfs, has gone down ill. So at the last moment two players are catapulted into the team. Firstly we will have the services of a new face – a fly-half called Jamie Guy who, according to those who saw his debut in a green shirt for the Foresters last week, is a Good Thing. He's currently a law student in Leeds, having come down here from the North East. And here comes the first irony: as a junior up there his previous club was today's opposition, Blaydon. That irony is compounded because his fly-half mentor up there, Andy Baggett, began his career down here at Wharfedale. Predictably, we're expectant about the new face. But we're also excited that an old face will be making his return – our little grenade of a flanker, Dan Solomi. The word is that Dan had to be persuaded to play. Without at least a run-out for the Foresters, he doesn't think he's yet ready to come back at this level. Perhaps Dan would feel inspired if he could pop out of the changing rooms to hear Adge's build-up.

"We're all looking forward to seeing Dan again, flying off from beneath the studs of the Blaydon boots, and swerving between the blades of grass as he runs down the field. Welcome back, Mr Salami!"

So how come we should all be not just surprised, but amazed, when within minutes of the game starting, Dan does his trademark trick. Like any good dodger, he hides the sleight of hand (in this case getting hold of the ball at the back of a ruck) from all his observers: the first we know about it is when he's already away. He doesn't seem to bother with an acceleration phase – he's just straightaway at top speed, eating up the yards towards the Blaydon line with a machine-gun stride. We on the touchline have seen Dan's trick a hundred times, and even we are caught unawares. Likewise the Blaydon forwards, who are left swirling around as the thief gets away. Sadly, Dan's team-mates look as surprised as anyone else. Dohers is the first to fly off after him, but can't quite get there in support before the Blaydon full-back. The move ends just short of the line, but the effect on the crowd is electric. We have something to cheer about.

Make that two things. On quarter of an hour Jamie Guy charges down a kick, picks up the rebound and flies past a straggling defence to score. The last of the morning's rain clouds have been blown away, and even though we're playing up the slope and into the wind, we're 10–0 ahead. More than that, we're actually *playing*.

As usual, when things are going well it is the backs who catch the eye. But for as long as we can remember, when we play Blaydon we're shunted off the ball at every scrum. This afternoon, even though Blaydon's granite front row is the same one we've made no impression on in the past, right now we're steadily chipping away at them.

Blaydon are no push-over, though, and although they're starved of their usual possession and position, as the match progresses they come back at us, so much so that with ten minutes to go they have managed to get themselves a seven-point lead. Despite this, the momentum is more and more with the Dale. Blaydon are holding out in desperate defence. We have the slope, and despite the small crowd, increasingly we have the roar. Not surprisingly, it's the hard core of our support that makes all the noise. The Green pack is virtually on the Blaydon line when its progress is halted. Illegally! Not just a penalty – quickly converted – but a yellow card for… who's that? Irony of ironies – it's our ex-player Mr Baggett.

Now the wind is in the Dale sail, and with four minutes to go it is the will of the club to carry our scrum onwards. It's the old refrain, and this, as the pack scrunches up and over the Blaydon line, is roughly how it goes.

riverrrrrrrrrrrrrrrrRRRR**RRRR!**

Try. Job done. As Tom Davidson lines up the conversion, the rest of the team troop back to half way, and I see Jake Armstrong applauding the crowd. Nice. It's almost as if the team want to have a roar too, because in injury time, as the pack set down for a final scrum, Dan Solomi is vocally braying a final bit of steel into his colleagues. So much for his diffidence about playing. We win the scrum, the ball goes out, and we've won the match.

Jon had written in the match progamme that 'the roar from the crowd makes *the* difference', and today at least there really is no arguing with that. Or is there? As the final cheer subsides I hear the diffident-sounding gentleman behind me. He's nominally talking to his friend, but I suspect that since I have one of the louder voices, what he says is also intended for my ears.

"I mean, I can see the sense in calling out 'river'," he says, "but shouting 'river' like that really makes no sense at all."

Sense. I'm wondering what sense, if any, the eight men in the Wharfedale pack have of what we call out. Do they hear the word 'river' at all? If so, do they really notice – *tut, tut!* – that some of us in the crowd are erroneously throwing the emphasis onto the weak syllable of the word? Come to think of it, are they really bothered about the literal sense of whatever it is that we shout? I mean, if they actually hear the word 'river', do they really think they are being encouraged to drive the opposition back over the try-line, through two wooden fences, through a field of sheep, down a steep bank and into the waters of the Wharfe? I somehow doubt it. Perhaps their understanding of 'river' is a little more figurative. Perhaps, in the maelstrom of the pack, they really hear no word at all, but just sense our sense.

Sense. An odd word. Let's just take a step back. We've spent the last hour and a half watching thirty grown men, wearing fancy dress, throw around a mis-shapen simulation of a pig's bladder. That might seem a nonsense in itself, but the really nonsensical part of our charade is that its outcome has mattered, to varying degrees, to all of those present.

And that makes me wonder: what, of all that human beings do, makes *sense*? Here is a fairly comprehensive list of things which I think, on balance, sometimes make sense.

Food. Health care. Irrigation systems in sub-Saharan Africa. Law. Sex.[29]

And now a very selective list of things which might make no sense in themselves, but which help make sense of people's lives

Armagnac. Baudelaire. Cannabis. Dancing. Embroidery. Faith. Gaudi. Hermès. Inspiration. Jewellery. Koala bears. Love. Monty Python. Narcissism. Optimism. Parties. Quince. Rock climbing. Sex. Topiary. Unicycling. Vacations. Wagner. Xylomancy. Yorkshiremen. Zabaglione.[30]

---

29 Philosophers might take issue with all of these except the last: let's face it, they wouldn't be doing much phi-losophising without that one.
30 Can I recommend this A–Z as a useful game to while away a tedious car journey?

I'm happy to say it's that second list into which rugby – playing it, watching it, shouting about it, and even writing about it – fits. Sense, I reckon, can be vastly overrated.

Chapter 15

*~ in which we venture west to Fylde, to see the lights go
on and off, and on and off, and… ~*

With a few minutes to go before the scheduled start of our match away
to Fylde, the players have run out and, unusually for a club match, have
formed two respectful lines facing the stand. The crowd hush, and a bugler on
the clubhouse balcony starts up. Heads bow. It is one of those moments where
we are asked to put our present recreation into perspective. I don't think there is
a person here who does not respect the sacrifices we are marking. But does this
small ceremony trivialise the game we are about to play? That depends.

The previous day I had been hospital visiting. For Geoffrey, the elderly
gentleman recuperating in the hospital bed, he was finding this to be a tricky
time. As an ex military man he should, by rights, have been lining up alongside
his former comrades at various Remembrance Day gatherings this weekend.
And he wanted to see the ceramic poppies down at the Tower of London.
Still, as a selfless stoic, rather than dwell on his own inactivity, he wanted to
know what I had been up to. I told him about our rugby travels, and when I
mentioned my inability to find suitable words for a gutted captain after the Old
Albanian match, I saw Geoffrey stiffen slightly.

"I could think of something," he says. "How about 'get over it – it's only a
game. It's not important'."

"Of course it's not important," I fire back, "and maybe that's why it's so
important."

Geoffrey gave me a puzzled look. With some hesitation, I started climbing
onto a little hobby horse of mine.

"Look at this way, Geoffrey. In last Saturday's game thirty-odd grown men
got together and chased round a field for two hours. I admit, it sounds pretty
ridiculous. But as they did it they got rid of every aggressive atom in their
bodies, and yet nobody got maimed, let alone killed. No lands were annexed,
and no-one was exploited to a state of poverty. Actually, bridges were built –
everyone shook hands and had a beer together afterwards. As I see it, anything
with that kind of function makes sense – it must be pretty important."

"I see what you mean, sort of… just so long as they don't take it too seriously," Geoffrey says.

"Sorry, but it doesn't work if they don't take it seriously. How can they get rid of all the aggressive stuff if they don't put it out there and let it go? It *has* to be serious."

There was a pause. We weren't exactly going to fall out over it, but neither, I sensed, were we going to see eye to eye. Understandably, to a man like Geoffrey, who has known war, sport will always be just a bit of fun. To me, never having known war, sport is one of our prouder marks of sophistication. Oh, and I think it's fun too.

Fun? Now let's cut to the end of the Fylde match, and ask a question. Does the scoreboard ever lie? As the players troop off the field, through the mist and murk of a November twilight, across on the other side of the Woodlands the lights on the board are shining out with an unequivocal message…

FYLDE 35-3 WHARFEDALE

…which doesn't suggest that we've had fun at all. What we are being told, in short, is that we've failed abysmally, and have every right to be despondent. The scoreboard is telling Fylde, on the other hand, that they have succeeded, and should be celebrating. Yet these are not the messages that anyone present seems to be receiving. The Fylde supporters, who have been justifiably grumbling for most of the match, have now stomped straight off for the exit. Not us. As the final whistle goes Lynda says, "Come on, we should go round and cheer the team off." And it's not just a few of us. There's a sizeable Dale contingent here, and together we make an informal guard of honour to leave the team in no doubt about how well we think they've done.

Yes, on the scoreboard that counts, Wharfedale have registered only a single, paltry penalty, and been trounced by the opposition, but as far as we're concerned, they've played like real winners. What we've seen this afternoon, if it is replicated until April, should keep us up. There is no irony when I hear one of the committee describe it as "the performance of the season so far." And yet that scoreline still stands: 35-3. This, I admit, will take some explaining.

To account for how we feel about something afterwards, we need to bear in mind what were our expectations beforehand. Ten days earlier, if we had been offered a haul of four league points from our next two fixtures – playing Blaydon at home and Fylde away – we would have gladly taken them. Well, we had garnered all four points from the first of those matches, so anything that we get from the second will be a bonus. And let's be realistic. We're playing Fylde away and, err, they're good.

So we've driven over to the Lancashire coast with the feeling that we're on a bit of a jolly. Even the weather doesn't depress us. November has caught up with us at last, and as we take the dog for a walk on the front, there is a stiff breeze blowing up a very frigid-looking Ribble estuary. But in lovely Lytham the Christmas tree is up, and the lights are in place for their big turn-on later this afternoon. It's buzzing.

It's buzzing a mile up the road in the Fylde clubhouse, too. This could be an intimidating place for a Dale fan. At The Avenue we have relics and mementos in the clubhouse, yes, but nothing like this. The walls at Fylde are draped with photographs and old international jerseys from Fylde's past greats. It was only three years ago that Jason Robinson played his last game – in a Fylde shirt – and his British Lions and England shirts are there for all to see. Then, from an earlier generation, there are the outsize shirts of Roger Uttley and Wade Dooley. There are plenty of others, too, but one man overshadows all in this place. We're even standing in a bar named after him. Bill Beaumont was one of the first publicly recognisable figures in English rugby. He captained the national team, and the Lions too, but it was after he retired that he became something of a National Treasure, as an avuncular team captain on *A Question of Sport*. We see Bill at Wharfedale whenever Fylde come over the Pennines, and even though he's chairman of the RFU, when he's at The Avenue he comes over to watch in the Shed. That little act of humility always gets a nod of respect from the home support. Massive character, miniature ego.

Sadly, Bill isn't here today. His position with the RFU means that he has to be down at Twickenham for an England international. That match kicks off half an hour before ours, and is there for all to see on the big screen in the Fylde clubhouse. On dual-attraction afternoons at The Avenue the screens stay resolutely blank. Doubtless screening the international match pulls in a few wavering supporters, who can keep an eye on both their teams at the same time, but for me, it just doesn't work. People linger in front of the screen until the last possible moment, so a good number are not outside to cheer their team on to the field. Then, as half time approaches, they're already filtering back inside to catch up on events at Twickenham. Juggling two balls at once like this is perfectly possible. Yet to me, what these people are missing is the rhythm of the live act they've come to see: the slow rise in intensity before the curtain goes up, the suspenseful respiration in the interval, and that final exhalation when the drama is resolved. The Dale support, probably because they have made the greater effort to be here, are out earliest, so when the teams run on we pleasantly surprise ourselves on the decibel register.

Perhaps the team are pleasantly surprised, too, because they get the better of the earlier exchanges. And then things take a sharp, barely credible turn.

It's not just that over the next fifteen minutes we lose four players to injury. It's *who* those players are – all key men in their departments. First up Richard Rhodes, the sole remaining executant in our Department of Ball Appropriation, agonisingly dislocates a shoulder; then our expert in the Faculty of Breakdown Studies, Dan Solomi, is hobbling to the sideline; next comes a bad concussion to Jamie Guy, the new Professor of Strategy; and finally the young whizz-kid from the School of Velocity, Taylor Prell, limps off on one leg.

Although we quickly see a blue flashing light pulling into the car park to take Richard Rhodes to hospital, the really worrying injury is to Jamie Guy. He gets up after his concussion blow, but he's tottering, and can only flap, in a half-remembered gesture, as one of the Fylde centres barges past on his way to the line. I watch the incident later on *YouTube*, and it's disturbing. We hear afterwards that in the first concussion test on the field, Jamie was asked about the man next to him in the back-line: he looked at Tom Davidson, but claimed never to have seen him before. Funny, but not funny.

Miraculously, this is the only score which Dale have conceded by the time that all our wounded have been cleared to the various field stations. Even more improbably, we have scored one penalty, to trail by only 3–7. More than that, the balance of possession and position is definitely with us. How come? Although it is a team game, there is often one player who provides the galvanising focus for a good performance. Who could that be? It's not immediately obvious who is the real thorn in Fylde's side. And the fact that its not obvious gives me a clue about where to look. If it's a back, or even a back-rower, who is causing the damage, identification is easy. Whatever they do, they do visibly. But if it's not obvious, look at the small numbers. Although we can't see what's going on at scrum time, the referee thinks he can, and more than once points accusingly at the Fylde loose-head which – *aha!* – means that our tight-head must be doing a proper job for us. And now I come to keep an eye on our 3, I suddenly realise that he's omnipresent in everything we are doing well.

How, I wonder, does it feel to be Jake Armstrong in this team? He's still only 21, and has played for England at age-group level since he was 16. A similar biography to Taylor Prell, then, but whereas a running back will always garner plaudits on the touchline, the admirers of a good front-rower will be closer to home. I've noticed that whenever Jake's name is mentioned to anyone in or around the team, the reaction is always the same – a blowing out of the cheeks and a disbelieving shake of the head: in a word, *Respect*. Jake is very much the aspiring professional. The word is that he lives and breathes training and playing. Where would we have been this season, I wonder, if Yorkshire Carnegie had come calling for Jake? Certainly not pushing Blaydon around last week, or

Fylde this: although I very much doubt whether Jake will still be with us this time next year, just for now we're counting our blessings.

One way or another Fylde are feeling the heat, and after half an hour have accrued two yellow cards. There's a dark comedy to all this, though. Almost every penalty we win is out wide or back beyond half way. We kick for touch but, inevitably, with six squat front-rowers now in the pack, but nobody of any great height, proceed to lose every single lineout. Back we go, only to win another penalty and start the cycle again. We can almost laugh about it, albeit in a gallowsy kind of way, because we know that we're never in any danger of winning the match. Fylde, to be frank, are unconcerned. They knew they were better than us before we started, and now they have seen most of our key players depart, that knowledge has surely only grown. It all reminds me of watching Wharfedale play Otley back in the Yorkshire Cup Final: we knew we were better, but forgot that knowing and being are rather different states. Fylde have forgotten that too, and the locals aren't impressed.

On the stroke of half time Fylde are roused by the voices of discontent amongst their support. They wake up and score a second converted try. There are three more – unanswered – to follow in the second half, but from a Dale perspective, realistically we could not be happier. The spirit is fantastic. It is almost like a poker game between the players and support. Don't ask me which side started it, but every time the team lay down something for us to cheer, we on the touchline raise them a cheer back. They slap down something even more cheerable, and we raise them again. On it goes like this, until with about five minutes to go the Fylde supporters are bemused onlookers.

Inevitably, we've lifted the team so high that when it comes, the fall is from a tall cliff, and the result is messy. Most of the team suddenly have that stiff, cramped gait. We saw Jake Armstrong being treated for an injury early in the second half and thought *not him too!* But Jake is still there, even if by now he's virtually hopping. There are those, I know, who tell you that physical tiredness is all in the mind. I don't buy it. A lot of it is in the mind, I know, but eventually physical chemistry will have the final say. So in the final five minutes, our team's legs just won't play any more. Fylde run in two gratuitously wounding tries. One gentleman actually turns round to apologise to us: "You really didn't deserve that." It's a nice thing to say, but the truth is that in a game of rugby you only deserve what you get. And in truth, if Fylde had played to their capacity for eighty minutes, we would have got a good deal worse.

After the final whistle, and the cheers, James Doherty rounds up three of the Fylde players for a photo his mum wants to take. James was brought up just along the coast from here, and was in the same minis team as three of the Fylde players. James is grinning away in the middle of the group, but as soon as the flash has gone, the Fylde boys trudge off, heads down, to join the rest of their team back in the changing room. I may be wrong, but from their body language I don't think they're expecting too many slaps on the back. James, on the other hand, joins the rest of the Dale team, who are still outside. They're spent, but smiling. Someone has gone back to our team bus, grabbed a case of beer, and is handing a can to each player.

What on earth have they got to celebrate, you might ask? They have done their best, but it's more than that. A league campaign is a war, not a battle. They've clearly lost a battle today, but what they've found in the process is a spirit which, when the wind of happenstance starts blowing with us and not against us, may well see us through.

Chapter 16

~ in which we get to know Adge, head to Cinderford,
and enter a forest which is not enchanted ~

In September 1968 a rather exotic creature landed in Wharfedale. As it came north, this migrant from warmer climes was actually first spotted in a school car park in Skipton. It was Jimmy Harrison who made the identification.

"You must be Ian Douglass. Welcome to Ermysted's. First teaching post, eh? And I hear you play rugby. Well I hope you do, because Wharfedale are playing Otley tonight, and you're propping!"

'Ian' didn't last long at Wharfedale. Within a few weeks, this new arrival had become 'Adge', nicknamed after the cider-drinking lead singer of the Wurzels. The resemblance between Adge Cutler and Adge Douglass was more than just a Zummerzet twang: they were both charismatic frontmen. Despite being the only non-Yorkshireman, Adge says that he was instantly accepted by the team. And it wasn't long before he became Wharfedale's unofficial pack-leader. True, as a member of the Durham University side – top-dog back then – he already had some serious playing credentials behind him, but there was more to his status in the Dale eight than that. Again, it comes back to character. Len Tiffany played with Adge for ten years, and has stood alongside him on the touchline for the last forty. When I ask him about Adge, he throws his head back. Pause. Eventually comes the comment: "Adge – what a man!"

So what distinguishes Adge? After all, lots of rugby men can bray and bawl. That's only half the story with Adge, though, because when you catch him on his own, Adge's first instinct is inwards: he listens, absorbs, considers, and only then responds. Yet give him a bit of a crowd – it can be eight or eight hundred – and his first instinct is outwards: his antennae are still picking up signals – he's never happier than when he provokes "a bit of banter" with his audience – but he's always willing to provide the initial charge. It was this extrovert side to his character that made Adge a natural pack leader.

"There was nothing particularly tactical about what I did," Adge tells me. "I was made vice-captain to Clarty eventually, but as far as leading the pack was concerned, it was really just noise. 'Riverball' came from me, you know? It was just supposed to signal an intent. It was a rallying cry."

Adge stayed at Ermysted's for the whole of his working life. At one time there were four teachers in the Dale team. Mid-week they coached at school, and between them made sure that the pupils with rugby potential were pointed towards Wharfedale for their weekend fun. There, the boys were told, they would find a junior section without parallel in the area. Again, the club stole a march on its local rivals.

As for Adge, by 1977 he had to accept that his playing days were over. "My final demise came captaining the Seconds at Barrow-in-Furness, when I crawled off the pitch like something coming out of the sea. A bulging disc. It had happened over time, but by the end of that game I felt virtually paralysed."

Retirement from the team, then, but not from the club. Adge took on a formal role, as chairman of selectors, which he did for twenty-five years. But it has been his informal role, as The Voice of the club, which really marks him out. He speaks at club dinners, on the balcony before games, and since leagues were introduced, after home matches. Ah yes, Sports Report! The first we know of this regular event in the clubhouse is when we see Adge climbing onto a chair, and we hear the following song…

> *Di-dum, di-dum, di-dum, di-dum,*
> *Di diddley dum di-dum,*
> *Diddley dum di-dum…*[31]

…being started up. Adge conducts, and soon everyone is singing. This must be audible in the upstairs bar, since the next thing we sense is a rumble of feet coming down the steps. The room is suddenly full, but over the tops of people's heads we can see Adge, pint in hand, ready to give us the run-down on the day's events in National 1. Results, ups and downs – that kind of thing. This is, I have to admit, a highly selective broadcast. If we lose, it doesn't get aired.

"In the early days the crowds at matches were smaller, but more of the crowd stayed on afterwards: drink-driving was not such an issue then. It was the atmosphere that gave me the oxygen to do the reports. And Clarty would say to me, 'Don't do it now – wait half an hour!' because the bar till was still chinging. Before the internet there was a lot more secrecy involved – only *we* knew what the results were. Still, even now, the visitors seem to enjoy it. Mind you, they only have to listen to me once a year."

---

31 These, as most of you will have no doubt spotted, are the words of *Out of the Blue* by Hubert Bath, which for over sixty years has been the theme tune of BBC radio's Sports Report.

Adge has stayed up north with us. As he takes up the microphone on the balcony before a game, visitors may find themselves momentarily dislocated at hearing Adge's alien call. Locals regard him as habituated – although we never take it for granted that a species of such vivid plumage has chosen to make this his home.

And at this point we head south west ourselves. A few years ago, when Redruth and Launceston were in our league, we would travel as far as Cornwall. But the far South West, like the far North, has suffered from the geographical contraction of the moneyed game, and these days the furthest we head in that direction is Gloucestershire. Cinderford, to be precise.

Now, before I sit down to write about each game in this season, there is an emotional barometer that I need to tap. In due course I will need to recall the external conditions on the day, and obviously the elements in the game itself, but first and foremost I want to remind myself what the weather was like inside my mind. How it all *felt*. For the most part, when the needle swings round and reminds me of how I sensed each match, I can hardly wait to write up my experience – be it about that sunny victory away to Hartpury, the feeling of the wind in our sails against Blaydon, or even how the team's spirit lit up the November murk of Fylde. It's not like that when it comes to our trip to Cinderford. Yes, the sun was shining, but that is emphatically not how it *felt*.

And this is a pity, because of all the away games in this book, probably the one I would most like to shine out with a warming glow would be our trip to Cinderford. The tale I want to tell here is of a penniless but spirited club, a club defiant of rugby's moneyed realities, which represents a community hidden in the folds of beautiful country. In short, I want to tell a story about a club which may be a distant contact of ours in miles, but is a close neighbour in spirit. And I'm sorry, but I can't honestly do that. Another day, perhaps, but not today.

Let's get one thing dealt with first. We lost. *Again*. And this loss was a particularly bitter one to swallow. It was against a side second from bottom – almost certainly a rival candidate for relegation – and despite having taken at least a consolation point back from the strongholds of Coventry and Rosslyn Park, from lowly Cinderford we came away with precisely nothing. What made it particularly galling, though, was that with the final play of the game we were heading for an unlikely draw, the significant consolation of two points, and then… well, I'll put off reliving that ghastly moment for as long as I can.

I wonder what you know about Cinderford? Perhaps you know where and what it is, but a lot don't. And to understand Cinderford RUFC, you really do need to know something about Cinderford the place. At this point I could come over all poetic, and say that Cinderford lies in the heart of the Forest of Dean, a knotty whorl of ancient woodland between the sylvan Severn and the winding Wye. Or I could just say that it is roughly equidistant from the M4, the M5 and the M50. They're both true, but I'll stick with the prosaic motorway locator, since most people I know seem to have driven round Cinderford but not to it. Major roads, or rail, have never really penetrated the Forest, leaving it relatively isolated and under-developed. And if by now you are imagining a rural idyll, think again, because beneath the glorious oaks of the crown forest lie coal and iron.

For all the beauty of its surroundings, Cinderford itself is really a mining town, with all the cultural baggage you might expect – brass bands, miners' clubs and rugby. Except that now, of course, it is largely an *ex*-mining town. When the industry declined fifty years ago, a virtual dustsheet was thrown over Cinderford's town centre: the bloodless architecture and absence of chain shops there now take us back to another era completely. Driving into Cinderford is a shock, if only because the approach to it, through the knolls and hills of the forest, is so beautiful. I have been here before (we lost that day too) and I wondered afterwards if I had imagined the smack to the eyes of Cinderford. But no, it hits me in exactly the same way today.

I've noticed that trips down to the Forest of Dean raise a few eyebrows amongst the Wharfedale die-hards. To them, Cinderford is regarded as positively genteel compared to the club ten miles down the road. Nowadays Lydney play in the division below us, but they used to crop up on our annual fixture list in National 1, and visits there were an Experience. Gordon has told me of a Dale visit there a few years ago, when a late decision cost Lydney the match, and nearly cost the referee his well-being: "A few of them came down the tunnel and tried to kick the referee's door down. Our president tried to calm them down and was very colourfully told to mind his own business." Before the days of league rugby, the London clubs would occasionally come down here to play in the John Player Cup, and on one famous occasion at Lydney a Saracens player had his throat grabbed by a spectator *during* the match. Perhaps that Lydney fan had misconstrued the word *hospitality*.

By comparison, Cinderford is a sociable place. And at least until the game starts, it is. The clubhouse welcome couldn't be more warm. And I should report what my notes tell me – that when we arrived at Cinderford the sun was shining. But my notes also tell me that, despite the sun, and one of the driest autumns on record, I had wet feet by the time I'd walked round the touchline to the far side.

I can only explain this by pointing out that the ground is carved into a hillside above the town. It is a design which might be effective for a reservoir, but for a flat pitch is a design asking for… well, a reservoir: the pitch looks wet and heavy. A fair few of the spectators at Cinderford look like retired props. Good mining stock, perhaps, but is it a coincidence that the pitch here responds best to those who move forwards with the resolution of pit ponies?

In theory, this heavy going should have suited us down to the ground. Didn't we finish last week's match with nearly half a team of front rowers? That might be one way of looking at it, but another is just to say that last week's match nearly finished half our team. All last week's injured are still out, and after the team sheet has been posted for Cinderford, two more backs pull out with illness. Even during the warm-up I can hear coughing and spluttering, and as he walks off Jon confirms that there are two or three more out there who would be better off back in bed.

The saddest news, however, is that one of our most popular players, winger Scott Jordan, has given up the unequal struggle of travelling from Chorley three times a week, and signed for Preston Grasshoppers. Scott has a young family and another child on the way, and for all the hole it leaves us in, from the club there is nothing but goodwill to him.

The team are all square pegs and round holes, then, and they look like it. Cinderford put the kick off high in the air, and our two make-shift locks dutifully move right underneath it. So far so good. But I'm almost beside them on the touchline, and notice that as it sails in their direction neither calls for the ball. Down it comes and – *bong!* – hits one of them smack on the forehead. Oh dear. The referee, back on the half-way line, calls it as a knock-on. Those of us closer to the action know that it isn't, but not even the errant player demurs. I think he's too embarrassed to complain.

Allow me to give just the briefest gloss to the grim eighty minutes that follow. Cinderford start poorly too, but gradually it dawns on them that it's only our low numbers that pose any serious threat. By half time Cinderford are 19–3 up, and it's not just their players who are growing in confidence. Next to me on the touchline is a cubic man who seems determined not to win gracefully. I've tried to break the ice, and have a benign laugh with him, but his own humour is a bit more spiky. He hears me shouting for the Dale, gives me a little dig in the ribs, and points down at the team sheet.

"Which one of your team is called 'Dale'? Sounds like you call them all 'Dale'… one big family up there, are you?"

Now that must be a first, I'm thinking. Someone from the Forest of Dean making this old joke, and not just being the butt of it. *Ho, ho!* When Cinderford are penalised at the breakdown at the far end of the pitch from us, he turns round to me and asks whether the referee travelled down on our team bus. *Ho, ho, ho!* Frankly, he's a good bit bigger than me. I'm not going to kill with anything other than kindness, so a while later I fling him a titbit of flattery. Alright, *spiced* flattery.

"You know," I say, with a big smile on my face, "I think your team have done *amazingly* considering that the ref has been against you throughout the game."

Does he taste that I've laced my titbit with irony? Perhaps later he might, but for now he's too busy tucking in.

"We've not done badly for a second team, have we?" he says.

I can't resist.

"Really – your Seconds! It's been quite an odd match, hasn't it then? I mean, your Seconds against our Thirds!"

But then events on the field in front of us take over. During the second half Wharfedale have fought their way back into the match, and with a minute to go cross for a second try which, once it has been converted, leaves us only seven points adrift. As things stand, we have a losing bonus point to take away from this dire match. Could we have more? Cinderford kick long, and we start moving up the field. We're just daring to believe that if we score again, we could come out of this trial with the most unlikely of draws. Two points. And then, another clanging calamity! As the ball is moved along the line, the same player who began the match with a knock-on lets his desire for structural symmetry get the better of him: he knocks on again. Worse, one of his fellow forwards dives straight on the ball – *ugh!* – meaning that we give away a penalty for offside. So, with the final kick of the game Cinderford duly knock the ball over, taking them to ten points out, and taking even our meagre bonus point away.

Does it get worse than this? I really, really hope not. Every supporter, once in a while, will ask themselves whether it is worth it. There, on a damp and chilly touchline at Cinderford, having been demoralised by the opposition and derided by one of their supporters, I had my doubts. It was a long way to come for less than nothing.

Last week, roared on by a large travelling support, the team put in a monumental effort. This afternoon, our support has been thin on the ground, and the team look like they have been out there on their own. For the first time this year, we choose not to go round and cheer them off. We've kept on shouting for them during the match, but now it seems better just to leave them alone. We climb straight into the car and edge our way out of the car park.

Sometimes, when we leave The Avenue, the queue of traffic is held up at Toft House Farm by cattle being driven back up the lane for milking. However much this typical Dales scene might engage the rest of us, the cows themselves just nudge obediently forward, nose to tail. Their heads stay down, and their hooves clacker and splash through the slop. I'm reminded of this familiar scene as we drive out of the car park at Cinderford, and have to pause to let our own team make their way off the pitch and over the lane to the clubhouse. I can hear the players' studs, scuffing heavily over the tarmac, but other than that, they are silent. They look ponderous. And we have much to ponder.

Yorkshire Cup Final 2014

A tale of two scrum-halfs — Woody wings it, Doherty waits

Winners!

The club is...

The Shed – a lonely place
for an opposition winger

The Tin Man –
Chris Baker

Adge and Tiff

Jill

...the people

Sports Report –
Spencer and Adge

The coach looks down

Clarty

A rocket lights up The Avenue
Taylor Prell goes the length of the field against Richmond

Launched

Landed

Lynched

Riverball: a game within a game

Dohers points to the river...

...and the pack find it

Dan's darts

...ewer see how they start...

...than how they end

In all weathers

Rugby Football — the Foresters
in the rain against Darlington

Jamie Guy skates away
against Coventry

Pink socks for Tom Slater

Badger as water boy

Ball boys

Young Tom in the pink

One of our forwards meets one of theirs: Jack
Barnard proves that size isn't everything

Result! — Dohers leads the team off after
a victorious end to the league campaign

Chapter 17

~ in which we explore the club's mystic runes, host Richmond, and see a spectacular rocket take off ~

You know that feeling when you have to steal yourself to study your bank account? Well, since we played Tynedale two months ago, and our league account was blooming, I have been hiding the reality of our slide towards bankruptcy. Enough. Time to take a deep breath and see how things stand.

23 November 2014

1	Ealing Trailfinders	12	57
2	Rosslyn Park	12	53
3	Coventry	12	48
4	Fylde	12	45
5	Richmond	12	40
6	Blackheath	12	34
7	Esher	12	33
8	Tynedale	12	28
9	Blaydon	12	27
10	Hartpury College	12	26
11	Darlington Mowden Park	12	22
12	**Wharfedale**	**12**	**21**
13	Old Albanian	12	20
14	Loughborough Students	12	20
15	Cinderford	12	15
16	Macclesfield	12	5

Not good, eh? Right now we need something to galvanise the club. How timely, then, that the night before our next match, at home to Richmond, we have the members' dinner, upstairs in the clubhouse. In more ways than one this gathering has the feel of being in an Upper Room, and it is here, for the first time, I realise that the language of the club shares something with the language of a religious cult. From amongst the committee and wives on the top table David, the chairman, rises to intone the grace and then, at the end of the dinner, offers a concluding meditation on the club's three mottos.

First there is the official motto – *vis ex montibus venit*, or 'strength comes from the hills' – which reminds us that what we are is where we are. Simple.[32]

Then there is the unofficial motto – 'keep the faith' – which sounds trite, but in this context is layered with history and identity. We all know where we sit in the league right now, and how the mindset of the whole club will be key to our survival. The importance of keeping the faith has already been addressed by the evening's main speaker. This is Daniel Harrison, sometime scrum-half of this parish and now Deputy Headmaster at Sedbergh School. Oh, and son of Clarty. Daniel tells of key moments in the club's history, when only the dogged conviction of a few individuals kept the light burning.

Every club has its Days of Destiny, but Wharfedale's list is far too long to digest at one sitting. We'll come to them in due course. The more instances that Daniel cites, the more it becomes clear that Wharfedale's repeated escapes from fate must have something more than continued good luck behind them. Dice just don't fall that way so regularly. No, only something as irrational as a faith – one strong enough to move hills – could explain Dale's long litany of deliverances.

The third and last motto David and Daniel talk about is the pithiest of all. Just two words: 'get it'. If you 'get it', whoever you are, you are welcome into the club. What, you might ask, is to 'get'? Simple – the club is bigger than you are. You may be an ex-England international, but if you turn out for the Firsts you will receive exactly the same tiny match fee as the ring-in from the Colts lining up beside you: there are no stars. You may be the season's top try scorer, but you will wait in vain to be awarded Player of the Year, because there isn't one: there are no stars. If you buy into that mentality, then you 'get it' – and you're welcome.

The speeches at the dinner, then, are like a renewal of vows. A necessary renewal. After two successive defeats, and a perilous slide down the division, it's a vital reminder of why we are all here. And even though the team are not present in body, when the last drinks have been drunk and we step out into the cold night air, it feels as if in some way the club is resolved.

As for the players, when they trooped off the field last week at Cinderford, at least they knew the great consolation of league sport – that in a week they would have a chance to make amends. That said, in this case there are certainly no guarantees of consolation. Next up are another London team, Richmond.

---

32 In the manner of inter-faith borrowings, we have of course taken this motto from the Christians. They, in turn, had taken it from the Jews. My own hermeneutical study of this text, though, leaves me in no doubt that the psalmist ultimately had in mind the Green Machine.

Currently they lie fifth in the table, but the really sobering statistic for us is that a few weeks ago they ran in seven tries whilst drubbing Coventry. Still, when we turn up at The Avenue on Saturday we're all buoyed by last night's event, so...

...bring on Richmond! Here we have another of the great antiquarian London clubs, another 'F.C.' In fact, Richmond claim the kudos of playing the first game of football of any sort – an *Association* Football match against Barnes in 1863.[33]

Richmond's first rugby match was the first ever inter-club game, against... that's right, Blackheath. Any other firsts? Ah yes, the first club ever to play under floodlights, and the first club ever to play at Twickenham. In recent years it also had the honour of being the first professional rugby club in England. They were bankrolled by a tax exile who took them up into the Premiership, took them up the road to the Madjeski Stadium in Reading, then took them in one long slide down to administration. Bankruptcy. For Richmond, the professional era has been a game of ladders and snake. But the amateur club was reformed in 2000, since when they have been steadily climbing back up the board. And now here they are, back at the highest level of English national league rugby: The Theatre of Bleats.[34]

In relating the essence of the game that followed, it's mighty tempting to fast-forward to the final minutes. What we witnessed then was, without a doubt, the most spectacular finish to a Wharfedale match that anyone at The Avenue can remember – a firework display that lit up the November gloom. Yet that would be to miss out on the essence of rugby itself – that finding empty air for the shooting rockets late in the game is only possible when the grim groundwork has been done first. So, the early contender for man of the match is again the young prop, Jake Armstrong, who at the first scrum drives through the Richmond loose-head to win two equally important things – a penalty from the referee, and a huge roar from the crowd. *Game on!*

The next player to catch the eye is another youngster, Josh Burridge, who is growing in stature by the game. We're still missing both of our regular lineout jumpers, so it seems that Josh, at back-side, has taken on this responsibility himself. There he is, calling the calls with a perfect poker-face, then executing his leaps immaculately, and after eight minutes he's driven over by the rest of the pack for the first score of the day.

But let's get one thing straight: Richmond are better than us. Once they wake up to the realisation that to win this match they are going to need to *play*, they should make life very difficult for us. And they do. With the slope in their favour, they cross the Dale line twice before half time, so we go in to oranges trailing

---

33 Though this, I note, was two years after the club was founded, which must make the intervening period the longest spell of pre-season training in history.
34 My yardstick here is, of course, altitude. On this scoreboard, we even beat Cinderford.

5–14. What do you think the prediction is in the clubhouse, then? Do we all just do the simplest of sums, multiply by two, and settle for a 10–28 defeat? Not so fast. In the second half we have the slope, but after last night, we also have the faith. No-one needs a reason to have a faith, but in this case we do have a reason. We've shown that we can match Richmond up front, and if, *if* the chance arises, we know we have a special weapon at the back.

This, at any rate, is what I say to a friend of mine who has turned up. Dave is a soccer man, really, but he's heard enough of me talking about the Wharfedale experience to try it out for himself. And, imagining the atmosphere of the gentleman's game up in the balm of the Dales, he's brought his three-year-old boy, Aaron, to soak it up. Poor lad. I hope he's now recovered. All the way through the first half I've been aware of him staring up at me, transfixed by this *adult* behaviour. But when the second half starts, and Wharfedale rip into things with winger Oli Cicognini scoring out wide, the little fellow beside me doesn't know where to look. Around him now, as he stares up through a forest of legs, the adults are thrashing around, being violently swayed by sudden gusts of passion that Aaron can hardly see, and certainly can't comprehend. And as for the noise in this storm! Dave, his dad, looks disconcerted too. All through his life, he tells me afterwards, he's been fed the line that rugby is a game of respect and quiet decorum. Well respect, yes: but quiet decorum – *no way!* When Tom Davidson kicks a penalty to nudge us in front, the clamour reaches a new level.

With ten minutes to go Dale's one-point lead is blown, though, when Richmond rouse themselves again and score a try. If we're going to win a match like this, the usual method is that the pack and the crowd come in close, and in one tight and taut unit we drive down towards the river. Not today. When we next get our hands on the ball, deep inside our own half, it finds its way into the hands of young Taylor Prell. Hold your hats – he's off! Round one defender, round a second, then a kick over the head of the Richmond full-back. It's a race for the line out wide, which the poor Richmond winger can only halt by blatantly tackling our man without the ball. Taylor just about grounds the ball anyway, but the linesman is already flagging furiously. Penalty try and a yellow card! Delirium!

All we have to do now, against fourteen men, is see out the remaining five minutes. But what's this? Richmond come again, and a driving maul takes them to the Dale five-metre line. For us on the touchline, our blood drains as we watch it's momentum. Josh Burridge's blood is pumping, though, and he heroically holds the ball up so that the referee gives us the scrum. We can breathe again, but only just.

Although this is a time for calm heads and percentage rugby, the adrenalin is obviously flowing through the Dale midfield. Right in front of our posts we needlessly fling the ball out wide again, and the Richmond winger races up for the intercept and what would be the simplest of tries. In the Shed, with not a single heart beating, I think most of us would pass as clinically dead at this moment. But Taylor Prell dives inside the Richmond winger to clutch the ball, jinks past him in the same movement, and he's away again. Up to speed in the flash of an eye, he beats another flailing Richmond defender on his own 22, and with a feint to kick and sidestep to the left, a third. He's still only at the half-way line, but now he's flying in clean air with only the full-back to beat. Surely he won't try the same trick again? Why not? Sure enough, up goes the deftest of chips, and when it comes down, this time … *bong, bong, bup!*… it flips straight back into Taylor's hands for him to run unopposed to the posts. He checks behind, leading to a minor collision with the upright, and an unscripted pirouette as he crosses the line, but the ball is safely dotted down.

Does that description sound suspiciously glossed and gilded? Did he *really* take the ball under his own posts, sidestep, then beat four defenders? Was the chip *really* that perfect? Well in this case, you are welcome to check out the details yourself. Wharfedale video each match for the coaching staff, and although normally the recording is kept private, this snippet of Taylor's skill has made it into the public domain, via a national Try of the Month competition. And there it is, now appearing on a computer screen near you. There's no sound to the clip, but you can gauge the mayhem in the crowd from the way that the camera is nearly rocked off its tripod up by the stand. They're jumping over there, and they're jumping over here in the Shed. Unbelievable.

The kick goes over, the whistle is blown, and the crowd erupts for a final time. We've shown faith, and we've witnessed a little miracle. One of the very, very best.

Chapter 18

*~ in which we head off to Macclesfield, where we meet
our prodigal son ~*

When it comes to keeping the faith, there really is no substitute for the wisdom borne of experience. Outside the Macclesfield clubhouse before the next match I bump into Steve. He's talking to our president, John Spencer. Now, both Steve and John are in their sixties, and both have played for, and watched, various rugby teams since they were tots. But when it comes to experience with Wharfedale, there is no comparison. John was born in Grassington, and although he played for Sedbergh School as a boy, for Cambridge as a student, and for Headingley, the Barbarians, England and the Lions as a man, Wharfedale was always the club in his blood. Steve, on the other hand, has been watching Wharfedale for only the two years his son has been coach. There's no doubt that Steve believes in Wharfedale, but is his faith yet firm? Right now it seems to be wavering.

"It's alright beating Richmond last week, but if we can't follow it up with a win against the club at the bottom of the league, it'll count for nothing. And look what happened down at Cinderford. I'm *nervous*."

"Me too," I admit.

John laughs. It's a polite but paternal laugh – the kind of laugh children might hear when they question whether Santa will be able to get down the chimney. It's not that John knows we will win here: he's a smart man and a realist, and he has seen Wharfedale lose enough battles to be aware that anything can happen on the day. But what he also seems to know – *know* – is that if our purpose is sound and our belief strong, we won't lose out in the end. I can only envy John his calm surety.

I dare say that some stellar talents, when they move on from their first club, have no wish to involve themselves in it again. It must be difficult, if you've graced the biggest stages, to raise your act for local rep. Even as a player, John was never like that. He knew that when he returned he would find players like the Harrison brothers, Jimmy and Clarty, and a fizzy scrum-half called John McGuinn: they might play for a small side, but they were major talents in their own right. And they liked to play in the way that John did – with verve!

It's probably no coincidence that Spencer and 'Dai' Duckham were admired by the Welsh, and that Wharfedale were one of the first sides in Yorkshire to play a free-flowing game, with a Welsh-style running full-back. Even without Spencer, who was by then an England star, in the 1971–72 season the first team scored over a thousand points. 'Nipper' Sugden, on the wing, had a personal tally that year of more than forty tries. Ridiculous numbers. What would it be like if Spencer came back to join in the fun? At the end of that season he did return for one match, bringing with him an 'International XV' to raise funds for the club. There was something heartfelt in the way Tom Slater wrote to thank John:

> *We all hope you will once again make the international team in the coming season, but we also look forward to the day when you return to club rugby which I'm sure you will enjoy for many years.*

In the meantime, at least the club could enjoy the success of its prodigal son. When Spencer played for England away to Scotland, Wharfedale arranged a mini tour up to Gala in the Borders. They were at the match, and proud as anything when Spencer scored a cracking individual try. The following morning, John came down to see them at their hotel. He hadn't forgotten his roots.

And eventually, in his late twenties, John did return to Wharfedale. Clarty tells me, matter of fact, about a match down at Keighley around 1980: "By then John's shoulder was damaged. I remember it popping out twice in a match, and both times I wound it back for him so he could play on." As Clarty relates this he gives me a casual demonstration of the technique. I'm thinking how extraordinary this all must have been, until I remember that I'm listening to a farmer talking about his prize specimen.[35]

Creaking body or not, John played on. In the changing room for one New Years' Day match Adge remembers John sitting on the bench reading the paper. Eventually he put the paper down and got up with a bit of a groan: "I see Duckham's got an MBE: all I've got is bloody arthritis!" But on he went, down into the Seconds. And when John McGuinn wanted to mark his fiftieth birthday with his friends, John and Clarty joined him in the Fourths for a day.

Spencer was elected president when he was still playing, and he's still fulfilling that role more than thirty years on. But this afternoon, aside from glad-handing Macclesfield's committee men, John has another job down here. Pictures of today's match are being broadcast Live to the World, and John is acting as pundit. Broadcast? To the world? It's true, we could have stayed at home and watched the whole match live (and free!) on the internet. Please don't ask me quite

---

35 I'm wondering if an inside-centre ever had better service from his fly-half?

how this works, but the host broadcaster is not local to Macclesfield. No, it's a community broadcaster back in the Yorkshire Dales, Drystone Radio, which has obtained the rights – if that's not too grandiose a term. Still, being on the internet means that you don't have to be back within sight of the Skipton radio transmitter to enjoy the coverage: you can be anywhere on the planet. And anywhere, of course, includes Macclesfield, which probably accounts for there being fewer than three hundred people (many of them wearing green) present at the game.

Yet once the players run on, I begin to see that the broadcast is only part of a wider imitation game – one mimicking the kind of experience found at a Premiership ground. So, the teams run out, and "Let's hear it for The Blues!" screams the MC. Or should I call him the DJ? He pumps the music right up as his voice trails off, so it's impossible to tell whether or not the crowd are letting us "hear it." And whenever Macc score, he quickly spins the same jaunty jingle you hear at big grounds up and down the country.[36] With Sale Sharks playing just a few miles up the road, Macc probably feel that they need to offer the same kind of package. Fair enough. And I have to say that off the field the imitation of top-flight rugby is convincing. But on the field? I hate to spoil the illusion, but this is not the Premiership. It's not even close.

It is, in fact, a rather scrappy encounter between two minor teams, one of which is desperate to avoid relegation (that's us, by the way) and another who I suspect are already resigned to the drop. Last season, Macclesfield carried all before them in winning the league below. A tremendous effort, for which their reward has been that, so far this season, they have only a solitary win to their name. That victory came away at Loughborough, which means that here at Priory Park their support has seen them do nothing but lose. A wincing thought. If Wharfedale fans need faith, right now Macclesfield fans must need blind faith. And yet, by half time, Macc are five points up on the scoreboard. Could this be their day? Their followers are almost beginning to believe. As for the Green support, well, if some of us were nervous before the game, by the interval all but our seers and prophets are whittling their nails.

Yet we also know that there are times, in sport, when it pays to be in second place with a while to go. Distance runners like to be 'on the shoulder' as they round the final bend, and rugby coaches probably find their half-time team talks easier when the opposition is just ahead. In this case, other than point at the scoreboard, Jon must need to do little else today. After all, the Dale team know

---

36 The little saxophone earworm in question is called *Tom Hark*, by The Piranhas. To be fair to Macclesfield, there are even more popular options they could have gone for but, bearing in mind their league position at the time, Tina Turner's 'Simply the best' and Queen's 'We are the Champions' could only have been played with the heaviest sense of irony.

that they have dominated possession and territory, and that all they need to add is the killer instinct for the match to be ours.

Normally that instinct would be instilled by our captain, but to judge from the way Dohers is coughing and wheezing his way around the field, that looks unlikely. With his professional rugby career over, James is training to be a primary school teacher. It's early December, and his mum tells me that he's on teaching practice: close contact with little mites has brought him a series of bugs. When the ref pulls him to one side for a talking to, James subsides into a fit of coughs and splutters: there's no doubt that he's poorly, but he's also a canny operator, and the message here seems to be 'go easy on me ref, I'm just not myself today'. It's the referee, though, who really has something to say. When James is asked about this conversation later he laughs it off.

"He just told me that he appreciated my efforts at refereeing the match so far, but if it was all the same to me, he'd do the rest of it. It was nothing, really – he's being refereeing me since I was in minis, so we know each other well enough."

James is not the only one in the referee's ear. Even before the match has started one Wharfedale supporter is muttering to me that his chief worry is the ref – who I'm told we 'know.' And sure enough, after he has awarded three scrum penalties against Macc on their own line but (despite a very visible warning after the second) has not seen fit to award a penalty try or yellow card, I can see hair being torn out over on the Dale bench. But it's not just Wharfedale that are grousing. Macclesfield arms are being thrown in the air too, and one of their staff tells us how we wouldn't even be in the match without the referee on our side.

Right. Let me state a shocking truth: this referee is third rate! But here's another shocking truth: the players are third rate as well! Literally. We're watching a match at the third level of English rugby, in which every single person on the field is performing less than perfectly. If Wharfedale and Macclesfield ever come close to flawless rugby, we will inevitably head up to the Premiership, where doubtless we would attract a better class of referee. But even if that happened – oh, and pigs flew – presumably we would still make the occasional mistake, and so would our officials. I know it's a controversial stance, but as I see it in any rugby match the thirty-three people on the pitch are all humans doing their human best.

Well, with or without the referee's help, Wharfedale step things up after the interval, and Macc start to creak up front. Matt Beesley, another of our young props, barges over for a try. In their desperation to stop the tide, Macc lose two of their players to the sin-bin. As last week, the Dale pack has won some fresh air for the backs to run into. Taylor Prell is itching to have a go, but this week the penetration comes from a less likely source. Only a few weeks back, young

Lloyd Davies on the right wing looked callow: he would run into contact with an upward lift, almost inviting the opposition to hold him up in the tackle. The offer was frequently accepted. Of late he's been going into contact stronger and lower, getting the ball to ground so it can be recycled. *Good.* But here at Macclesfield we see another development. With fifteen minutes to go, when we have scored three tries to lead 25–17, we see Lloyd running the ball from deep, fast, swerving and veering past flailing defenders. *Very good.* He links up with Dohers, who jinks his way past the full-back to score under the posts. *Brilliant!* The game has hardly been transcendental, but for us at least, that moment, and the result is. Another win, and another five points. *Hallelujah!*

The moment when we clap the players off is the time when all the parts of the club – players, committee and supporters – come together. John Spencer is there, patting backs. He's far too benign a man to admonish Steve and I, but right now, if he addressed us as *ye of little faith*, we could hardly quibble.

Chapter 19

~ in which we travel to Darlington to enter a surreal space, come face to face with a reindeer, and hear the sleigh bells ring out ~

It's late on the Saturday morning before Christmas, and we're up at Cam Head, high on the tops above Kettlewell. It feels as if civilisation is a world away, rather than the half a mile we've walked across the limestone edge from the head of the little pass over into Coverdale. For miles to the south, Wharfedale stretches away beneath us, down to where the river kinks around Grass Wood. To the east, on the other side of the pass, snowy streaks slope upwards into the cloud at the top of Great Whernside. If you come this way in summer, for all its remoteness, when the weather is smiling it will feel like an active place: a steady trickle of walkers will be heading up the track to Buckden Pike, and above will be the busy skirl of skylarks. Right now, though, we have the place to ourselves. No people. No birds. Just us, and a few sheep in the lee of the wall, sheltering from the volleys of wind and showers being fired over from the Three Peaks country to the west. This is a place I link with the light of summer, and yet although it's cold and grey this morning, it's a privilege to stand up here. How many sporting fans, trudging around the country in today's December gloom, will have the chance to pass through a place like this? Granted it's not the most direct route we could take to Darlington, but for an extra few minutes and miles we can take in the length of the Dales – up Wharfedale, over into Coverdale and Wensleydale, and down Swaledale to Darlington.

This little intimation of paradise is ironic, because all season I've been grumbling about going up to Darlington Mowden Park. It's not the journey I've been dreading, admittedly, but the arrival. How will it feel to play in a huge, largely empty, echoing stadium? For Wharfedale it will certainly be a first. As things turn out it turns out to be the best away fixture of the season so far. Since the venue turns out to be every bit as vacuous as I had imagined, this is glorious evidence that when the spirit is with you, you can party anywhere.

I'm getting ahead of myself, though. Our match-up against Darlington really began three days earlier, when the second teams of both clubs were slated to meet at The Avenue. A mid-week evening match a week before Christmas? That seemed improbable enough, but the fact that one of the teams was travelling seventy miles for the fixture, suggested that the concept of 'social rugby' holds no sway with our reserve teams. And there was undoubtedly going to be a little edge to this match. Our Foresters don't lose often, but when they visited Mowden earlier in the season they didn't just lose: they were whupped. Beaten by over forty points. So this return fixture at The Avenue promised to be *interesting*.

Still, at half-past six last Wednesday evening, even down the Dale in Ilkley the weather was filthy: driving, driving rain. How 'interesting' would 'interesting' have to be to drag us out on an evening like this, when the fire lay before us in the grate, cooing the words *light me!* We tossed a coin: heads we went, tails we didn't. Heads! Two minutes later we were in the car, not without some misgivings from Caroline: "You know that apart from a few parents and girlfriends we'll probably be the only people there, don't you? People will be starting to wonder about us." That thought had occurred to me too, but as we pulled into The Avenue I realised that we weren't the only ones to have been lured. Remarkably, there was a real crowd, despite the weather up at Threshfield being even worse than it was at home: there was water standing on the pitch, rain driving down the ground, and steam rising from every scrum – of which there were many. With clattering challenges arriving whenever the wet ball was passed, the early part of the game was a succession knock-ons. After a while one Dale old-timer turned around to give me his two penn'th: "It's all well and good that modern players are taught to handle the ball rather than kick it. But horses for courses, eh? What's wrong with a bit of hacking and harrying when the weather's like this? These lads should know that it wasn't long ago Ireland got to the semi-final of a World Cup with a bit of that."

And 'that,' eventually, was the game the Foresters opted for. It may not have been a pretty sight, but it was a terrific one. For a 'meaningless' friendly, both teams played with a ludicrous level of intensity. And Dale – *just* – won. An unexpectedly great night.

In theory that result can have no bearing on what happens at Darlington, but it certainly has had a bearing on our mood as we travel up. We are, in a word, buoyed.

And then we arrive, and have to confront the reality of the stadium.

What do I find so awful about Darlington Mowden Park? It's this. The great thing about rugby at our level is that at every other venue there is a distinct sense of place. Whether it is urban or rural – the planes cruising down over Rosslyn Park, or the wooded hills around Cinderford – we know where we are. We look around us, and know that we've journeyed *somewhere*.

At the Northern Echo Arena there is just a sense of unplace. Of vacancy. Only twenty minutes after leaving the Dales behind us, we have pulled off the busy A66 and straight into the ground's vast car park, without having come close to the town of Darlington. From the outside, the stadium itself looks as if it has been decaying from the moment it left the architect's computer screen. There is moss on the sloping roofs and mildew on the painted steelwork. It looks to me like an old fridge – impersonal and unloved. Once inside the ground we're unable to see out, and since the stands are entirely uniform, there is not even a sense of place within the place.

I dare say that it would all feel different if the stadium was full, or even half full. Today it doesn't even feel half-empty. The attendance given – 1,300 – means that the arena is about five percent full. Around us there is a vast acreage of faded red seats. No-one can accuse Mowden of not pulling out all the stops to draw a crowd. Underneath the stand they have laid on a 'Winter Wonderland,' complete with a small choir singing carols, a few stalls, and a single reluctant reindeer.[37] A good effort. Out in the stadium there are cheerleaders before the match, and an MC doing his best to thrust us all into the middle of next week's festivities. Perhaps in ten years time Mowden will be up in the Premiership, Darlington will be known as a rugby mecca, the arena will be rammed, and all these trimmings will feel right. For now, I have to say, it looks like a plate with chestnut stuffing and cranberry sauce – but no turkey.

There are a good number of Dale fans here, but even with 25,000 places to choose from, few of us seem comfortable with the seating arrangements. Of course, we could sit back in the stands and have a birds-eye view of proceedings, but that would mean spectating, and that's not really what we come for. We come to be a part of the game. The closest we can get to the pitch is the tarmac track which separates stands and touchline, but I don't like this: presumably to help with drainage it is just below the level of the pitch, offering only a worm's-eye view of proceedings. So I head off to one corner of the ground, well away from anyone else, and stand in an aisle a few rows up. All those years of singing in churches and concert halls tell me that this should be an acoustic sweet-spot in the stadium. It is. When the match starts, a few of my strident cheers ring around, and down on the touchline a couple of heads turn. Not that mine is a lone larynx by any means. Down in front of the one occupied stand I can hear familiar voices cheering on the Greens. Half our support is standing down by

---

37 Just in case that reindeer should happen to be reading this, I think I should apologise for the startled, prob-ably rather hostile look my wife and I gave you. Thing is, on our way down to Cinderford the previous month we'd stopped off on route at a small town in Shropshire where, at their Christmas market, we saw a reindeer in a pen. Well, we went on to lose that match, so when we saw you we wondered whether reindeer had now replaced Anglo-Saxon churches as an omen of bad luck. So, sorry about the look.

the advertising hoardings. Caroline and Lynda are there, complete with their Christmas sleigh-bells, which they frantically jingle whenever the Dale pack gets momentum. It sounds like we're watching the downhill at Wengen, but all told it has an effect. Jon later says that in the changing room at half time one of the players commented that the noise of the Dale support was making it feel like a home fixture.

Whatever the reason, the fact is that Darlington start as if they're half asleep. Wharfedale are straight into them, and within the first ten minutes flanker Dan Solomi manages to cross the line twice. There is a swirling wind in the stadium (not a problem, I imagine, that Tom Davidson has encountered before) so neither try is converted. Still, 10–0 up in as many minutes is a great start. This, we have to remind ourselves, is not a match which anyone is expecting us to win. For those who dabble in forecasts, there are many benchmarks for the qualities of any two teams. But for Dale fans here, there is one fact which speaks volumes: Aaron Myers, one of our outstanding players over recent seasons, moved up the road to Darlington but couldn't make any headway and left: their players *must* be better than ours. How about their team, though? That is what we are here to find out.

Only once in the first half do Darlington manage to rouse themselves and score. When the *Eye of the Tiger* music has subsided the MC urges the home support to get behind their team. A dutiful cheer goes up. It's difficult not to feel that the home fans, otherwise mute, are being shamed into voicing their support.

Amongst the Wharfedale fans who are pacing around, Alec has wandered up to join me. As Darlington's conversion sails over, he points down at the enormous speaker through which the MC is bludgeoning the supporters again with more exhortations and jingles. This is the second week running we've been deafened like this, and Alec is getting fed up. "If I could change one rule in rugby," Alec says, "it would be to ban use of that bloody thing once the game has started. If supporters can't make their own minds up about when to shout, what on earth are they doing here?" At which point the music fades out for the restart, and Alec unleashes a great steely cry of "*C'MON THE DALE!*" which echoes round the whole stadium. This one voice, personal and intense, is more galvanising than any number of amplified decibels: I see a couple of the Dale team look up in our direction. If their spines were stooped just a moment ago, as they stood under the posts, they are splint-straight when play starts again. They rip back into the opposition, and with a third try just before the interval, and Dan Solomi's hat-trick try just after, Dale have established a 24–7 lead.

We're now assured of our four-try bonus point at the least, but none of us is going to settle for that meagre return now. A win and five points look like they are ours for the taking. In the stands we are looking at each other in blinking disbelief.

Fast-forward thirty minutes, and we are looking at each other in winded disbelief: we're now 24–26 *down*. Mowden have suddenly woken up and played to their potential. We might be wondering how the turnaround happened, but this is no time for gloomy backward glances. There are still nearly ten minutes left. By this time most of the Dale support has moved down to the touchline, and once we have regathered our selves, we loudly compel the team not to throw in the towel. We might not feel optimistic, but we can at least *pretend*.

Now it is Mowden's turn to feel chased. They give away a penalty and Jamie Guy, who has taken over the kicking duties, steps up. Is this his moment? The stadium falls silent until he begins his run up, when a couple of voices – perhaps ghosts from the soccer crowd who used to come in here – loudly boo. That *never* happens at our level of rugby. I don't know whether Jamie is as shocked to hear this as we are, but he misses. With only two minutes left on the clock he gets another penalty chance. Is *this* his moment? Again the boos come, but this time he's not distracted, and calmly sails the ball over between the posts. We're back in the lead, and time is nearly up.

The final play of the game is over on the other side of the pitch. Over there, under the gaze of ten thousand empty seats, the players are beyond any support we can offer. Yet they keep their composure, and when the ball pips out of a ruck on our side, Dohers whams it high into the vacant stand. We've won! Only by a single point, but we've won! Three victories on the trot, and the goal of surviving in National 1 for that landmark twentieth year is suddenly looking like we might – *might* – realise it after all.

The last eighty minutes have been a sensational experience for us – intensity and passion in a surreal space. But ask anyone from Wharfedale – player or supporter – what their lasting memory of that day is, and I suspect that you will get the same answer: the moments after the final whistle. By the time the players have made their way over to the touchline, the Darlington team and support have mooched off towards their exits, and the Wharfedale congregation has gathered together.

It's the last match before Christmas, and even without the excuse of mistletoe, there is a fair amount of embracing going on. I'm in the throes of a filthy cold, and trying to keep my distance, but Maria, the captain's mum, is having none of it: "who cares after that!" she says, and gives me a big hug. The men are a bit more reticent, but when I suggest to Ed that he will enjoy writing his match report, he shrugs his shoulders: "I'm not so sure – I was so excited I didn't take a single note." I notice that even the older supporters, who have seen their team play out this scene many, many times before, are happy to join in.

"'Ey, Clarty," I hear one of them call out, "you'll have to sing for the team on the bus home now!"

"What's that all about?" I ask Alec.

"Tradition. The team always sing on the bus home, but there's one song that they only allow themselves to sing when they've won. *Poor Little Angeline*. Normally Dohers leads the singing, but Clarty has to start that one off. Tradition."

Then a great cheer goes up as the players make their way towards us. The team let their game faces relax into smiles, grins and laughs. They may have looked like men for the last two hours, but right now they look like kids, plain and simple. So does the coach. I'm stood beside his dad – a proud man if ever there was.

"Steve," I ask, "what's your best Christmas present likely to be?"

"Five points from Darlington."

"Right answer. Mine too."

Chapter 20

~ in which we pull festive crackers with North Ribb and Tynedale, find a local rare breed at the gate, and catch sight of another exotic migrant ~

A fortnight has passed. Christmas. New Year. A time to take stock.

Back up in Darlington, when the team closed up shop for their Christmas break, shares in us were on the rise. Three months before that, when Rob Baldwin hobbled out of the Ealing game, we were a definite *sell*. And when our Dale-Lite team had been rag-dolled by Cinderford in November, shares in us had reached rock bottom. But after a few injections of experience and belief, and the small matter of three wins on the trot, by the time that we drove away from Darlington we were a clear *buy*. How our stock value had changed! Or that, at any rate, is how it felt as we enjoyed our Christmas turkey and fizz.

There must have been something positive in the air, because when Boxing Day came, and with it the traditional Foresters fixture with North Ribblesdale, a great bubbling crowd turned up at The Avenue. We were welcomed on the gate by an unlikely pair of ticket sellers: the club captain – "Well, everyone has to do their bit, haven't they?" – together with Dan Stockdale, the hooker. Also there, standing incognito with his parents in the Shed, was Jon Feeley. I'm sure that the coach, the hooker and the skipper could all have found plenty of reasons not to be back at The Avenue during their Christmas break, but with wind in the Dale sail, like the rest of us I suspect they all wanted to enjoy the feeling while it lasted.

These days, the players on the field might take it seriously, but to most of us the Boxing Day match is still a social event. And a family one. Take the Stockdales. They were all there for the North Ribb match. Dan was down at one end of the Shed side, selling raffle tickets on the gate. His dad was a little way further along, next to us. At the far end were the grandparents, John and Jane, and in between them all stood Richard's brother, Jim.

If that makes the Stockdales sound dysfunctional, nothing could be wider of the mark. The truth is, since they all still live and work together around the family farm down in Burnsall, the rugby club is one place they can come and spread themselves out a bit. Mix. As Richard says, "The club has been our social life for as long as I remember." Longer, actually. Richard's granddad, James, played in the twenties and thirties, and was later president. Richard's dad, John, played in the fifties, until down at Ilkley in 1962 he broke his leg.[38] John never played seriously again after that. When I asked him why, he just rolled up his trouser leg to reveal a still-visible lump: a bad set, as they say. Still, John nudged his sons towards the club, and they both played a bit in their time – all of which makes young Dan the fourth generation of Stockdales to play for Wharfedale. Richard tells me that as Dan was making his way from the Colts through the senior teams, his great motivation was that he wanted his grandad to see him run out for the Firsts. Family pride.

The game against North Ribb is the oldest in Wharfedale's fixture list. Like any relationship it's had its downs as well as ups. Back in 1934 the Wharfedale committee received a letter from the Settle club, alleging 'rough play' in a recent match. The Dale committee considered the complaint 'not at all justified', but all the same sent the letter on to the Yorkshire RFU to arbitrate. Could they ask the referee for his thoughts? They also sent a response to North Ribb, which hints that the bad feeling may have been more on the touchline than on the pitch:

> *If it is the wish of your players, as distinct from your supporters, that we should cancel the fixture arranged for next season, we shall be pleased to oblige you in the matter.*

Nobody took their bat and ball home, though. Later that year all parties met on neutral territory in Skipton, and although there are no details of the complaint and how it was resolved, evidently it did end amicably, because twelve months on we were back in Settle to play.

Things gradually relaxed. Richard Stockdale has told me about an event in this fixture in his playing days. "It was all a bit more social then. Back in the eighties I remember one year when a lad was so drunk that the ref wouldn't let him take the field. The player was having none of it, and the ref ended up actually having to send him off – before they'd even got on the pitch!"

By the time we reached the ninetieth anniversary of our fixture with North Ribb, on Boxing Day 2014, we were definitely playing a friendly. What litmus test told me that this was a 'friendly'? The test certainly wasn't on the pitch, where players were bringing the pride of their tribe into each contact. No, the

---

38 In a typically Dale-esque turn, John was lining up that day alongside his son Richard's future father-in-law. It was Richard's future mother-in-law that admitted John to Skipton Hospital that evening. Got that?

real test lay off the pitch where, for most in the crowd, matters on the pitch seemed secondary to seasonal goodwill. When the first team are playing a league match here, the noise often veers wildly from a taut silence to a racketing bedlam. On Boxing Day, the decibel needle hardly moved, reflecting an easy burble of bonhomie: mid-winter tries were greeted like mid-summer boundaries. Oh yes, and the Foresters won.

In every respect, the Christmas period is a significant staging post in the season. The away match against Darlington marked, in golfing terms, the turn. We're now on the homeward stretch, playing return fixtures against all the sides we have met so far. Sitting in mid-table, we're happy to be about par, but we're aware that the course can play unpredictably from here on in. In the past, teams who have been in danger of missing the cut at Christmas have pulled miraculous new clubs out of the bag in January, and marched steadily up the leader board for the rest of the season. And (it is as well that I mention this now) after our next match we have what look like four bogey fixtures in a row.

All of which should explain why, despite a maximum points from our last three games before the break, we are in a state of some anxiety about Tynedale visiting us on January 3. Given, they lie below us in the table, and have an injury list like the one we had a few weeks ago, but it was this time last year that we contrived to lose at home to the bottom side in the league. If there is one time when Wharfedale supporters know not to feel complacent, it is when we have every reason to feel complacent.

But the Boxing Day bubble doesn't feel as if it has burst when we arrive at The Avenue straight after New Year. Far from it. The biggest crowd of the season so far is here, still hanging on to the last of the festive spirit. Much of the talk is about team news, and for once it has nothing to do with the First XV. No, on the back pitch the Foresters are playing Tynedale's Seconds, and amongst the rugby-twitching community, a significant spot has been made. He's a flitting little fellow with a distinctive straw-coloured plumage: our old friend Aaron Myers.

Aaron who? It might not be a name on everyone's lips, but ever since Nigel Melville saw him as a seventeen-year-old and tipped him to play in the back row for England, rugby watchers have been following his career with interest. Or at least trying to follow it. Not always easy. Frustrating, in fact, and so much so that on the National 1 message board, a few months ago, someone posted a new thread: 'Whatever Happened to Aaron Myers?' It became a Lucanesque mystery. Over the course of a few weeks, in rolled page after page of cocksure (but curiously second–hand) sightings: he was variously reported as working off-shore; playing Sevens in Dubai; on his way back to the West Hartlepool club; playing in a charity match in Newcastle; labouring on a wind–farm in Scotland; about to join Ealing. Aaron himself didn't post an answer, although it was reported (hearsay! hearsay!) that he was 'amused' by the debate. Actually, there is a suspicion that any or all of these sightings could be valid, since Aaron has more than a hint of Peter Pan about him. Let's just say that he is evasive, on the field and off. Anyone looking on the website of his most recent club, Mowden Park, would have found this elliptical autobiography:

> *I like food and water. Oh, and I also sleep on a night time. I am fond of wearing clothes and shoes. I am really into breathing at the moment. I have a car that I drive to work, and a house where I live.*

Thanks, Aaron. Yet the same entry includes a listing of 'Previous Clubs', and here Aaron can't quite slip the leash of reality. It's an extensive list. Even at just twenty-five, he could garland a whole clubhouse wall with the various jerseys he's worn: West Hartlepool, Westoe, Newcastle Falcons Academy, England Under-18s and 19s, Durham, London Welsh, England Counties, Wharfedale, England Sevens, Great Britain Sevens, Suzuki Wailers, and lately Darlington Mowden Park.

In the weeks before Christmas the trail seemed to have gone cold. Was Aaron taking wing for his customary hibernation in Dubai? Then, just before New Year someone from Wharfedale posted the news people had been waiting for:

> Found him!!!!
> The Foresters side this Saturday will feature the familiar figure of Aaron Myers, the formalities of whose registration once again for Wharfedale have just been completed; the management points out, however, that Aaron's availability for the remainder of the season is dependent on his work commitments.

And, sure enough, there he is on our pitch again – ripping away at every breakdown, and generally being a legal (*just*) thief. So, Myers is back in a green shirt! And not just Aaron, but his brother Nathan too. A few days later, the report of this match on the Wharfedale website is almost doey-eyed:

*What a heart-warming sight it was to have the Myers brothers back in
the Green shirts, and they both performed to the standard we have come
to expect from them. Let us hope that they continue to play with such
enthusiasm.*

Is there a hint, there, that no-one at Wharfedale is getting carried away by
Aaron's reappearance? Certainly. But (and it's a big but) we're quietly proud that
of all the clubs he could have chosen, he has come back to one that is not local,
and offers him only a fraction of the money he could earn elsewhere. Ironically,
although two months ago he could have walked on one leg into our threadbare
backrow, even if he now pledged us his undivided loyalty, it is tricky to see quite
where he would fit in. Out on the main pitch, with Dan Solomi back from
injury and in top form, Jack Barnard freed to us from Yorkshire Carnegie, and
Josh Burridge improving his impersonation of Badger with every week, the
back row suddenly looks plushly upholstered.

With that significant drum-roll having been sounded in the Foresters' match,
at half time most of the crowd swap pitches for the main event. The opening
minutes of the first team game are an epic battle. Wharfedale don't lay their
hands on the ball once in that time, and are consigned to grim defensive duties.
And the Dale support, champing at the bit to put its own shoulder to the wheel,
is similarly consigned to the rearguard action of cheering repelled thrusts. Some,
it has to be said, are 'helping' by offering the officials advice. Through green-
tinted monocles they see things the officials evidently don't.

"*OFFSIDE!*" I hear someone yell out as the first passage of play goes on and
on. "Come on ref – he's been at it all game!" Everyone around hears the words
"all game," and I can see a hundred thought balloons float up, all reading the
same: *hang on – we've only been playing two minutes!*

More than once during this opening salvo from Tyne I hear the Dale team
yelling "no pens!" to each other, reminding themselves to defend with discipline.
In the sixth minute a Tynedale player drops the ball forwards, the referee signals
a Dale scrum, and with the prospect of actually holding the ball, the crowd
offers an ironic – but huge – cheer. And that, as a contest, is just about it. What
follows is, frankly, a let-down. Not that we Wharfedale fans have any complaints
about the quality of the rugby. And the result (34–14, and another five points for
our league tally, thanks very much) we can only celebrate.

As the match progresses it all feels great. It is only at the final whistle when
I realise that for a Dale fan there has been a complete absence of the drug we
have become dependent on: tension. This is a match which we should have

won comfortably, and which we have won comfortably. Predictable. Historically, though, *predictable* is not part of our lexicon. Yes, we are sometimes predicted to win comfortably, and sometimes we do win comfortably. Rarely, though, do the two combine. Usually, between the calm rationale of the forecast and the cool reality of the result, lies an eighty-minute period of white heat and volatile reactions through which all solid bets vapourise.

Not today. We dominate possession and territory enough to assess our current style. Wharfedale, however people from the outside may see it, has always been a club of change. I wonder whether, this season, it is changing again. For decades, Wharfedale's game was quick and cavalier. Even as late as last year, with Philip Woodhead at scrum-half, the plan from the off was still to fracture the field with quick taps and snipes. Once the neat defensive line lay shattered, and before the opposition could reform, Dale backed their wit to run through what remained, in strafing, mazy lines. At its best it was intoxicating to watch, partly because the clubs most likely to be confounded by it were the bigger, professional, steady-as-she-goes teams: Dale's splashy paint bombs resembled a Jackson Pollock, and this was not a picture opposition players recognised from their defensive coach's chalkboard. But (and it is an enormous 'but') ours was never a percentage game: it could turn out like a masterpiece, or a child's splatty daubings. Playing like this, we could turn over the team at the top of the league, but could just as easily come crashing down against the team at the bottom: and as for the ones in the middle, well, that was anyone's guess.

It was, if you like, Barbarian-style rugby. Only thing is, we weren't – *aren't* – the Barbarians. We play in a league, and to stay in it we need not just to entertain, but to win games. So this year, with James Doherty firing the shots, we have been playing with a bit more savvy. There are those in the Shed who, if that ball is left to gather dust at the back of a scrum for more than a nanosecond will yell at James – *just play the ball!* – and if he puts a box-kick up for the forwards to chase, will berate him – *don't kick, it's not the Dale way!* – but they're in a minority. The rest of us think that the Dale way is to flourish in the modern game, and we accept that just occasionally that might mean playing the modern game.

How about Woody, though? I wonder what he must think. How must it feel to be the heartbeat of the team, and overnight find yourself out on a limb? At the moment an injury has taken him out of the equation, but the way things have gone for Woody this season, won't he feel a little jilted anyway? Even at this level, we hear plenty of stories of players who throw their toys out of the pram when their names don't feature on the teamsheet. But if Woody does feel like that, he's certainly an impressive actor. When the final whistle goes, there he is amongst the crowd gathered to clap the players off the field – looking as pleased as anyone. For all his individuality, Woody has always seemed the epitome of a team player on the field, and that is exactly how he appears off it.

There is one last moment to savour today, before the festive bubble must deflate. Adge's Sports Report. On a day like this, we're more than happy to hear how the others have fared, and how we stand. Are we gloating? No. After all, there are still a large number of Tyne followers in the bar, and with their noses now stuck firmly in the relegation mire, the last thing they must want to hear about is how the league lies. Yet Adge is a skilled operator, and he always uses his post-match soapbox as an occasion to bring opposing clubs together, and to send us off as one. In this case, his message to Tynedale is clear: *if we could choose any team to stay up with us... it would be you.* Right now, as things stand, the mid-term share values of our clubs could hardly be wider apart. Interim reports, though, count for little.

Chapter 21

~ in which we find out who we are, trail down to
Ealing, and introduce procial rugby ~

January is here, the festive season is over, and like all responsible types, we should take a look at how our account now stands. Let's see:

4 January 2015

1	Ealing Trailfinders	17	78
2	Coventry	17	72
3	Rosslyn Park	17	68
4	Fylde	17	62
5	Blackheath	17	50
6	Richmond	17	49
7	Esher	16	45
8	Hartpury College	17	42
9	**Wharfedale**	**16**	**41**
10	Blaydon	17	38
11	Darlington Mowden Park	17	33
12	Old Albanian	17	31
13	Loughborough Students	17	31
14	Tynedale	17	28
15	Cinderford	17	25
16	Macclesfield	17	7

What a relief! To some, our position will look like mid-table mediocrity, but as far as we're concerned, we're flying high. It's not just that we're elevated above the relegation cut. We also have a game in hand, and if we win that fixture against Esher we will heading into the league stratosphere! And if we wi… *Woah!* Steady on, because if we start looking ahead, we see that standing right in our way are four matches against top-five teams. We've won everything in the last month, granted, but all the matches in the next month we could just as easily be about to lo… Hmm. Maybe some debits are due, and our account isn't so rosy after all.

First up is a trip down to the league leaders. This is the team formerly known as Ealing. Presently they are Ealing *Trailfinders*. If tinkering with the name of your club seems trivial to some, it doesn't to us. In Wharfedale this is something we know all about.

At this point, let's step back in time for a moment, and imagine ourselves at the bar of a Grassington pub in the sixties and seventies. Chances are, you wouldn't have to wait too long before the talk amongst the locals turned to the etymology of the word 'upper'. After a while the talk may embrace the geographical implications of the word 'dale'. And as the discussion moved on, you might well notice that the conversation had become more of an argument, and its temperature was rising out of all proportion to what, on the face of it, was a rather cerebral piece of semantic wrangling. Yes, this was a hot topic under debate, because behind the discussion of words and meanings lay a much weightier question: *who are we?*

From 1923 onwards, 'we' had been *Upper* Wharfedale. As long as we were playing *North* Ribblesdale and *West* Craven, *Upper* Wharfedale seemed just fine. But by the early sixties, the Greens were thrashing these traditional opponents, and wanted to test themselves against better teams. And that, to some, meant change. Jimmy Harrison, a great mover and shaker, voiced the opinion of many of the players: "We'll never get any decent fixtures with 'Upper' in our name. It's like 'Lesser Snodbury'. Why don't we just get rid?" It seemed so simple. And to start with, it was. The club's minutes for May 1966 suggest the smoothest of passages for the change:

> *It was proposed J.A. Harrison seconded R.S. Spencer that the name of the club be amended to Wharfedale R.U.F.C. There was no amendment and the motion was carried unanimously.*

According to Chris Baker, things didn't flow quite that easily: there were some rocks hidden below the surface. "I remember someone saying at the meeting, 'Mr President, it's just not constitutional to change the name,' and Jimmy getting up, quick as a flash, and saying 'Well if it's not in the constitution we'll change the bloody constitution too!'" Jimmy had his way, the new name was put in place, and the deal was done.

No it wasn't. When word trickled south down the dale, not surprisingly Otley and Ilkley objected to what looked like the annexation of a Wharfedale that was as much theirs as ours. Nor was the change popular further north. In a beautifully florid hand, the landlord of the Falcon in Arncliffe, Marmaduke Miller, wrote to the president with his reservations:

> *The name 'Wharfedale' might open the doors to this and that… it certainly breathes sophistication, is 'smooth' and 'with it' I'll grant you, but is that what Upper Wharfedale wants?[39] Is that what she deserves after all the glories of the past; to have her name decimated and to share what's left with every club the length of Wharfedale; all semblance of individuality gone. Upper Wharfedale to me suggests a tougher breed, men of the uplands and men who can play 'rugger'.[40]*

And never mind the disputes within the dale's environs, down in Leeds the Yorkshire RFU bigwigs were affronted that they had not been consulted. They ruled that the name must be changed back again. End of story? Not likely. The discourse just got tastier. When Adge arrived, he took the argument of his new friend Jimmy on another tack: "I gave the geographical slant to it: that a dale isn't an urban thing, but a rural, steep-sided affair." Gradually, local opposition was worn down. But as late as 1973, when the club was still voting for change, the YRFU was still refusing to accept it.

Ultimately, the blazers were wasting their time. If the men of Wharfedale were gaining a reputation for one thing it was for tenacity. In 1974 opposition around the county was finally quelled. From then on, the locals in the pubs of Grassington knew who we were: Wharfedale. In Ilkley and Otley we could know (if we chose) that we were Wharfedale too. In truth, though, it wasn't about geography. Jimmy, Adge and the others knew that there was something special about their club, and they wanted to spread the word. They did. It went out way beyond the watershed of the Wharfe.

How far? Well, a while ago I was making my way down The Avenue after a home game, and I overheard a conversation just behind me. A visitor from South Yorkshire had come to find out what we were about, and had fallen in with a group of four regulars.

"You certainly get good support," the visitor said. "Whereabouts in the dale do you come from?"

"Ha! Well, I come from Haworth," one of them answered, "he's from Skipton, he's from Lothersdale, and she's from Silsden."

---

39 So, Wharfedale is 'with it' and breathes 'sophistication,' eh? This might come as news to some of the metropolitan teams we play today.
40 These words have a fine ring to them, granted, but let's pause a moment: where exactly was Mr Miller making his passionate plea for the tribal identity of Upper Wharfedalians? Ah yes, Arncliffe in *Litton*dale.

"Are they around here in the dale?" he asked.

"Not quite!" the not-quite-local said, and went on to evangalise the wider attraction of Wharfedale, and the loyalty of its support.

"I see. If that's how it works I think my part of Rotherham might just become part of Wharfedale too."

What on earth is 'social rugby'? I dare say that we all have a picture of what that term means. Personally, I have a scene in my mind of about a dozen men fancying a run-out at the weekend. Yet with a couple of days to go before an arranged match, a quick tally tells the skipper that they are a few men short. A few telephone calls... *go on, it'll be a laugh!* ...and the disparate group of men is now a Team. Well, at least come Saturday afternoon they are all dressed in more-or-less the same kit. In the side there will probably be a couple of teenagers, dreaming of the future, along with at least a couple in their forties who are dreaming of the past. All will be dreaming of an earned beer later.

That, at least, is how I see it. But driving back north on the day after our Ealing Trailfinders match, I realise that how we view 'social rugby' depends entirely on where we are viewing it from. On the radio is a feature about London Welsh, who are currently winless and hopeless, dangling by one fingertip at the bottom of the Premiership. The question being asked is whether this once-great club should abandon its aspirations, go back down to the Championship, and just accept the realities of 'social rugby'. I have to laugh. Only yesterday we were being humiliated by a team whose aspiration is to go *up* to the Championship, where we think their unashamedly professional approach will find its true level. Perspectives! Ealing, I suspect, look down at the way Wharfedale operate and see it as the upper end of social rugby. And in a few weeks' time we, in turn, may find ourselves running rings around clubs in the Yorkshire Cup: we will put their deficiencies down to the realities of social rugby – and they will curse their luck in being drawn against a team of professionals.

Here's a question, then: is your own team professional or social? If that's a tricky one to answer, perhaps it is because I have posed what linguists like to call a false dilemma. In other words, your team is not necessarily one *or* the other, but more than likely *both*. Every team is social[41] and hundreds of them – literally hundreds – are paid for their efforts. So Wharfedale and Ealing are

---

41 And if it isn't, in what way is it a team?

somewhere in the middle ground of... let's see... how about calling it *procial* rugby. Dialects differ, however, and in Ealing there is definitely a stronger emphasis on the 'pro'.

Ealing are slick. The *Trailfinders* advert now clipped onto Ealing's name gives a clue to the club's ambition and funding. Everything about them, from their new stand and the two-story team dug-outs, to the change kit they have to use when playing us (we don't have one), is impressive. Against the rival sporting attractions West London has to offer, Ealing can only muster a crowd of five hundred for today's game, but lack of public support has not dented the ambitions of their owner-cum-sponsor.

To us, the Trailfinders look distinctly professional off the pitch. And on it? Their artificial surface is fast and firm, and so too is their rugby. Shiny. There may not be much of a following for them here, but the team do their backer proud. Any flickering hopes we might have that we can extend our winning streak are doused within the first twenty minutes, by four crisp, clean (and unanswered) tries.

Everything – *everything* – which Ealing do is just a little quicker, a little stronger, and a little more assured than anything we can put together. They reverse our scrum, unpick our lineout, and outfox our midfield. Just before half time the Dale support has something to cheer about, when Dan Solomi leaves his calling card – the bolt over the try line from a ruck twenty metres out. And then Jack Barnard muscles his way over for a second. Does this give us cause for hope? We're not kidding ourselves, trailing 40–12 at the break, that we are in any danger of winning, but our losing bonus points at Coventry and Rosslyn Park are still fresh in our memories, and perhaps...

...or in this case, perhaps not. Following the break Ealing show why they will probably win the sole promotion spot this year. Unlike the teams chasing them, against us they never let up until the final whistle blows. By then they have run in a further six tries, and despite a huge effort, we have added precisely nothing.

After their fifth try of the half, I hear one of the Trailfinders forwards shout out to his team mates with a salutary call-to-arms I haven't heard before on a rugby field. He calls out one word: "*Process!*"

This is what Ealing want, and what Ealing have: processed rugby. They know that if they follow every aspect of every single drill and routine they spend their time rehearsing, the result will take care of itself. It does. Like a prize sausage at the end of the machine, out it eventually comes: 78 tasty, meaty points for them, against a twelve for us which barely account for the skin. Scant consolation that this, their coach later comments, has been the performance they have been striving for all the season.

Later, as the players leave the field, I overhear one of their committee talking to David, our chairman: "That's what we pay our players for," he says, with a shrug of the shoulders. He's not embarrassed about their superiority, but he's certainly not crowing. David later comes over in our direction, his eyes still watering from what he has learnt of our respective playing budgets. We're all agreed that, whatever the scoreboard suggests, there was no humiliation for us today. However flawless the Trailfinders pitch, the truth is that we haven't really been on a level playing field. And if that was social rugby we just came up against, I think we'd prefer not to be processed by the real pros.

Chapter 22

~ in which the snow descends, Coventry skate into The Avenue, and the game goes on ~

It's that time of year. Will it be on or off? From the middle of the week, down the dale in Ilkley I'm peering out of the bedroom window first thing each morning, seeing how much snow has fallen overnight. Not much, but whatever thickness is lying on the ground here, we can safely double it to gauge what depth of blanket is covering the pitch up at Threshfield. Nor is the forecast promising: more snow, and only minimal thawing during daylight hours. I hear that, come Friday, Gordon has decided to print only a single sheet of paper for the programme: fair enough – what's the point in printing the whole thing if it's only going to be pulped? The air of pessimism is hardly countered by a tweet from the club:

> Weather report. Friday 16 January: 10:30 am. Very little thaw overnight, but only a sprinkling of fresh snow. Beautiful sunshine, pretty as a picture, but no sign of fast thaw. Pitch inspection scheduled for tomorrow morning.

It's a later inspection than normal, presumably because Coventry's travel and accommodation has been booked, and we hear that they are going to travel up on Friday on the off-chance: they're on a fourteen-match winning streak, and presumably don't want to lose momentum. Come Friday evening, though, and with snow flurries in the air, and prospects for the match bleak, I am imagining that the Coventry team will be finding it hard to resist the bright lights of Skipton. I'm hoping that they are succumbing, anyway. In the unlikely event of tomorrow's game going ahead, I reckon that our best chance of getting a result is to play against a bleary-eyed team with no real stomach.

The referee's inspection is scheduled for 10am on the Saturday. We wait in to have the postponement formally confirmed, before heading out to look for a new sofa in the sales. And just as we're discussing styles and colours, in comes a tweet from The Avenue:

IT'S ON!!!
With a slight thaw in the air, the referee has passed the pitch as
fit. Thanks to the volunteers who turned up early this morning to
clear the snow off.

Ha! So much for predictions! We're momentarily dislocated. Once we've
realigned our mental compasses to point north up the dale, off come the
respectable clothes, and on go the thermals. And fleeces. And waterproofs. We
really can't quite believe that the match will go ahead – the forecast for this
afternoon is still for wintry showers blowing in – so I think the question is not
if the match will be called off, but *when*. As long as it isn't ten minutes into the
second half, when we're fifteen points up, I'm fairly phlegmatic about whatever
the day may throw at us.

"My bet," Caroline says, "is that we'll have pie and peas in the clubhouse,
catch up with a few people, and then be heading home."

I can't argue with that, but once we're there, as kick-off time approaches the
sky above is still clear. Then, when we've taken up our positions in the Shed,
someone points up the pitch to the western skyline, from where a thick grey
drape is drawing towards us off Threshfield Moor. It hits us a minute later, a
great shacking lash of sleety snow. Is our day about to end before it has started?
The roof on the Shed doesn't run the whole length of the pitch, so those on the
outside scuttle for what cover there is. Through the snow we can barely make
out Adge, who's just taken to the microphone across the pitch. He, on the other
hand, has clearly spotted our little winter migration.

"Look at them over in the Shed! They're like a colony of king penguins,
gathering together and taking it in turns to stand on the outside and bear the
elements."

And as we hear this, we look at ourselves, and a grim little chuckle of
recognition goes round. He has a point. We have that forlorn look of stoicism,
huddled together as if fate has handed us this role, and as if we really have no say
in why we're stood here in the vilest of vile weathers.

But the snow doesn't settle any deeper, and by the time the players are out the
squall has blown through. We can see it moving across the dale, combing over
the bare branches in Grass Wood as it scuds on eastwards.

From that moment, I have no particular memory of the weather. I suspect
that anything short of a white-out would not have registered, because the match
was thunderously gripping from the off. At the first scrum, near half way, we
push Coventry back and win a penalty. What a cheer! With respect to Rachel's
pie and peas, *that's* what we came for! It's not that we're straightway deluded into

visions of victory. No, we're very aware that we have the wind and slope in the first half, and at scrum time in the snowy mud that advantage counts for a lot. But we cheer anyway: today, we cheer simply because we have a game to cheer.

And, after our catastrophic first half when we played Coventry away, as the game progresses it really does seem as if we're going to give them a game. In the first half the play is almost all down at the river end, and despite Cov breaking up field to score first, the Dale heads do not go down. First we knock over a penalty and then, with the last play of the half, Jake Armstrong charges down a clearance virtually on the Coventry line. He's first to scoop up the bouncing ball, and touches down in front of an ecstatic Shed. When Jamie Guy lands the conversion, the cheer carries the players right back to the changing room.

We're still not getting carried away, but the simple fact is that we've reached half time, and we're not just still playing, but we're actually winning. And when, five minutes after the break, we kick another penalty to lead 13–7, we're just daring to believe. Coventry, for their part, are now realising that idle hopes of easy wins with bonus points can go whistle. The snow has now been stamped into the moraine, and it looks as if progress in any direction will be glacial at best. Inch by inch, Coventry grind down towards the Dale line, and eventually the referee spots an infringement which merits a penalty try. They now have the lead.

Is that it? Not quite. First we have the little comic scene which is inserted into all great dramas. Some people in the Shed, having now decided that the officials are in the pay of Coventry, are freely offering their 'advice'. Well, I have as loud a voice as any in the Shed, but the one direction I don't raise it is towards the referee and his acolytes. Sure, they make mistakes, but so (emphatically so on a day like this) do the players. Anyway, at one ruck right in front of us, a number of voices in the Shed are baying at the officials about Coventry being offside. A moment later the ball finds touch, and the linesman swings round to have a word. With Me!

"Hey!" he says, fixing his eyes on me, "you know exactly what the offside law is, do you? Do you want to tell me what it is?"[42]

For some reason, he's decided that I am his most vocal critic.

"Eh! Hang on a minute," I say, "you've got the wrong guy – I didn't say a word."

---

42 Just out of interest, I wonder if you know 'exactly' what the offside rule is at rucks? I don't. Even if could recite it (Law 16.5, sections (a) - (d) if you want to test yourself, by the way) that wouldn't mean that I necessarily knew it. Not in a practical sense. In theory, the lovely clear drawings on the IRB website should help, but in application I suspect they are no help at all. The trouble is, those little two-dimensional figures are *static*, and one thing I've noticed is that real three-dimensional players tend to be *mobile*. More than that, at each ruck these inconsiderately active players are not just treading the fine lines of law 16.5, but if they have anything about them they'll probably walking a similar tightrope for laws 16.1–16.4 and 16.6–16.7 as well. Refereeing, anyone?

He's not listening.

"Come on then," he says, still eyeballing me, "I'm waiting – tell me what the offside rule is." He cups his hand over his ear for a response.

Well, he certainly gets an earful back, but not from me. I'm just laughing at how ridiculous this all is. I can't even blame it on the person standing alongside me: Steve is so racked with nerves during a match that his larynx is virtually paralysed. I might be firing nothing back, but the linesman's real critics in the Shed have now got some proper ammunition: the game has now restarted, but the flagman is still carrying on, flipping round to keep up his monologue to me. Up and down the touchline I can hear voices wading in.

"Watch the bloody game, linesman!" they yell. "Just do your job!"

It could go on for ages, this scene, but play is taken away from us in the most spectacular fashion. As Coventry pass the ball out to their wing, our fly-half reads the opposition semaphore, and leaps out of the line to take an intercept pass. And he's off! Jamie is over half way in a flash, and heads straight up our wing towards Coventry's try-line. We lean out across the hoardings and crane our necks. He's running up the slope, through thick, slushy mud. With the Coventry defence in pursuit, to Jamie it must feel like that classic nightmare running away from a bear. Even with the whole of The Avenue hollering him on, this is a marathon *and* a sprint. The distance is telescoped, but with the try-line seemingly only a stride away, the Coventry winger flings out an arm and lassoos Jamie to ground. Just short! Their support flies in behind, and the moment has passed. *So* close.

We're still in the Coventry 22 five minutes later, when the referee blows the final whistle. As losses go, for most of us on the touchline this is one we can take. We have a losing bonus point, against a top team, and the effort from the players has been faultless. As we clap the team off, I'm standing next to Alec. He nudges me and points down to the sloppy ooze of mud beside the Coventry bench. It looks like a herd of restive cattle have spent the afternoon tromping around there: "Coventry were *nervous.*"

Right now, though, Coventry and their healthy support are pretty pleased: not completely, because they have not secured a winning bonus point. But when, a few minutes later, news comes through that Ealing have *lost* at Cinderford, the Coventry cup is suddenly overflowing. The faces of the Dale fans drop a little at this news: the top of the table may just have closed up, but so has the bottom. Still, when he clambers up onto a chair for his Sports Report, Adge manages to make light of this unlikely result in the Forest of Dean by "the greatest team of bog-snorkelers in the Western Hemisphere." He's probably right not to worry. He points out that England's tenth largest city has just been taken to the wire by one of the largest villages in Upper Wharfedale. If we keep playing that way, chances are we shall be seeing each other next season. This gets a huge cheer from the Coventry fans: they may fancy promotion, but I don't think they would mind another dose of this entertainment for another year.

The clubhouse is rocking. It is one of those rare occasions when both sets of fans have something to celebrate: they have stolen a march at the top of the table, and we have gained an unlikely point in our annual scramble away from the bottom. Bearing in mind the prospects for play twenty-four hours ago, we're also celebrating the fact that we've had a game at all. More than that, we're celebrating because we've had a *great* game. Proof, if you like, that there's rarely an unfit ground for a game of rugby – only an unhealthy air.

The banter is still bouncing off the walls when we eventually step out into the dark. An hour and a half has passed since the game ended, and the lights in the clubhouse are gleaming over the snowy patches on a pitch which is now repining, silent and deserted. The breeze has dropped, the sky has cleared, and the moon has come up. Out and above us, where the snow lies thicker, is the glowing dome of Threshfield Moor. Another day out of this world.

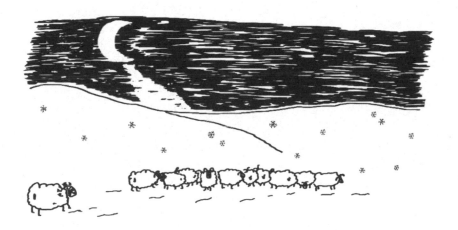

Chapter 23

~ in which we meet Pythagoras, go on more distant
adventures, and come back to reality ~

Time for some digressions and diversions.
Do you remember a character we met back in Chapter 1 – the sheep
in the Wharfedale clubhouse? Let me now introduce an even more remarkable
creature, who came into the bar more than once. This was a large Burmese python:
we'll call him Pythagoras. Now, Pythagoras was owned by a cameraman from
Skipton: we'll call him Philip.[43] In the 80s and 90s Philip travelled everywhere
videoing the team, and in those days that meant not just home and away, but
home and abroad. Tours. Most clubs like ours toured in those days, but few can
have embraced the digressions of rugby travel quite as readily as Wharfedale. In
a way, touring had always felt part of the Wharfedale way.

Chris Baker tells me that when he first played, a lot of farmers in the
team had never been beyond Skipton, so for them a fixture away to Hull was
a journey to new found land. Then, when the bigger local teams wouldn't
give us a game, Wharfedale started to travel up to the North East, across to
Cumbria and down to Cheshire in search of better opposition. From those
trips, it was a only a minor extension to go up to the Scottish Borders, or
down to Essex, make a weekend of it and play a couple of fixtures. Next came
an invitation from Willie John McBride's club, Ballymena, in Ulster. Then
came Dublin, Europe, Canada and America. We'll come back to Europe (and
Philip the snake-handler) in a moment. First let us go off on an even bigger
tangent. To North America.

In Canada, where Wharfedale toured twice, the club was a welcome guest. The
Dale team played in the warm-up game for an England B international against
Canada, and were fêted. And they took every opportunity to fête themselves,

---

43 Certain names have been changed in this section. I'm not worried about misrepresenting the humans, but for
all I know that python is still alive, and I don't want him slithering through my letterbox to correct me on any
points of detail. And I'm not the only one in the club to have concerns about that snake. When Philip brought him
into the bar, he would look for an unsuspecting player, approach from behind, and drape Pythagoras around his
shoulders. Dan Harrison, who was scared to death of Pythagoras, tells me that half of the team took to drinking
with their backs hard up against the wall of the bar.

because these were sociable club tours, more than competitive team fixtures. A lot of the Firsts couldn't spare the time to tour, so Seconds and Thirds came in their places. Snake-handlers too, but not their snakes.

In the States, Wharfedale had a more mixed reception than in Canada. On a day off in Washington, a few of the team decided on a cultural visit to Fredericksburg. A minibus and driver was organised for the journey down south, and off they went. Having taken in the town's historic sites, the players repaired to a bar in the old colonial part of town, close to their arranged rendezvous with the bus. Come the appointed hour, one of the party (we'll call him Billy) nipped out to liaise with the driver. Time passed, but Billy didn't return. Eventually the players made their way outside, and looked down the street to see their minibus surrounded by police cars and any number of gun-toting state troopers. At the centre of the action were Billy and the driver. Evidently there had been a dispute about the cost of the transport. First, voices had been raised. Then fists. Quite who had done what was not clear. One thing was clear, however: Billy and his buddies were no longer welcome in Virginia. They were escorted from the state under police escort. Wharfedale didn't go to America again.

Yet they did still go touring. To Italy, Slovenia, Poland, and Prague. And it is in Prague that we again find Philip the photographer. He's feeling a bit lonely. He doesn't have Pythagoras with him. Nor, more to the point, does he have his wife: we'll call her Phillipa. Anyway, Philip wants to phone home. Trouble is, not only is Philip deaf and dumb, but so is Phillipa. She works at The Duck in Skipton, so after-hours on the Saturday night, a well-oiled Philip decides that the time is right to make contact. For this, of course, he needs assistance. Dan Harrison gamely offers to act as Philip's go-between from the phone in the hotel lobby. In the same role at the other end of the line stands the landlord of The Duck: we'll call him Donald. Don. So this is how it works: Philip scribbles, Dan reads to Don, Phillipa lip-reads Don and scribbles a reply to Philip via Don and Dan. And so on. Clear? To start with – *How are you? How are the kids? How's Pythagoras?* – all goes well. Dan finds himself a little more uncomfortable with Phase Two of the conversation, as he finds himself whispering sweet nothings – *I love you! You know how much I miss you!* – to a pub landlord he's never met. But when the conversation moves into Phase Three, Dan baulks. He looks down at the scribbled sheet in front of him, and his eyes pop out at the anatomically specific plans Philip is hatching for their re-union. He turns round so that his lips cannot be mis-read: "Philip! I'm not saying *THAT!*"

Oh yes, Wharfedale beat whoever it was they played in Prague. No-one quite remembers who they were, or what the score was, but then rugby wasn't really the point of these digressions, was it?

These days, now that leagues have come to dominate our thinking, club tours are a thing of the past. Blackheath is about as far as we get from The Theatre of Bleats. But even though the outing may only last a day, the cultural shift from the Dales to the City gives us the sense of being on tour. So too does the warmth of the reception.

For the big clubs in our league, I imagine that there are two ways to view a visit by Wharfedale. At one extreme it can be a mild embarrassment: if yours is a historic club, or a big city club, or just a desperately ambitious club, then entertaining a rural village side can be an unwelcome reminder of your present station. At the other extreme, a visit by the Dale can be a cause for celebration: whatever you may have been, or may aspire to be, right now you are being offered one of the genuinely feel-good quirky realities of modern sport.

On our travels round the country we meet both responses. Often we meet both within the same clubhouse, but at Blackheath – *praise be!* – the reception gets full marks across the board. As soon as people spot the rams-head motif, or the green scarf, they step out of their way to offer words of welcome. A fair few have been up to Wharfedale, and speak about it with the glint of the river still in their eyes. Others have heard the tales and want to come and see for themselves.

Of course, it could all sound a little patronising, especially in the case of Blackheath. Lest anyone has forgotten, when they came north in October they ran eight tries past a Wharfedale defence that, on the day, was more lie-down lamb than wham-bam ram. You might think that Blackheath are simply rubbing their hands at the prospect of another try buffet, but I suspect not. Over the years we have beaten them enough times for them not to take anything for granted. The last time was here, on Blackheath's famous Rectory Field ground, only last year. Yet Club are clearly a stronger team twelve months on, and the general feeling amongst the travelling support is that first and foremost we need to restore some respectability. Would a losing bonus point be too much to ask?

It is. Just. We lose 7–17, just missing out on a league point. Still, the Greens play well, and are still giving it their all when the final whistle blows. This effort, and the welcome from Club, allow us to leave feeling not quite empty-handed. Oddly enough, the scenery helps too. Last week the snow-covered hills of the Dales acted as a balm on the frustrations of our match. This week, the view could hardly be more different, but acts similarly as a tonic. Blackheath's ground is perched on the hill above Greenwich Park, and as we walk over to the car park, the lights of the City start to reveal themselves. They're not all below us, though. The Shard and his surrounding giants are way above, their airplane warning lights silently winking at us across the void of a dark January sky. Doubtless to those who live in Blackheath this urban, urbane view is just part of their scenery. To a club which started out its journey playing small towns and villages in the rural North, it is a reminder of just how far we have come.

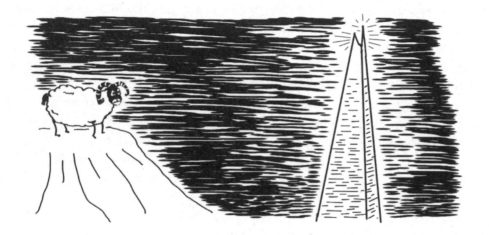

Chapter 24

~ in which Va'aiga is revealed, Rosslyn Park come to The Avenue, and Dohers whacks a ball but has to apologise for it ~

For most of us, the game down at Club ended with the final whistle. That was that – Club were better than us, and deserved their win. But to some, the game had not quite finished. I heard a Dale fan, in the clubhouse afterwards, start the ball rolling. *What if* that gust of breeze hadn't blown Jamie's first penalty attempt off course? – we'd have had a bonus point. Maybe so, a Club man countered, but *what if* our fly-half hadn't been injured? – we missed most of our kicks too. Ah, but *what if...*

They were still at it, wrestling with reality, when we left Blackheath, and it hadn't finished. On the *rolling-maul.com* forum, the following day 'Greenpower' questioned why a 'dubious penalty try' was awarded against us.[44] The answer, from 'Local Person', a Club man, took only minutes to arrive:

> Scrum going forward and a deliberate collapse?

Three minutes later and another Dale fan, 'Backrowboy', was wading in:

> Well it would have been had the scrum gone down. The penalty
> was given for James Doherty pouncing on the ball after it seemed
> to have left the scrum.

And on it went. Every five minutes someone posted a new angle and a definitive verdict. It was all polite enough – the Dale fans were happy to thank Club for

---

44 As with all matters Blackheath, when it comes to dubious tries, history trumps the present. Try this one for size: back in 1889, when the first New Zealand international team (a team of 'natives') played at Rectory Field, an English player had his knickerbockers disrobed in a tackle. He then put the ball down, and some of the New Zealanders gathered round him to 'preserve his modesty' as he reaccoutred himself. Meanwhile, another Englishman picked the ball up and touched down between the posts. When the referee awarded the try, three of the Natives walked off in protest and could not be persuaded to return for several minutes. England scored three tries in all, to win 7–0. (With point inflation, I make that 17–0 in today's currency.)

the welcome, and the Club fans were all happy to have seen us again – but in the tit-for-tat about the penalty try, the temperature was steadily rising. By the time that 'LHTT', 'Alcazarcat' 'Longtime' and 'Happy Gumbos' had had contributed their observations, it felt as if more points had been scored than in the match itself. Except they hadn't. The points tally for the match remained 7–17. After a while, some clever-dick calling himself 'Va'aiga' couldn't resist a little dousing contribution:

> It WAS a penalty try... I know that, because the ref stuck his hand
> up in the air, and the scoreboard went up by five points.

Not surprisingly, this attempt at applied Wittgensteinian philosophy was ignored. Let's face it, whoever Va'aiga was, in the endlessly entertaining game of *what if*, he just wasn't playing.

We've turned up at the Avenue for the next home match, and although Lynda's only just said hello, and although she's half-laughing, she's already swiveling the interrogator's spotlight into my eyes.

"Now then, tell me: are you that Va... Vi... Viagra Man?"

"Come again?" I ask. I realise I could have answered more delicately, but really, I haven't a clue what's she talking about.

"Are you that man on the rolling-maul forum called Vi... Va... I don't know how you pronounce it."

"Ah! You mean Va'aiga! Er, I *might* be."[45]

"Ha! I thought it must be you," she says. "Well don't be a kill joy, with all this 'I know it was a try because the ref awarded it' rubbish. For some people, armchair refereeing passes as entertainment."

In the Shed, waiting for the teams to come out, we're trying to warm ourselves with whatever humour we can find. The conditions are unspeakable. The ground may have less snow on it than it did for Coventry's visit a fortnight ago, but all that water has sunk in, and the surface now looks like a stud-sucking swamp. And the air! Today it is no silky caress from the west, but a vicious stabbing dagger from out of the north. Its thrusts are piercing us face-on in the Shed,

---

45 I don't really know why I chose this nickname (pron. Vy-inga, incidentally) other than that Va'aiga Tuigamala is as close as I have ever come to having a sporting hero. Amazing man.

and although most of us look like the Michelin man, clothes feel like a useless armour. And we're here (we tell ourselves through chattering teeth) for *fun*.

Before the match, looking out at the pitch, we're all in agreement that if ever there was a match to be won up front, this is it. So, when Rosslyn Park push us back *uphill* at the first scrum, the writing is on the wall. True, we were not expecting much out of this match, but there was always a chance that the conditions could be a leveler. Evidently not.

But what's this? Five minutes later, from the back of a ruck on Park's 22, Dan Solomi does his thing. As usual, the first we know of it is when he's already flying for the line. *Go Dan!* He arcs out of a last-ditch tackle, stretches for the line, and bangs the ball down by the post. 7–0. Nice. We're not in a position to retire on the strength of one try, but a little credit in the points bank never did a team any harm. Especially when Park thunder back up the pitch and begin their payback. Within ten minutes they have sliced through for two tries of their own.

The one consolation for standing in the Shed this afternoon is that the wind encourages each kick towards our touchline, so most of the play takes place right in front of us. Throughout the match the action is a whirling skirmish, moving up and down one side of the pitch: the ball is often the only static thing, planted in the mud, with flying bodies and boots converging on it. You could close your eyes, but you would still *hear* how brutal the contacts are. In rugby, though, these are the rules of engagement. No problem. But at one of these melees, right under our noses, the unspoken rules are broken. It's not deliberate – in fact, the actual incident is not seen by the officials or any of us in the crowd – but it is evidently real: James Doherty has inadvertently whapped the Rosslyn Park winger, Kiba Richards, in the tackle. I mean, in The Tackle. The ball[46] has dribbled into touch, and Mr Richards has stumbled off, bent-double and gasping, back to his position. It's Dale's throw into the lineout, and the forwards want a quick instruction from our skipper. Yet before he can do that, James dives round past the linesman, puts his arm round the winded winger, and whispers a word. It takes only a couple of seconds, and even though the ball isn't in play,[47] for those of us that spot it, this is sport at its best. Here, in a nutshell,[48] is proof of the adage that rugby is a game for thugs played by gentlemen.

Once he has his breath back, Richards and his colleague on the other wing, Joseph Ajuma, prove to be a real thorn in Dale's side. It's no day for speedsters, but time and time again they still manage to wrong foot our defence, making mannequins of them, before powering off down the wing to gain more vital

---

46 The *rugby* ball.
47 Sorry about these puns.
48 Sorry *again*.

yards. Actually, Rosslyn Park win just about every face-off. They're more powerful up front, their lineout is flawless, their moves are slick, and (most impressive of all on a day like this) they play as if the ball is coated in glue. When we have it, by contrast, the ball looks to be sculpted in wet ice. Adam Howard is having a particularly bad day. Time and time again he charges towards the Park defence, the crowd cheer, and – *ugh!* – the ball plips forwards out of his hands.

"I hope Adam hasn't completely forgotten how to hold something important," Alec mutters. "His wife is expecting another baby next week."

Even when Dale do hold the ball for a while, only once during the first half do we again progress downfield. Still, at least we take that opportunity to cross Park's line. That brings us level, but straight afterwards they score again, so we go in to oranges trailing 12–17. As things stand, we're in range of getting at least a losing point, but no-one trying to thaw themselves inside the clubhouse is in danger of getting carried away.

"If Park can score three tries running up the hill," I hear someone say, "what will they do to us going down the slope?"

"And if we couldn't hold a lead against Coventry," someone else chips in, "what chance have we got when we're already down by five points?"

Rhetorical questions. We troop back out into the Baltic blast inwardly unwarmed.

Still, at least the team haven't given up. From the restart they kick deep and manage to keep Park pinned back. And after a few minutes an odd thing happens. Very odd. We win a penalty at a scrum. A minute later we win another. Someone points to a replacement Jon has made. At prop he has brought on a big lad called Matt Freeman. He can't be the most mobile front-rower in the world, but on this pitch he's worth his weight in... well, he's worth his considerable weight, and let's leave it at that.

All the play is up at the top of the field, in and around Park's 22. Obviously it is only a matter of time before Park break free and roll us downfield – they still want another try for the bonus point they need in their push for promotion – but this period of Dale pressure is heartening as long as it lasts. And lasts. And lasts. After twenty minutes of the half it's starting to dawn on us that Wharfedale haven't established themselves in enemy territory by a single lucky break. No, they are there because they have earned it. Are earning it. Park give away penalties out wide, but with an evil gale gusting across the pitch, ready to sadistically humiliate kickers, attempts on goal would be literally pointless. No, what we need to do – and what we can't quite do – is cross the line. Never mind getting their bonus point, Park know they are within one missed tackle of actually losing. Their defence miraculously balances organisation with desperation.

Eventually they break the stranglehold when we drop the ball again, and off they fly down the slope. Their attack is eventually bundled in to touch, but now they are down in our 22, and their fourth try looks an inevitability. Except it isn't. Our defence is more desperation than organisation, but it works. Somehow we repel them. More than that, when we get possession again, phase-by-phase the Greens work their way back up the field, so that on eighty minutes we are camped back on Park's line. Again – agonisingly – we just can't quite make it over. Still, when the final whistle goes we have an unexpected bonus point for our league tally. Who knows how vital that point may prove?

When the end comes, we've been so absorbed that it takes us a moment to realise that, remarkably, we've just witnessed a 0–0 draw in the second half. To most of us it feels like a minor victory. Not to our captain, though. When the players get in to their huddle, arms round each others' shoulders, I can hear James's voice bawling at his team.

"I'm getting fed up with losing these matches – never mind a losing bonus point, we should have *won* that match."

Really? I love James's mentality – always driving his young and inexperienced charges towards expecting more of themselves – but to those on the sidelines, the side that should have won *did* win.

"We had no right to be even on the same pitch as them," Steve says in the clubhouse afterwards. "They had players that were faster, stronger, fitter and smarter." He thinks for a moment, then adds a significant caveat. "All we had was a team."

Chapter 25

~ in which we travel to Planet Luffbra, and come home
for a glimpse of the future ~

W e've now reached that moment in the season when, after a succession of losses to all the top teams, we take the field against opposition further down the table than us. Loughborough. Presumably we can chomp through them as we did the other lowly teams around Christmas. And, replete with our fill of league points, we can trot back into the secure folds of mid-table. If only.

By the end of the day we're feeling utterly hollow. It's daft. For us, leaving Loughborough unfulfilled makes no sense: coming here should be fulfilling, whatever the result. The town has an impressive, long-established community rugby club, with six senior, one women's, and eleven junior and mini teams: a thriving club in one of rugby's heartlands. But sadly, that's not where we're heading. No, Loughborough *RFC* play down in Level 7 of the English game. We're playing Loughborough *Students* – a team of much higher quality. What kind of club are they, though? In what sense are they a club at all?

The answer is that they are a perfectly legitimate club. More than that, in their own galaxy they burn very bright. The problem is that their galaxy is nothing like ours. No, they are a student club, and we are not. In large part we have a student *team*, but we're not a student *club*. During the match it strikes me that a visit to Loughborough Students will cause more qualms to the Dale's supporters than it will our players: most of the Dale lads speak the language of the modern campus. But for a lot of us on the touchline, old enough to have student-aged children, arriving here feels as if we have stepped out of a spacecraft into an alien world.

On Planet Loughborough, one of the first cultural differences I notice is that our old-style financial dealings have no place. The pitch is surrounded by angular campus buildings and walkways, and it is quite possible – probable, even – to arrive on the touchline without having seen anyone interested in the contents of your wallet. One Dale supporter inadvertently does this, and the first he knows of his transgression is when a chap wanders across from under a gazebo in the corner of the ground to ask if he has paid: cue needless bristling from both parties. I think pinning tickets on foreheads may have been mentioned. Not the ideal start.

But even during the match I notice that hundreds of students are wandering along the roads which border two sides of the pitch. Are they paying? Are they even here? Some pass by without a glance. Some give the match a quick look. Some stay a while. But are they *here*? Next to us, for a while, is a young lad with earphones on. He's texting someone on his phone. Is he really here? Or, amongst the nowhere architecture of the campus, is the concept of *here* an outmoded one too? There is no stand, and no clubhouse. No sense of an event. It feels as if we are playing in the void of a various orbits.

The soporific soundtrack to the game doesn't exactly help place us in a real space. Compared to the adrenalin and testosterone-fuelled MCs we are pumped by elsewhere, the student with the microphone at Loughborough certainly won't stand accused of over-hyping things. His welcome to Wharfedale has all the passion of a man reading from a timetable of late and cancelled trains. Alec turns round to me:

"Blimey! – I've been welcomed to the front of a post office queue with more passion than that!"

Then the music starts. It's shatteringly loud, but what on earth is going on with the playlist? Before the match kicks off we have a series of mournful ballads. It's a bleak, cold day, and the music wails out to nowhere and no-one. I'm suspecting that the MC might just have relationship issues. Perhaps the music will turn more upbeat when the game starts. It doesn't. After one Loughborough try, I hear a solo violin enter with a high, keening lament. It spirals downwards into yet another love-lorn incantation just as the kicker is knocking the conversion over. I really don't get it. Whatever planet we're on here, I have to remind myself that I'm just a visitor.

But yes, mention of the word 'try' reminds me that however much it may have felt like a non-event, a rugby match did indeed take place and – how did you guess? – we lost it. We arrived to the news that Adam Howard, our ball-wrecker of a forward, has been on paternity leave from four-o-clock this morning. We knew this was coming, and we're delighted for Adam and Natasha – but couldn't she have waited! Oh, and Josh Burridge has broken his hand.

I'll spare you the details of the match itself. The gist is that Loughborough are terrific – slick and well-drilled. We are… well, I hate to admit this, but we are *witless*. In all the years I've been watching them, even when Wharfedale get outmuscled and overrun, they have rarely been outwitted. Quite the opposite. We've always been thrilled by their nous for doing exactly what the opposition think they won't. Not today. When we get the ball, almost without exception it is simply shoveled along the line in the hope that the flying machine at the end, Taylor Prell, can somehow be sent off into space. Except that space on a rugby field always – *always* – has first to be created. And creation needs wit. We don't have it, and lose 15-29.

When the match ends we spare the team the embarrassment of looking us in the eye as they troop off. We head up the road to the anonymity of the Student's Union bar for a gloomy post-mortem. Twenty minutes later, to our surprise, the team walks in. Most of them have their post-match meal in a quiet corner. They're subdued. This is no time for gnashing of teeth, let alone for slashing recriminations. This match is not an end in itself, but part of a season. With next week to think positively about, the players are keeping a lid on things.

But as we leave the bar, we find the chimney where the team's steam is quietly escaping. Stood outside the door is James, the skipper, jabbing his fingers into his phone: "I'm keeping my distance," is all he says, although to judge from his expression someone will soon be receiving a splenetic text. James has told me that "99% of the time" he gets the team to sing on the bus home – even if they've lost: I think this might just be the 1%. Alongside James stands Jon: he's texting too, but looks up to share two words. "I'm *livid*."

If there is any good news to come from Wharfedale's visit to Loughborough, it lies on the reserve team pitch. There, our Foresters have come down to take on the students' Seconds, and have been soundly thrashed. 7–82. And that's *good* news? Well it is – and here's how. Year in, year out, the Foresters win Yorkshire's Second XV league. Come Saturday afternoon, and if they're not winning by a cricket score, often as not the Foresters are twiddling their thumbs when yet another side has cried off. One way or another, local tests for Wharfedale's Foresters are few and far between. They could sit back, of course, and baste themselves in the glory of superiority, but that has never been the club's way. That way has always been to seek out challenges – and to improve. Back in the sixties and seventies it was the first team who travelled far and wide to get meaningful fixtures. Often they were beaten, and sometimes thrashed: they were taught lessons but, as the Dale's steady rise up rugby's greasy pole testifies, they learnt from them. In those days, Clarty was one of the players who learnt. Now, he's the man arranging our lesson schedule, pestering other National 1 clubs for reserve team fixtures. He does it because he knows that if the club is to preserve its cherished link between the minis and the Firsts, it will need the youngsters in our Foresters to make the improbable jump from local reserve team level to National 1. To do that they will need an intermediate step. This afternoon, they've found one.

So we head off almost hopeless, but not quite. And, as we leave James and Jon outside the bar, we can take some solace from knowing that the two men who are key to the club's survival in National 1 are still together.

On the Sunday morning after the Loughborough match we're in need of a pick-me-up. Clarty has been telling me that I should head up to The Avenue on a Sunday morning to see the minis and juniors: "It's so vibrant it's untrue," he says. And Len Tiffany, who was instrumental in establishing the junior section, just chuckles when I ask him about it: "There's *nothing* like it!" I'm intrigued. After all, I've seen these Sunday sessions at clubs before. It's just youngsters throwing a ball around, isn't it? Some want to be there, some don't? That kind of thing? Not quite.

The first thing that strikes me, driving into The Avenue, is the sheer number of kids here. Hedley Verity,[49] who runs the show, later tells me that there are more than 250 kids in green shirts here most Sundays. Grassington and Threshfield, let's just remind ourselves, have a combined population of 2,500. When we walk round the age-groups, though, the really striking thing isn't so much the quantity of players, as the quality of their play. They're all having fun, that's plain to see, but they play with a level of intensity that stops us in our tracks. Caroline and I stand there watching, jaws dropped, both thinking the same thing: *how?*

Well, minis rugby should be strong at The Avenue, since the RFU's head honcho for 'game development' is none other than John Lawn, an ex-Wharfedale skipper who coaches our Under-17s. But to understand how this thriving hive got buzzing, we have to go back much earlier, to the early seventies. It was Clarty's brother Jimmy, the teacher, who extended the Colts side into a major operation. A few weeks after Jimmy and his friend Norman Whitaker had made a start, Len Tiffany turned up. Len was an ex-player who had heard about what Jimmy was up to, and in the back of his van had brought up his own sons and their friends from the farms around Bolton Abbey. Len was no teacher, and no coach. He thought he was just coming to watch.

"'Ey Len!" Jimmy said, "don't be standing round – take these lads over there and get them started."

---

49 No, he's no relation to the legendary Yorkshire cricketer. "My dad was cricket mad. I think he'd have liked me to be the next Hedley Verity, but I couldn't bat and I couldn't bowl." He could play rugby, though: 300 games for the Wharfedale Firsts.

"Well," Len says, remembering that moment, "what was I supposed to do? I hadn't a clue. But d'you know, after a week or so I started to get a feel for it. My wife even bought me a tracksuit for Christmas! And that was that."

Mr Tiff, as he became known to the kids, had found his vocation. To start with he coached the Under-9s, and followed this group up until they became the Colts. When I ask Tiff about his coaching, he shakes his head: "I don't know about 'coach', he says — I was really just 'coach driver'." I don't believe a word of it. I've heard men at the club talk about Len with real reverence for what he gave them — fun, savvy and passion in equal measures. When I told Sam McGuinn, who coaches the current Colts, that I had been speaking to Len Tiffany, he paused to think, then just said "in which case, you've been talking to the best human being I know." Len's own boys graduated, but he stayed on — "eventually I had a few lads come back with their own kids — full circle you might say" — until time called time. Tiff still comes up occasionally, and I can see him over the far side of the ground here this morning.

This afternoon the Colts are playing an important match, but in the morning Wharfedale are hosting all the junior sides from one of the bigger clubs down the dale. Caroline and I first alight on the Under-10's match. It's an eye-opener. The smallest lad on the field, wearing a green shirt, looks as if he has been given a new toy for Christmas — and that toy is The Perfect Tackle. He runs round with this toy, giving a masterclass in how to use it: down by the ankles, both legs together, and *WHUMP!* — another one bites the mud. We can't take our eyes off him. I ask Hedley later about this little threshing machine, and he nods: "That'll be Oli Riddiough. Promising lad. His dad played alongside me when we beat Worcester down at Sixways." In other words, he has pedigree.

Hedley has the grand title of Director of the Wharfedale Academy. In other words, he is the club's payroll. He goes round schools the length and breadth of the Dales, giving kids a taster of the rugby experience. The ones who show interest and talent, and who aren't attached to a club, he points towards Wharfedale.

After a while we walk over to the back pitch. There, Dale's Under-12 team are busy trouncing their opposition. At fly-half is one of Hedley's own sons, Beau. He looks classy, too, but since Hedley is married to one of Jimmy Harrison's daughters, his sons have pedigree down both blood lines. And there's a bit of horse-breeding in the way Hedley answers my question about the positions his sons Louis and Beau play. Hedley was a flanker — in most people's judgment the best Wharfedale have ever had — but he says his lads are both midfielders: "They've the Harrison gene, you see, and the Harrisons have always produced backs." Then he ponders his own contribution to the gene pool: "maybe they'll end up at centre." For those of us holding form books, these are players to keep an eye out for.

The event we've really come to see, however, takes place a little while later. The Wharfedale Colts have already tied up the Yorkshire Premier league for this season, but now they have their eyes on a much tastier prize. They have made their way through to the last sixteen of the National Plate competition. The writer inside me thinks that this could be interesting. The supporter inside knows it will be interesting. By the time they kick off in their match against Dudley Kingswood, the weather has turned vile. Within a minute, Dale show that they have a canny weather vane, in a rolling maul which takes them uphill from their own half to the Dudley line. An awesome statement, from which Dudley never quite recover. Soon the Wharfedale backs start flying around too, and by the end they have run out 38–0 winners. For those of us with the future in mind, this is a team to keep an eye out for.

Chapter 26

*~ in which we come across a player with no arms or legs,
we're invaded by Albania, but we show the virtues of
heads-up rugby ~*

We're nervous. After five losses on the trot, we're feeling decidedly shaky, and can sense the relegation trap door rattling beneath our feet. Look:

8 February 2015

1	Ealing Trailfinders	21	95
2	Coventry	22	93
3	Rosslyn Park	22	91
4	Blackheath	22	70
5	Fylde	22	68
6	Hartpury College	22	66
7	Richmond	22	60
8	Darlington Mowden Park	22	52
9	Esher	21	50
10	Blaydon	22	47
11	Loughborough Students	22	46
12	**Wharfedale**	**21**	**43**
13	Old Albanian	22	39
14	Cinderford	22	34
15	Tynedale	22	31
16	Macclesfield	21	13

Since we're playing Old Albanian today, one more loss and we will be in danger of the hinges opening up. We're *really* nervous. All of us are – supporters, coaches, and even the players. Our prop, Jake, has been on edge all week, his mum tells me: "He knows they've just *got* to win," she says. Hell's teeth! If even the front rowers are worried, this really must be serious.

So as the match approaches we're reading the tea-leaves, desperately looking for any reassurance we can find. When our team sheet comes out, on the credit side we're relieved to see Adam Howard already back in action. As long as his new baby hasn't been keeping him up all night, it will be good to have his kinetic energy back in the equation. On the debit side is the Old Albanian teamsheet. I compare this to the team we faced back in November, and I gulp: only five names appear in both starting fifteens. We all feared that the sides with strong Premiership connections, like Albanian, would be able to strengthen their teams if the drop started to threaten, and I'm suspecting that this has happened. Since they have beaten Fylde and Blaydon in their last two matches, they are probably eyeing us with something like relish.

That's certainly how they start the game. Within five minutes, despite having the advantage of the slope, we're already 0–7 down. And we've barely even touched the ball. The visitors do indeed look unrecognisable from the faltering outfit we played in the autumn. This lot look slick and powerful, and when they cut through us to score, along the length of the Shed there is a moment of stunned stillness. The Shed is without doubt the loudest piece of real estate in our league, but it can also be the most profoundly silent. The kick goes over and the silence only seems to deepen. Our minds are suddenly full of negative thoughts, but we can't afford these to filter down to our larynxes and out onto the pitch. Right. Deep breath, and… *"C'MON THE DALE!"*

Shout by shout, gradually the decibel count starts to rise, and gradually our tackle count starts to rise too. Adam makes one particularly walloping challenge in midfield, and the ball is spilt forwards. As the scrum sets itself, we have our first collective roar of the day. Perhaps business can begin. And sure enough, from then on, moment by moment the pendulum of pressure and possession starts to swing our way. Albanian resort to giving away penalties. We kick one of them, but even that, and a warning from the referee, can't stop them from infringing. Before half time Albanian have collected two yellow cards, and we've collected a penalty try.

Truth told, it's a ragged affair. It's the kind of match – more tension than skill – which might euphemistically be described as better for radio than television.

In fact, the classiest action on the field comes not from one of the players, but from our physio, Jill. James Doherty is the last person to feign injury, especially whilst the ball is in play, so when, in the middle of the first half, we see him go down clutching his leg, all our worries come crowding back in. Jill has seen him on the floor, and starts sprinting across the field. She will be as worried than us. But as she runs out, away to her left Will Magie, the opposition fly-half, falls to the ground in contact. How does Jill sense that this is serious? I can hear no screaming and shouting, and I can see no waving. The Albanian physio certainly hasn't rushed on, but Jill senses immediately where her priorities lie, and veers off at ninety degrees to the immobile Magie. It's fully a minute before she feels able to leave him in the hands of his own physio, and head over to James. I know she's a health professional, and all she has done is what is ethically expected of her, but I'm still wowed that anyone's wiring can be at once so clinical and so human.

It's a long stoppage. After a while James gets to his feet and limps back into position. Good man. Will Magie is not so lucky. Eventually he's carried off on a stretcher, arms strapped in so he can't even acknowledge the conciliatory applause. At The Avenue it can take an age for an ambulance to wind its way up the road from Skipton. When it eventually slides up to the back of the clubhouse it's half time, and I am stood nearby chatting with Steve. Magie is brought out. As we look over, all we can see is his head. His limbs, reined into the scoop of the stretcher, have vanished beneath a blanket. There's a respectful silence, broken only by a whisper from a young boy next to us, who looks aghast.

"Dad… have they… have they had to take his arms and legs off?"

Later – when we hear that Magie is fine – this will make us laugh. At the time, we're too concerned for him to be laughing. And I'll be honest, we're also too concerned for ourselves. At the break we're losing 10-12, and we have to play uphill in the second half. That's bad, and it soon gets worse. Moments after the teams come back out Adam Howard is sin-binned for a swinging high tackle – "Misuse of the cradle-rocking arm", as Alec puts it – and whilst he's off Albanian cross our line again. 10–17.

Are we staring at the end of our nineteen years in National 1? Are we about to take our first downward step in the club's history? Looking dispassionately at the situation, the answer to both those questions has to be 'yes'. Well, I know what the old-guard say: *believe!* I even hear someone shout out this single word as Dale prepare for the restart. They need to, and we need to. And here's the odd thing. I think we do. Bizarre. Like all faiths, it involves a leap into the unseeable, but once we have convinced ourselves that we are still only one score away from parity, there is no stopping us.

We kick deep from the restart, the defensive line hares up the pitch, and we keep the opposition pinned there. When we get possession we just won't let go, and Albanian's frustration at our tenacity is palpable. Soon it's their turn to see yellow, and our turn to have numbers and territory in our favour. But can we cross the line? The pack take us ever closer, but our back line still look unlikely lock-pickers. Someone needs to do something unpredictable.

Cameron Hudson decides that he is the man. As James grabs the ball from the back of a ruck, just five metres out, Cammie cuts back inside. There's no doubting that this is an unpredictable line. James, for one, evidently has no inkling of what's coming. He fires the ball up and out, looking for the wide runners, but it gets no further than the on-rushing centre a couple of yards away. The pass is so fast that Cammie can't even get his hands to it. It thunks straight into his forehead, and bounds past the defence, to land over the try-line between the posts. Cammie's momentum takes the same route, and when he gets there first he collapses on top of the ball. In the Shed we're groaning. This is exactly the kind of bungled back move which has been costing us all season, and now it has surely cost us the ultimate price. Except what's this? The referee has gone over to consult with the linesman. As they confer, it slowly dawns on us that we haven't actually broken any rule. Heading the ball over the line may be farce, it may be slapstick – unless you're an Old Albanian it's funny one way or the other – but it's not actually against the rules. And yes – *YES!* – the referee is suddenly running back under the posts with his arm aloft. Try![50]

So the sides enter the last quarter level on points. Yet the force is with us. In particular, since Jon brought on Matt Freeman as a replacement prop, the scrum has been grinding up the hill like a traction engine. Wharfedale's forwards have been traditionally small and nuggetty, but let's just say that Matt breaks the mould. A solid citizen, as Bill McLaren would have said. A citizen of where, though? He's only just flashed up on our radar in the last few games. From? Someone tells me that he is a Kiwi. And sure enough, when I go away and check later, I see that ten years ago he was lining up alongside Israel Dagg and other future World Cup winners for the New Zealand Under-17s. Since then, disappointment must surely have been a leitmotif of Matt's rugby career. But even if now it is The Avenue rather than Eden Park, and even if the reward is likely survival in National 1 rather than the Webb Ellis Trophy, I hope that Matt takes something from this match to put on his mental mantelpiece. Surely at least the noise must imprint itself on his mind, because as play-by-play the Greens creep ever closer to the line, it's *bedlam*.

It's too much for some. When Albanian get their hands on the ball and hoof it into touch, I see a member of the committee, Howard, scurry off across the car park to fetch it. Later, Howard tells me that after he had lobbed the ball back he looked up and saw someone with a yard brush sweeping the drive behind the clubhouse. It was David, the chairman. Howard tells me that David just shrugged his shoulders: "Too tense."

David's spent half his life at the club, and even if he can't bear to watch, he will be able to interpret every roar and groan from across the car park. But I've often wondered, at moments like this, what The Avenue must sound like from further

---

50 I have always maintained that one of rugby's great virtues is that there is no such thing as a 'lucky' try. Hmm.

afield, to those who don't know what is happening. After all, we're surrounded by some of the most tranquil land in the country, and to those ambling up the Dales Way, or through Grass Wood, our din must be…well, what? At this point in the match I'm aware of a lady I've never seen before, standing by my shoulder. She tells me she's come over from the caravan site – that's nearly a mile away – to find out what the commotion was all about: "It sounded like there was some kind of tribal war going on," she says. In other words, it sounds like it is.

The pressure on the opposition line is unrelenting. With five minutes to go, the scrum drives over, Jack Barnard falls on the ball, and we know we've won. There may still be time on the clock, but whereas the men in green suddenly look immense, the opposition look broken. To score, it seems as if they will now have to fight past giants and climb a wall of noise. If that sounds like a challenge straight from the realms of myth, then to meet it Old Albanian would need to believe in the impossible. They don't. We do. We win.

Chapter 27

*~ in which at last we find social rugby, then head north
to Blaydon to find another river ~*

I'm still looking for this thing they call social rugby. Does it even exist at The Avenue? Obviously I'm wasting my time looking for it in First XV games. I thought I might find it with the Foresters – they take their name from a pub after all – but I've given up on that, too. I need to dig deeper. As luck would have it, on one of the free days built into every National 1 season, I notice that our Thirds are slated to play at home. Here, surely, I will find a team playing just for fun. I should have known better, because the Thirds also have a name, and it's the 'Development XV'. These players are trying to head somewhere. They may be Colts making the hard yards towards the Foresters and Firsts. Or they may be established players on the fast track back to the top. Today, for instance, last season's First XV captain, Chris Steel, is coming back from injury, and making life hell for Bradford & Bingley Barbarians' pack. And in the centre is Huw Morgan, a promising centre who had just made it into the Firsts around Christmas, only to come down with an injury. He's been offered a recuperative run-out: he grabs the invitation and runs with it, scoring four tries in a 75–5 win. Social rugby? Not in these green shirts. I'm still looking.

At half time in that Thirds match, I walk round onto the reserve pitch at the back of the clubhouse. Here, the Dale Fourths are playing Old Otliensians Seconds. Surely, this must be social rugby? After all, they are managed and captained by Mick Greenwood, who is a man of a... well, I was about to say of a *certain* age, but that wouldn't be right. Mick is of an *un*certain age, mainly because he won't tell anyone in the club how old he actually is.

What Mick has told me is that he first played for the Fourths – after a few years out of rugby altogether – in 1984. Your guess is as good as mine – but he's no Colt. Once Mick got back into playing he worked his way up through the Dale teams, eventually managing twenty minutes off the bench for the Firsts. But he was – and is – quite happy with the Fourths. After all, even in that team he's played alongside an England international, back in the day when a veteran John Spencer was drafted in.

For the Fourths, playing on the back pitch at The Avenue is a bit of a treat.[51] And yes, they're undoubtedly having fun. Both teams. Towards the end of their match, when Dale are 17–7 up, a huge opposition prop takes a quick tap and charges forwards. This, he must be thinking, is the moment to have *his* fun. Only thing is, in his way stands Mick. Now Mick may be – well, whatever age he is – but Clarty likens him to Popeye, and he's still a *specimen*. And proud of it. He doesn't just stop the ball-carrier in his tracks, but – *BOOOFA!* – knocks him several yards back. The prop releases a winded groan. He also releases the ball. It bobs free, a green shirt sweeps it up, and runs off beneath the posts.

There's time for one last play. The big prop has just about got his breath back, and as the teams line up for the restart, he shouts out across the no-man's land of the half-way line.

"'Ey Wharfedale… you'd better give us a proper feed after doing this to us."

To which Mick, quick as a flash, shouts back: "The way you lads have played you'll be lucky to get anything!"

Thirty men laugh. Social rugby at The Avenue. *Found it!*

Previewing our next league match, in Newcastle's *Evening Chronicle*, Blaydon's director of rugby, Micky Ward, offers an appraisal of our team: "Wharfedale are typically a bunch of tough farmers, and they are always difficult opponents." To some, we will always be known as a team of farmers, just as the Welsh tight five will always be miners, and Harlequins will be investment bankers. But whereas the pits of the Valleys no longer exist, and the City makes time-demands that no modern pro could realistically meet, Wharfedale still keeps a connection with its farming roots. True, when I count the farmers in our line-up I can only find two – Jim Mason and Dan Stockdale – but I doubt that many players pull on the green jersey without occasionally finding themselves on a farm – even if it's only a swim in the river on Clarty's land during summer training, or Sunday morning breakfast at the Mason's farm in Appletreewick.[52]

---

51 The Fourths often have to play on our old pitch out on Wood Lane. As the crow flies this pitch is only a few hundred yards from the clubhouse, but short of wading through the Wharfe, getting there entails driving the best part of two miles through Threshfield and Grassington. For the tourists they pass on their way, the players' journey must be an astonishing sight, since the *char-à-banc* provided is Mick's tipper truck – into the back of which both teams crowd, heads peering over the top. Locals are probably more phlegmatic about this sight, since they regularly see similar transportation methods – on sale day at Skipton Auction Mart.

52 An example of how infuriatingly, fantastically understated the Dales farmer can be: when I met Jim Mason's brother, Ted, I asked him if he played too. He'd given up, he told me, but nowadays did 'a bit of fell running'. When I checked later, I found that Ted's 'bit' extended to twice being crowned national champion.

In the old days, when half the team really were farmers, the bus for an away fixture often could not leave until after milking. A few of the old-timers have told me tales of having to get changed on the bus, and running straight out onto the pitch. Well, in those days warm-ups were unheard of, and as for running through set-plays and codes – *pah!* These days, though, that couple of hours between the team arriving and kick-off is vital: on the touchline we may be clueless about what '*puma play!*' means, or what '*3-7-4-aardvark!*' might signify at a lineout, but after their final revision session, hopefully at least the players will know. Not today they won't. The A1 is stationary for miles around Newcastle, and the team bus chugs into the Blaydon car park with barely half-an-hour to go: the officials will only defer kick-off by ten minutes, so it looks as if the team will have to revise during the exam. Not ideal.

Still, at least the little delay allows us to absorb the Blaydon experience. Now, supporters of any club – in any sport – can always find cause for complaint. It might be where you play, or the way you play. It might be the mercenaries on the pitch, or those pitching the merchandise. I'm aware, however, that only those curious fans who value peripheral matters such as trying to win their league, or having ample seating with uninterrupted views of a flat pitch, are offered much to gripe about at Wharfedale. I hate to admit it, but most of us are happy about how things are.

It would be easy to crow about our advantages, but the club itself can take very little credit for our chief virtue: geography. Never mind the view, think about the practical details. When the club moved to The Avenue, back in the sixties, the single pitch ran parallel to the river. The current arrangement (to accommodate a second pitch when another farmer's field became available) came not from the genius of an architect, but from the concrete realities of old trees and old walls. This, remember, is a National Park, and permission for removing anything more substantial than sheep-droppings constitutes a significant planning issue. So, although geography may have dictated that we have a sloping pitch, which is on the small side, and has an unyielding stone wall just beyond one dead-ball line, geography has also led us towards a great asset: small stands on both sides of the pitch, and an atmosphere you just can't escape. In a word, *intensity*.

Nowhere should Wharfedale count our geographical blessings more than when we visit Blaydon. Like us, they are a community club: aside from our First XV, both the Wharfedale Foresters and Under-12s are up here to play their Blaydon counterparts. In most respects, then, we could be back at home – a clubhouse with chirpy minis and friendly seniors everywhere, a pitch with a feisty home team, and even a river beside and view of distant hills beyond. But somehow, by some quirk of inhuman geography, at the heart of the Blaydon

RFC lies a great passion-sucking void. I can't believe that anyone at the club chose to place a vast car park in between clubhouse and pitch, but this is the physical reality. And although two hundred yards might not sound much, the spirit in the bar really does seem to dissolve on route to the single stand on the far side of the pitch.

The home support is quiet. Then again, do they really need to make much noise today? In truth Blaydon haven't got much to play for. They're stuck in mid-table, as they are most years: too steady to be in much danger of falling down the crevasse of relegation, but never quite with the financial power to barge their way up to the solitary summit perch of promotion. Still, this afternoon's hike amongst the foothills they should be able to take in their stride, and to start with they do.

I don't know whether it is because of their late arrival at Blaydon, but in the first hour of the game the Wharfedale team might as well be at the races as here at the rugby. It's almost comical. Take one example: there's a stiffish breeze blowing across the pitch, but when we win a penalty in the middle of the pitch, Tom D plants his kick for touch windward. On the sideline we can all sense what is coming, and the ball duly bananas round to go dead over the end line: cue a collective sigh from everyone in green. Five minutes later, when the same opportunity presents itself, all the Dale support to leeward frantically wave and shout at Tom – "*OVER HERE!*" – but although he heeds the advice, it comes to nothing: the ensuing lineout throw isn't straight. The effort's there for all to see, but sadly not the execution.

So it's a comedy of errors, and with quarter of an hour to go in the match we're behind by 15–34, and we're staring straight down the barrel: it looks as if maximal humiliation and minimal league points are about to be fired in our direction. It should make us feel better when someone reports that in the earlier kick-offs the bottom three have all lost. But it doesn't. Not really.

We're being played off the park, and that feels *bad*. And then our friend Mr Freeman. With his significant fresh legs, the scrum starts motoring forwards. The Blaydon pack are conceding penalties, and with three minutes to go, Dohers takes a quick tap and, before the defence can align itself, goes over. At least we have a measure of respectability. But what's this? From the re-start we're heading up-field again, eventually winning a scrum wide out, just five metres from the Blaydon line. We're glancing at the scoreboard, totting up the possibilities. All of a sudden things are a bit tense. In goes the ball, and after a moment's stability the Dale pack takes our shouted cue – to head for the river: they duly munch their way through the opposition as they head for the Derwent. The Foresters have finished their match and have come over to lend their support. And in addition to the bellowing adult voices, Wharfedale's Under-12s are down by the corner, screaming the pack onwards. Facing the inevitable, Blaydon collapse the scrum on their line, and without warning the ref runs under the posts to award us a penalty try. Perhaps he just can't bear the noise. For our part, we can barely believe it.

It's all happened so fast that I can hear the maths being done on the field as Jamie Guy is tapping over the simple conversion: with that one act we now have a league point for scoring four tries, and another for being within seven of Blaydon. $1 + 1 = !$ And time will be up when the ball next goes dead. "Just get it to me!" James shouts as the forwards prepare to receive the restart. They do, and James bangs the ball straight into touch. Not for the first time this season, we have somehow lost a match but won a march on the bottom clubs in the league. We can't help celebrating.

Right then, on the woodland path which runs above the pitch, I see a couple of walkers. They have stopped to look down at the cause of all the noise. What must they think? From the cheers and handshakes they will be able to tell that it is the end of the match, but who do they think has won? Surely not the team in red, who are quietly making their way off the pitch, looking mildly irked. No, it must be the men in green, who are hugging each other and punching the air. And look how they are being greeted! The walkers will see some young lads in tracksuits forming a guard of honour: as the greens trot down the tunnel, they hold out both arms to touch hands. All are grinning from ear to ear. Without doubt, to those passing by it is the greens who must look like the winners.

And yet we've lost. I know there are those to whom a loss is a loss – an unequivocal negative in the simplest of equations. Yet this match is part of a much bigger calculation – a league. Viewed in that light, it feels as if on the touchline at Blaydon we're left looking at a plain positive: two more points.

One thing is for sure. We may have lost, but there will be singing on the team bus back. James has told me that "a double-up trip with the Foresters is always a big one for the singing". I'd been imagining, when I heard about the team sing-songs, that they probably involved just a few bored players at the back of the bus, with the youngsters further down, playing on their mobiles, or with their headphones on. Not a bit of it.

"The lads are asked to sing a song on their away debut," James says. "After that, then, all the team have 'their song' that they like to lead. Hedley used to be the human jukebox – loads of Elvis classics – but now it's more Richard Rhodes. If they don't know the songs, the lads are encouraged to listen and learn. Dan Stockdale's told me that he practises them all when he's driving round the farm on his tractor! The singing's really a highlight of any trip. The quality might not be that great, but no-one could fault us for effort."

I could say much the same for the game they've just played. And that, for me, is why they're such an easy team to support.

Chapter 28

~ in which we travel forwards in time, meet Roger the Groundsman, then share a trip into the past with Esher ~

A modern game. It's already about thirty points to twenty-something when I switch on the television, and the clock and scoreboard are still ticking. The scores keeps flipping over as if it's a basketball game, which is about right, since both sides in this Super Rugby try-fest are razzing the ball around like the Harlem Globetrotters. Under the roof and lights of the Highlanders' Forsyth Barr Stadium, it's Sonny-Bill Williams and the Chiefs who are melting zig-zagging lines through the artificial turf. And it's being beamed live into our living room as I chomp through my breakfast toast on Saturday morning.

In almost every way, the techno-rock of the Chiefs and Highlanders is a world away from the classical fayre I can expect to see at The Avenue when we play Esher this afternoon. But my ears prick up at the name of the Chiefs' captain. Matt Symons. Sounds familiar, but... surely the man bossing these global superstars around can't be the same man – *English*man – who just three years ago was playing for Esher. Can he? I google his name to check, and it's true, packing down alongside Brodie Retallick, the current World Player of the Year, is an ex-Esher second-row. How did he get there? How on *earth*? It's like looking at a polar bear in a Salvador Dali beach scene, but occasionally it takes something faintly surreal to make a connection between here and there, or between then and now.

So I start my day pondering Matt Symons and Esher, and individuals and clubs, and how shared trajectories can part directions. There's no doubt that since he decided he was going nowhere slowly in the English game, the career of Symons has taken off. There's also no doubt that Esher, from the stratosphere of the Championship, have come crashing back to earth and National 1.

Plenty of teams who make this fall bounce straight back up without so much as getting their undercarriages mired, but Esher have become well-and-truly rutted in. In fact, this is their third season back with us, and they are melding nicely into the scenery, nestled down amongst the mid-table clubs. Do they mind? I suspect they don't much like having their noses wiped in it by the current crop of ambitious clubs – the Ealings and Hartpurys – but when it comes to the mud of Wharfedale, Esher seem positively to wallow in it.[53]

Yes, mud. It's that time of year. Late February. The snow is still lying in streaks on the moors, blown up in drifts against the limestone walls, and whilst the floor of the Dale may no longer be white, when you walk on the turf you realise where the majority of the snow has gone: down, not up. We're still in February, so the turf has no prospect of rejuvenation for weeks. Looking at the fixture list in the days after the Blaydon match, as I see it the only thing the pitch can look forward to is three home fixtures on the trot – three more weeks of rotivating packs and pounding mauls. But hold on a moment! What's this about the pitch *looking forward* to things? I realise that if I'm feeling sorry for the pitch I'm getting into the curious territory of attributing feelings to a patch of vegetable matter. It's a worry. Before I find myself fully pledged to the teachings of the Buddha, I think I should at least get to know the pitch a little better. I phone the groundsman, Roger, to ask if I can keep him company when he's marking out during the week. No problem, he says, Friday is most likely, although he can't guarantee it: "Weather dependent," he says, ominously.

As it happens, Friday dawns fairly dry, and when I get to The Avenue I see Roger already rolling his paint trolley up the far touchline. I duck under the perimeter rail and wander over to join him, realising as I do so that I've never actually set foot on the pitch. It answers a few questions even before I reach the groundsman. It tells me, with every scrunched and sunken step, why it seems an age since we saw Taylor Prell leave a defence for dead, and why most of Dan Solomi's recent bursts from rucks have been snaffled before he's started. Sand. The runner inside me finds this as enticing as brown sugar ladled over stiff cold porridge. Still, as Roger points out when I reach him, without the sand, by this time of the year we would be knee-deep in a quagmire: by comparison, ankle-deep in a sand-pit sounds like a good deal.

I must admit, I have been led up here the day before the game partly through curiosity about the ground, but also through curiosity about the groundsman. I'm intrigued. Hang around the club for any length of time, and however much they try to avoid it, eventually the spotlight picks out most of the key figures. Not Roger. I suppose it is the nature of the job that the groundsman stands in the shadowy wings, vacating the stage before the actors and audience turn up. But in Roger's case, from the snippets I've picked up he sounds to be nothing less than the Prince of Darkness. I've heard how he loudly castigates

---

53 It's not just Esher's chairman of rugby, Mr Inverdale, that enjoys the *terroir* of Wharfedale. The club always brings a healthy support, who exude enjoyment of what we have to offer. Perhaps we remind them of their own roots. Esher were founded in 1923, shared their first field with cows, and in the early days (tell me when all this sounds familiar) had to get changed in a local pub.

children who dare to play on his pitch without permission, how in his youth he was an irascible fast bowler, and how (here comes the genuinely scary part) in his professional life he was a senior tax inspector: so, an ogre, right? Except that I've walked five yards with Roger before I've ripped up that notion. Or, rather, I've remembered that there can be a distinction between what you do and who you are.

Roger couldn't be more friendly, although he makes no bones about how outspoken he can be as the advocate for his voiceless pitch: how – to the squirming discomfort of others on the committee – he recently gave a piece of his mind to the match official who passed a snow-covered pitch as fit for play. "They have no idea what those decisions mean for the grass," he says. I must admit, the grass cover looks sparse. Walking alongside Roger, from six feet up the view reminds me of the Australian outback from 30,000 feet, in which tiny tufts of greenery are major landmarks.

"You wonder how it ever recovers from this," I say.

"You'd be surprised. Mother nature is a much better groundsman than most people give her credit for," Roger answers.

So *that's* who his co-worker is! Otherwise, it looks a job for a man who enjoys solitude. Most of the time, out here under the open sky, that solitude must be a boon. Roger tells me that being alone has, just occasionally, caught him out. Like the occasion he took it upon himself to do a spot of maintenance on one of the floodlights.

"I hoisted myself into position on the cherry-picker, and was up there working away quite happily when I heard the engine cut out below. Hmm. It was a bit lonely up there, but it could have been worse. I knew that the players would be turning up for training, and when they did – and after they'd had a good laugh at my expense – they rang someone to come and fettle the engine." Roger pauses – I imagine he's pondering how else this scenario might have played out. "Mind, I haven't done that job again on my own."

Roger is eighty now. He looks healthy enough, but on one new knee, and after a heart scare last year, he is aware that nothing is forever. After each turn on the pitch he glances at his wrist to see what his heart-rate monitor is telling him. The news is fine, but it doesn't stop him wondering. "Who will do this job after me?" he asks. Good question. On one level, it is the most thankless of tasks. What pride is there to be taken in preparing a lumpy, sloping, poorly drained pitch? When I look down at the paint roller, daubing its blotchy lines on rutted wet mud, it reminds me of the sloppy mess of art classes at primary school: where's the pleasure there? At pitch level, I can't help thinking how much more rewarding it would be to be the chief manicurist at a modern stadium like

Twickenham, where laying down sleek stripes with the mower and acute lines with the spray marker must offer the satisfaction a silk-screen printer knows. But then I look up, and instead of a dark cavern of empty seats, I'm looking at a Grass Wood and Threshfield Moor. Somehow, I suspect that against this backcloth, the prospect of playing with old boys' toys – tractors and tools – will always find a taker.

Let's face it, the Wharfedale groundsman will never know the pleasure of tamping his pipe as he gazes out over an immaculate stretch of baize. For the players, the grass will always be too long in September and the mud too deep in February. For most of us, though, we see in what Roger does the same that we see in what the coach does: not just the best *he* can do, but realistically the best *anyone* can do. With both men, an injection of millions could transform the quality of their work, but sadly it would transform it into not being *us*. And, on balance, we are happy to settle for *us*.

As I leave Roger and drive back down the dale, the windscreen wipers come on. First intermittently, then continuously, then fast. *Poor pitch*, I'm thinking as the rain chugs down for the rest of the day. And sure enough, although the rain has stopped when we arrive back on Saturday afternoon, I can hear the tell-tale *clack-clack* of boots in the mud as the players run through their pre-match routines.

In the clubhouse the atmosphere is tense. Although we have home matches against lower-placed teams to come, we're unlikely to avoid relegation unless we win at least one other match. Esher, just above us in the table, look like our best bet. But that, in turn, tells us that they are still not safe, and will themselves have identified this as a crunch match.

Crunch is the word. No-one is expecting anything pretty. All the talk in the bar is of it being a day for eight-man rugby. Still, one thing I've noticed is how it always takes the players a while to realise what all the observers seem to know. Certainly as far as Esher are concerned, they start the game as if they can put us to the sword, rather than slowly clobber us with a blunt instrument. With the slope and breeze in their favour, they zip the ball around dangerously. After ten minutes of swinging our defence from side to side they find themselves with a two-man overlap. The Esher centre is under no pressure and could probably run in on his own, but with his wing in acres of space beyond, he takes the safe option and ships the ball out – and straight into touch. *What!* In the Shed there is a silence borne of disbelief.

"If I didn't know better," Alec says after a while, "I'd be suspecting the involvement of a Far Eastern betting syndicate in that pass."

The wings of Esher's confidence seem clipped by that one bungled move. From then on they are less sure of their ability to get over the line. Later in the half they win two penalties, and both times trust their kicker's boot rather than their runners' hands. 0–6. As for the Greens, whenever we get the ball we clutch it close, and head up the field with a tenacious grip that wouldn't be out of place in a greasy pole competition. Still, this method wins its reward, when after half an hour the pack rolls over. 5–6.

The crucial moment in the afternoon comes just before half time, when Taylor Prell fields a kick deep in defence. He runs back up towards half way, then hoists a towering kick to chase. Off he hares, roared on by the crowd. He launches himself up into the air to regather the ball, but finds the Esher full-back has beaten him to it. Taylor effectively takes the man out in the air, and both players land on their backs. There is a thud, the sound of the ref's whistle, and then a worried silence. It's not Esher's full-back we're concerned for – he's quickly back up on his feet – but ours. Taylor is still on the floor, and we're fearing that when he eventually gets up it will be to see a red card. It shouldn't affect the decision, but perhaps the fact that Taylor has come out worst from the challenge has bought the referee's sympathy: he only gets yellow. I can't help but think that if it had been Taylor holding the ball when the collision happened, the Dale mob would have been baying for Esher blood – or at least something red – and it would have taken a brave man to deny them. Anyway, rather than face more than half the match with a man down, we now only have to see out ten minutes. And we do.

When Taylor comes back on soon after half time, we kick a penalty to go 8–6 up. We now have the lead, the slope and the breeze. It should be all over, but the pitch is cutting up more and more, and for all our territory and possession, we can't find a way through the Esher line to seal the deal.

As for the periods when the opposition have the ball, the tension is palpable. I can hear Julia, the coach's girlfriend, muttering under her breath behind me – "I don't like it, I don't like it!" – and I want to reassure her that none of us do. Or do we? Sure, the story of the match, as we read it, is ugly, uncertain and prosaic. But the history of the match, when the referee blows the final whistle, is altogether different. We've won. Only 8–6, but we've *won*. Now, as the victors, we can write into the history of each brutal collision something ultimately noble, heroic, and poetic. And we *like* it.

Rugby is a game of many facets, and many styles. There are terms for most of them, but in the clubhouse afterwards the one I keep on hearing is that today we've seen a game of 'old-fashioned' rugby.

Old-fashioned rugby. What on earth was that? Was it 23–15, back in the hipster seventies, with Phil Bennett jinking through a concertinaed defence, or Serge Blanco and Jean-Pierre Rives riotously flinging around a light-brown ball in the Parisian spring? Well it was both of those, but more often than not it was something else. It was mud-caked men in rain-soaked jerseys, kicking a heavy leather ball with heavy leather boots: it was men slogging around with all the freedom of warriors in chain mail: it was medieval. It was 8–6. An old-fashioned game.

Chapter 29

*~ in which we get a taste of Fudge's medicine, Fylde
come to play, and we find the trail of a meteor ~*

This is what it's all about. With the vaguest hint of spring in the air, before the home game against Fylde we've come up to Threshfield early, but instead of turning right to go straight down to The Avenue, we've turned left through the little hamlet of Skirethorns, and climbed steeply up Malham Moor Lane to where the road ends. Where we park, up amongst the knuckles of limestone on the dome of the moor, we're less than two miles from the ground, but the dale below is out of sight. On this March morning, a few sheep are bleating in the distance. Other than that, the silence is vast. We often bring the dog up here before a match, and apart from the odd mountain biker making his way over the track to Malham, we rarely see anyone. We don't walk far – just a mile or so round the old lime kilns by Height Laithe – but even the briefest whiff of the high air acts as an opiate. It's better than any drug, though, because even if its effect crashes down during the game, it will somehow float back afterwards. Whatever the result, no game day that starts up here on Malham Moor is ever wholly bleak.

Today, aside from the sheep, the only sign of life up here on the tops is a trail of smoke coming from the chimney of Bordley House Farm. It is one of England's most remote dwellings, lying in the fold of the moor, overlooked by the limestone ridge of Proctor High Mark. When you walk through the landscape of Wharfedale, you walk through the history of its club. Take that name – Proctor. Back in the fourteenth century, a 'proctor' was someone who leased and managed a remote part of a monastic estate.[54] Most of the land around here was owned by Fountains Abbey, and from about 1350 to the present day Proctors have farmed and then owned the estate at Bordley. Over time the family name spread throughout the area, so it is no surprise to find it peopling the story of the club.

---

54 The English word 'proctor', as any self-respecting dead Roman would recognise, comes from the Latin *procurare*, meaning 'to manage'.

Nowadays, two Procter brothers epitomise the unsung, often unspoken strength of Wharfedale. Neither Brian or David played to any great level, but in different ways helped build the club's modern success. Brian, a gentle character, for years devoted himself to that most thankless of all tasks – creating a strong second team. Yet it's David who has literally helped build the club. Back in 1966, on farmland which Younce had made over to the club, a new pitch and single-story clubhouse were opened: all made possible by a local philanthropist called Mrs Coulthurst, who liked what the club was doing. But the upper floor of the clubhouse, the main stand, the Shed – all these were built later, on the back of David's sharpness as a fund-raiser and organiser. Estate manager. Proctor by name...

At the same time that David was growing the club off the field, on the field something even more significant was being built. A serious team. When leagues were introduced to English rugby in the eighties, they were the making of Wharfedale. For years, a persuasive man called Ron Booth had been improving the club's fixture list, but the bigger clubs around were still reluctant to take a team of farmers seriously. Now the leagues dictated a large part of every club's fixtures. The leagues, in turn, were dictated by results – and there was no arguing with them.

Starting at Level Seven of the English game, Wharfedale went into the final match of the 1987-88 season needing a win to be crowned champions. They were at home to their rivals for promotion, Rotherham, and a fifteen-year-old Daniel Harrison was standing down in the scoreboard corner. In the final play of the game John Stockton, the local vet, went over in the corner for what Dan describes as a "hotly disputed" try. When I quiz Dan about what he means, there's a pause: "To be honest, he dropped it."

No matter, Dale were on the up, and having climbed the first rung, they now set about Level Six: it detained them only a year. Dan Harrison was still at school, but by now he was on the pitch too. There has never been a time when the Dale side was not shot through with Harrison involvement, but during this period it almost became a family fiefdom. Dan was often lining up alongside his cousins Glenn and Michael, and occasionally his brother Tom. On the touchline Clarty, with his best friend Peter Hartley, was calling the shots as coach.

So to Level Five, where Dale spent a couple of seasons before a win away to Lichfield sent them up again.

The air became more rarified at Level Four, and another period of acclimatisation followed. Come the start of the 95-96 season, though, Dale started at a gallop, winning their first three matches of the campaign. But twenty minutes into their fourth, 0–20 down at Dewi Morris's Winnington Park, and with their fly-half hobbling off injured, Wharfedale's escalator seemed to have stalled. In the hasty rearrangement that followed on the field, a teenage wing called Andy Hodgson was moved to full-back, and Dale discovered that back there they had a star.

Clarty thinks that Hodge "in his prime was probably the best back we've ever had."[55] Dan goes further. He reckons that back then Hodge was "potentially the best attacking full-back in England." When Dan said that to me, my initial reaction was probably the same as yours when you read that – *pub talk!* – but from what I know of him, Dan follows the family tradition of calling spades spades. More than that, as head of rugby at Sedbergh, he's spent the last twenty years guiding young players on their way up to the top flight of the game. So is there something to what Dan says? And if so, why do we not all know the name Andy Hodgson? Dan's explanation is that the top of the English game was then dominated by forwards, and that game needed full-backs with enormous boots who could position the pack up-field. Hodge was primarily a runner, not a kicker, so when he moved on it was not in Rugby Union at all, but League. At Bradford Bulls his brief career was dogged by injury. On he went, to Wakefield Wildcats, eventually returning to Wharfedale and his Union roots.

It was back at Winnington Park that Hodge's talent was uncorked. He ran the home team ragged, and an hour after being 0–20 down, Wharfedale were blinking in disbelief as they left the field 31–23 victors. "I sat down with my dad afterwards," Dan remembers, "and just said, 'This guy Hodge can fly – we have to re-think things.' And we did – we ripped up all our existing moves, and started to channel everything in Hodge's direction."

From then on, there was no stopping them. Or the support. When I asked Len Tiffany if he had been there at Worcester, he said "Never mind just me – the whole of the Dale was there!" The Dale support at Worcester saw yet another Wharfedale win. On it went, and when the final game of the season came round, against Sheffield, the Dale still had a hundred percent record. They needed only a draw to guarantee yet another promotion. Yet for Dan Harrison, this was no gimme. The previous weekend, playing in a charity match at Sedbergh, he had severed his tongue. Badly. With ten stitches in, he rang his dad midweek and told him that he couldn't play. "Right," Clarty said: "Well, come down anyway." Needless to say, he ended up playing. By half time, even though Dale were leading, Dan says he felt dreadful. "Here," his dad said, "have some of this – George's Special Medicine." And Clarty passed him a water bottle containing Fudge's cure-all: Lamb's Navy Rum. That was the last drink Dan had that day. Dale won, and to mark the greatest achievement in the club's history,

---

55 "I don't count Spencer in that," Clarty says: "We never had him in his prime."

the celebrations began. Dan was normally at the heart of any team party, but not that day. He went straight home and slept for twenty hours.

When we get down to The Avenue for the Fylde match, things are buzzing. The visitors have brought a big contingent across the Pennines. The spring-like weather has brought the locals out too, and by the time the game starts it's clear that this is the biggest crowd of the season: the stand and the Shed are rammed, and patrons are spilling right round the bottom of the ground. The atmosphere is friendly, but as with any Roses match, it has a particular spice.

In most team sports, at most levels, there are games within games – personal match-ups which will be pivotal to the outcome. Perhaps a player on one side used to play for the other, or maybe particular individuals have a history of contest. There is something of both these factors at work this afternoon. At the heart of it is our skipper. Now, since James comes from near Fylde, he has played with and against plenty of their players since he was a boy. More than that, Fylde know that James is more than just good – he's central to everything we do. Anyway, the rumour is that James has been tipped off by a Fylde friend to watch his back: he's going to be a marked man. We hear these kind of rumours all the time, and normally they're not worth the paper they're not written on.

Today, it seems as if there might be something in the whisper. From the off the Fylde players are chirping away at James, barging him around when the ball goes dead, and generally trying to get a rise from him. Well, they do. After quarter of an hour, with Fylde already a try to the good, Cameron Hudson breaks free on the opposition 22. James sets off in support, but finds his jersey reluctant to come with him: one of the giant Fylde locks is attached to it. Rather than just try to break free, James turns round and flings an arm. At this moment, fortune smiles on James. Not only does the flail fail to land, but all three officials have their backs to him, as they hare off to keep pace with the ball carrier. Cameron goes over to bring the scores level, but whilst the rest of the Greens mob the scorer, James is being mobbed by Fylde players. It's only handbags, and he's giving as good as he gets – *no-one is saying we're angels* – but when the game restarts it is the Fylde players now thinking they have a score to settle. We can't foretell the outcome, but we can sense that this little tourney is about to reach some sort of conclusion. Just a couple of minutes later, it does: the play is over on the far side, so in the Shed we see nothing. What we hear, though, is an eruption of noise from the stand, and a significant blast on the referee's whistle. The linesman steps in, makes a gesture to indicate striking, and a moment later the referee pulls over Chris Briers, the Fylde full-back: *red card*.

As always happens at these moments, the crowd go virtually silent. We're all suddenly reappraising the game. The point is that, if we're honest, we know that Fylde are a better side than us, and we're calculating that having one man more for three-quarters of the match might just even things up. If we have any doubts about Fylde's superior quality, they are firmly quashed by two rapier-thrust tries they score before half time. 7–24. Never mind a single red card, it looks as if we might need a two-man advantage to turn this one round.

Still, after he's drawn the half-time raffle, Adge stands on the balcony, microphone in hand, and quietly takes us into his confidence.

"Do you know, I often stand here at half time when we're losing, and I have to try very hard to convince myself that we can get something out of the game. But…" – and here Adge pauses as he seems genuinely thoughtful – "…today I really think we can. In the second half we'll have the slope, we'll have a man advantage on the pitch, and if we all do our part, we'll have a man advantage off the pitch too." And here Adge gathers momentum and volume, quickly shifting through his rhetorical gears of peroration – *what will we do?* – and exhortation – *we'll bring them home!* – to leave the Wharfedale support flying down the fast lane as the teams run back out for the second half. All we have to do is scoop up the team and carry them with us. Now we have the sixteenth man in place, and what feels like a two-man advantage!

Despite the din, the Fylde supporter next to me doesn't seem worried.

"This one's an odd game, isn't it?" he says, as the teams take their positions. "I mean, normally when a side goes a man down they lose – simple as that. But not today." He's not crowing – just stating what seems to be the obvious, as he mulls over what he's seeing.

"Maybe, but have you seen the slope?" I ask.

"Oh I see, there is a bit of a tilt now you come to mention it." He still doesn't seem too concerned.

Within two minutes of the re-start he turns round and raises an eyebrow. We've scored and converted. All of a sudden, with nearly forty minutes to play, a ten point difference seems very little. And, inevitably, the fourteen men of Fylde start to tire. On the hour, Jamie Guy slots a penalty. All we need is a converted try to draw level. *All!* We go over the line once but are called back for a forward pass. We go over again, but fail to get the ball down. Still, possession and territory are all Green, and Fylde are pushed ever further down towards there own line. They get their hands on the ball but knock-on.

So it comes to this. With a minute to go Wharfedale have a five-metre scrum down by the scoreboard. Now, believe it or not there are matches at The Avenue when you will never hear a single cry of '*RIVER!*' It might be a day for the backs, and the pack might never get the scent of the line. This is not one of those days.

In truth, it must have been for a moment just such as this that Adge, forty-something years ago, first summoned his fellow forwards to drive on, down towards the Wharfe. Adge is still our real pack leader, and he's still at it. He's come over to stand with us in the Shed during the second half, and is leading the battle cry. We follow his lead, and the result on the pitch is inevitable. The ball goes in and slowly, slowly, the Green Machine starts to crank itself forwards. It's gaining traction – it's rolling now – and the roar soars higher. Soon it's at full steam, up to, and over the line. Jack Barnard falls on the ball and… well, what? Not *total* delirium. We've scored a try, yes, but we still need the conversion to draw level. This, we realise, will be the last kick of the game, and since it is only a few metres in from touch, it is not a given. We're always being told by the old guard at Wharfedale that we have to keep the faith – that we have to believe – and the strange thing is that for once, I find that I do. I'm absolutely sure that Jamie will do the business for us. He steps back to compose himself, and for the second time today I'm aware of a great wave of silence. Not complete, though. Earlier it was the sheep, and now it is the birds up in the trees at the end of The Avenue, twittering away as if home-building somehow mattered more than what is going on below: a man in funny-coloured clothes kicking a ball between two posts. Well, that ball matters to *us*. Jamie trots up and – *boof!* – belts it right between the posts.

With the final whistle, nine hundred people offer a salute: the players salute each other, we salute the players, and the players salute us. Yet together, we're all saluting *it* – that rare miracle of a sporting result where we know we have seen something special, and even rarer, all have something to celebrate. The first person to tap me on the shoulder is the Fylde supporter.

"You see, I was right – the team with fourteen men didn't lose!" he says, with an ironic smile.

Elsewhere on the ground, other gestures are being made. Chris Briers, I later hear, has gone over to our skipper and our coach – both of whom he knows well – and apologised profusely. Accepted.

As for James, he's quite recovered himself.

"The atmosphere was electric," he says. "Nothing beats hearing '*RIVER!*' being screamed in the last minute of a game like that. The players feed off it."

Yet the biggest gesture of all is made in the clubhouse, where it feels as if half of Lancashire and half of Yorkshire have shoe-horned themselves in to bury the hatchet. Eventually Adge climbs on to a bar stool. He delivers his Sports Report, running through the other results in the league, but as far as we here are concerned, it seems as if there was only one event worth mentioning. Adge moves on to talk about what we have just shared. For the lethal speed of the Fylde backs he has sincere praise.

"Traditionally," he says, "we've had powerful backs too. Just now, that's not where our strength lies. Today we won by other means; we had power up front; we had spirit; we had resolve; we had determination…"

"Aye, and you had an extra man!" a Fylde supporter yells from the back.

"Not true!" Adge darts back at him, eyes flashing at this opportunity for the final score of the day. "We had just the right number, and if your full-back hadn't mistaken Mr Doherty's head for a coconut shy, you'd have had that number too!"

At which there is an uproar of laughter – from both sets of fans – which nearly takes the roof off the clubhouse bar.

The sun has gone down behind Threshfield Moor when we eventually leave the clubhouse. Still, as we walk back down The Avenue, there is enough light to glance towards the corner at the scene of the game's final act. The turf here tells a tale. All over the pitch there have been scrums, rucks and mauls, but nowhere else is the ground much disturbed. Here, where the final act was played out, the surface is very different. Five metres out there is a great circle of rutted ground. From there to the line the footmarks form a small straight trench. It's like the scene where a meteor has crashed to earth, and even though there is no smoke or steam rising up, the ground embeds a great mass of spent energy. That, there, was what it was all about.

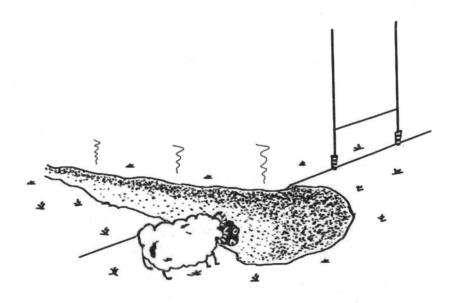

Chapter 30

~ in which we meet some gambolers, host Cinderford for
a party in pink, and say a farewell ~

It's now March, and heading up Wharfedale at this time of year is good for the heart. The daffodils on the green in Theshfield may have not yet flowered, the leaves on the trees down by the Wharfe are still only buds, and with no growth in the grass the fells remain a blanched beige. But never mind all that – peep over the walls, and it is impossible not to smile. In every field there are the first real signs telling us that winter is on its way out. Yes, the early lambs are at play, skipping up onto rocks, and scarpering around with their new pals. In time they will learn that their lives might not really be for living, but that realisation can wait awhile. Just for now they are rising to what is surely the highest attainment any sentient being can know: *being silly*. And that, of course, brings us back to grown men throwing an odd-shaped ball around.

In rugby terms, the only people who have traditionally found Wharfedale heartening in the spring are the opposition. Steve, the coach's dad, tells me that when he played for Bradford, each season when the fixture list was published he would scan down to see when they were down to play Wharfedale.

"If we played them during the lambing season I was relieved. We knew we'd not be up against the farmers, but probably the farmers' sons. Mind you, they were no push-over even then. If it was in the autumn or winter, though, we knew we were in for a hard match. I remember coming up here for a game in January once, and one of our props looked at the Dale team as they ran out, and said: 'Steve, if I leave this pitch with anything less than half an ear hanging off, right now I think I'd settle for that'. Actually, Wharfedale weren't really rough – but God, they were tough!"

It's easy to make light of the effect that lambing, and farming in general, have on a team like Wharfedale. But it's no cutesy joke. Starting around now, Clarty tells me, is a three-week period when sheep farmers are lucky to get more than a couple of hours sleep a night. Even if they can get away for a match, they're likely to be shattered by the time they get on to the pitch.

Nor is the rest of the year easy. For those with cows, the herd is always tapping its watch come milking time. When Richard Stockdale told me that he and his brother always played in separate teams – one in the Thirds and the other in the Fourths, I asked him if they didn't get on: "We got on fine, but we had a farm to run. Either Thirds or Fourths would always play at home, and that meant that one of us could always get back in time for milking."

With fewer farmers in the team, nowadays milking and lambing are lesser issues. But even without absentees for lambing, we had all been expecting that our survival in this division would hang in the balance until the last game of the season. Most years it does. Yet in the last month we have taken points from every game, and rapidly clambered up the table. And now we're like the breathless climber who comes over a little snowy rise in the ridge and unexpectedly sees the summit just ahead.

8 March 2015

1	Ealing Trailfinders	25	115
2	Rosslyn Park	25	106
3	Coventry	25	96
4	Blackheath	25	80
5	Fylde	25	80
6	Hartpury College	25	74
7	Richmond	25	65
8	Darlington Mowden Park	25	62
9	Blaydon	25	58
10	Esher	25	57
11	Loughborough Students	25	56
12	**Wharfedale**	**25**	**55**
13	Old Albanian	25	44
14	Cinderford	25	39
15	Tynedale	25	33
16	Macclesfield	25	13

We've all squinted disbelievingly at that league table this week, and had to pinch ourselves to check that what we see is true – that if we gain a bonus point win against Cinderford we will be guaranteed a place in this league next season – and yes, that is the reality. All season long the talk in the clubhouse has been about reaching the milestone of twenty years at this level, and we're almost there.

That said, however tantalisingly close our own summit may be, the penalties of a slip at this late stage are horrific. Cinderford would suddenly be hard on our heels, and their route to the end of the season has fewer potential crevasses than ours. One way or another, it promises to be a momentous occasion.

And yet the team's continuance in National 1 is not the most pressing issue for the club right now. One of the Under-10s side is facing a much more serious battle for survival. A young lad called Tom has a rare liver cancer, and has been receiving support from a local children's cancer charity, the Candlelighters. So, today is all about fundraising for the charity. Pink is the Candlelighters' colour, and as a visual prompt for the crowd to dig deep, the Dale team are all sporting bright pink socks. The buckets rattle.

The club, I suspect, would throw its weight behind this charity whoever the victim in its ranks was, but the name of this lad lends a particular significance to the collection. Tom is a Slater, grandson of the Tom Slater who first played for the club in 1949. Granddad, as I already know, is a realist. I have this in mind when I find him at the back of the Shed, just before the Cinderford match kicks off. He tells me that young Tom is responding well to the treatment. I'm inclined to believe him.

As for the match itself, once the whistle is blown Wharfedale show that they haven't lost sight of their purpose on the field. In the first half they are playing up hill, but this doesn't stop them running in three tries. Cinderford's only answer is three penalties. At the turn-around, then, we are 15 9 up. It's not a huge lead, but we have the slope favouring us in the second half, and so far Cinderford have posed no great threat. Nor do they have much support on the touchline.

All-in-all, there is little material here to get Adge excited as he takes the microphone for the half-time raffle. We get one good quip – "If Ray Mears wants to learn something about survival, he should come to Wharfedale: we've been at it for twenty years, not just eating snail sandwiches in Borneo for a couple of weeks" – but in truth, Adge sounds luke-warm. It really does look as if the team will be able to do the job on their own. We are having a rare glimpse into the psyche of supporters in the league's top clubs: not only is our victory predictable, but it looks as if our vocal backing will be ornamental: nice, but not necessary. It is a peace of mind which we always crave but which, like so many objects of desire, is in truth deadly dull.

Ten minutes into the second half, when the backs have run in two more tries and taken us out to a 25–9 lead, our confidence seems well placed. A win is on the cards, and with the four-try bonus point also in the bag, we can start to unfoil the champagne bottles. Except – inevitably – Wharfedale decide that the easy final step is not for them. No, they start to dance around, jinking this way and that. We've waited all season, and here it is: champagne rugby![56] True, it results in one of the tries of the season from the backs – *ppupp!* go the corks in the Shed – but it also results in a first, and then a second Cinderford try. Oh dear. The momentum has shifted.

Cinders are still eleven points behind with a couple of minutes to play when, in quick succession, two Dale players get yellow-carded defending on our own line. Cinderford now have a scrum right under our posts. If they push us over here, or if we give away a penalty try, we will be defending the last play of the game with an insignificant four-point advantage and a significant two-man disadvantage. On the touchline we're now trying to ram the corks back in. Our perch suddenly seems precarious, and the drop beneath is dizzying. Time for steady heads. After two reset scrums (for once no-one is complaining about the clock running down whilst this happens) the Dale pack rouses itself, pushes Cinderford off the ball, which is passed back to Jamie Guy who – *boooof!* – whangs the thing into touch. *Now* we can clink the champagne glasses.[57]

Truly, there is much to celebrate. Perhaps surprisingly, the team itself is not the chief toast. This afternoon they have done no more than assured our survival in the league. In other words, we're not going to be losers. But the absence of a negative doesn't in itself make much of a positive. Sportsmen are winners by nature, and for the team, I suspect that any celebrations can wait until the end of the season. The Yorkshire Cup may not mean what it once did, but perhaps if the team can retain it, they can indulge themselves in a winners' celebration. So those festivities can wait.

No, the celebrations today are for individuals. First comes young Tom Slater. Before the team leave the field they have gathered to have their photograph taken with the Under-10s. He looks a little wan, but there, hiding himself in the middle, is young Tom. Later, on their long journey home, one of the Cinderford physios posts a lovely photo taken with them and "this little Wharfedale hero" – a slightly bemused-looking Tom. He might be the centre of attention, but he's not exactly lording it. Definitely his granddad's grandson.

The other individual being lauded after the game is Matt Freeman, who we hear has been summoned back to New Zealand by his mum. He leaves the field to the applause of his team mates and the cheers of the supporters. Judged purely by his deeds on the pitch, Freeman has done relatively little for the team: only eight appearances, of which none were as a starter. It's true that he made a weighty impact in those games, but I sense that this is not what is being marked

---

56 *Champagne rugby* (def.): offers immediate euphoria, but more froth than substance, costly, and when indulged in to excess, inevitably a source of regret.

57 These references to champagne are – need I say? – metaphorical. To my certain knowledge the Shed is a Krug-free zone.

here. What I keep hearing is that 'Freeman' is a *club man*. He's been a stalwart for the Foresters, and never carped about only playing a supporting role for the Firsts. To use a word any self-respecting Kiwi would take as the ultimate complement, he's been *staunch*. The team have their own send-off planned for Freeman, but first comes the official one from the club. Clarty stands on a bar stool in a packed clubhouse, and thanks him for his contribution.

"When he did eventually come into the first team, I have to say we wondered why it had taken so long to include him. And seriously, it does make you wonder about what the selectors are playing at." Clarty pauses for effect here, as we all wonder whether we're hearing the unspeakable: dissent in the ranks. "Well, since I'm head of the selection panel, I could probably start by asking myself a few questions."

A few more words, and Clarty calls Freeman forward to receive his tie and tankard.[58]

The toast may be to individuals – to Tom Slaters past and future, and to Matt Freeman present – but through their selfless natures it comes back to the club and the community.

Doubtless for the team, tonight the games will go on. But for some, at this time of year, it is the work that must go on. When we leave, and drive back past Oat Croft Farm in Burnsall, I see someone zipping his overalls up in the yard. It's Richard Stockdale, ready to head up through the fields and check on developments.

---

58 Except it's not actually Freeman that receives it. The fancy-dress theme he's given his team mates for his farewell bash is ginger – I'm stood near a very fetching Highland cow, which I gather is Dan Stockdale. In this zoo-cum-freak show, Freeman himself is only one of *two* identical Honey Monsters present. When Freeman's name is called, one of the monsters dashes forward to take the goodies, and milk the applause. Amidst general confusion, in the middle of the room the other monster removes his head piece to reveal the real Matt Freeman.

Chapter 31

~ in which we meet some little people, experience déjà
vu in Richmond, and find ourselves playing canalball ~

All season long I'd been dreading this scenario. We've avoided relegation.
Early. *Early!* Can you believe it? It's still only March, and the team has
already done the trick. Over the years Wharfedale, the masters of suspense, have
ideally waited until the final play of the final game of the season to keep the
outcome in doubt. And year after year, as the team have toyed with us, I've stood
on the touchline thinking *if you put this in a book they'd never believe you.* And now
that I've started to put Wharfedale in a book, they've gone and chosen another
ending entirely. Damn them!

That, of course, is the writer inside me talking. The club man inside me
couldn't be happier. We can now enjoy that rarest of luxuries for Wharfedale:
we can *relax* and *enjoy* the rest of the season. There's just one problem: no-one at
The Avenue really knows how to do that. When I've spoken to the old-timers,
one theme which keeps recurring is how they are never happier than when
facing a test: how they would prefer to search out a challenge rather than just
take the easy option. Perhaps the club can create another, more climactic ending
to the story of our season. I suspect that they can.

The Yorkshire Cup. That's where this book began, and I'm hoping that it is
where this book can end. In years when Wharfedale's league season goes to the
death, our interest in 't'owd pot' inevitably gets marginalised. The Dale always
field a team, but instead of the Firsts, it is the Foresters. That team can take us so
far, but rarely to the final itself. So a proper cup run might just be our reward
for surviving early.

A couple of days after the Cinderford match I'm with Jon Feeley, and I put
in my request.

"No pressure Jon," I say, "but it would make my book a lot easier to finish if
you could get to the final of the Cup".

"Don't worry," he replies: "After last Saturday, we've got that in our sights now."

I'm speaking to Jon in the foyer of Bramhope Primary School. He's asked me
to go into his school and speak to the kids about being a writer. At the risk of

believing my own publicity, I've agreed. After all, how scary can the questions be from a group of infants? I give my little spiel – that writing books is really just like sharing your stories out in the playground – and straight away, up go the eager hands.

"Do you write narrative – like histories, or fiction – like stories?" *Woah! Throw her a sidestep…* "Er, perhaps histories are stories, and stories are histories!"

"Does being a writer pay well?" *Lie! Kick that one into touch…* "Well enough, thanks!"

"Do you write in a shed?"[59] *What? Remember, this is just a game…* "No, but I sometimes get the ideas for writing in a Shed!"

And so it goes on, with testers coming in from right, mid and particularly left field, until after twenty minutes of our fun run-around, Jon blows the whistle.

One reason I've agreed to this little examination has been that I'm *nosy*. I want to spy on Jon in his professional life. I want to try and join two apparently disconnected strands: rugby coach and primary school teacher. It's easy to joke about how similar they must be – how in both roles Jon is trying to impart wisdom to sometimes-petulant listeners who really just want to play – but at heart we know that the changing room is a man's world, and the infants' classroom isn't. The real similarity in Jon's jobs, I suspect, lies in one word: preparation. Jon has asked me in to school, he says, as part of a plan to prepare the kids for a real world which lies beyond the virtual one on their iPads and phones. But whilst we are waiting for the children to file in, Jon tells me that much of his time at Wharfedale is spent readying raw youngsters for the real rugby world which they are about to face – of gnarly old pros on their way down, and wannabe Premiership players on their way up. One thing I've gleaned about Jon is that he seldom raises his voice with the team: even when we were 5–43 down to Coventry at half time, I gather that Jon's method was to hold up an imaginary mirror, and get the players to be honest about what they saw.

There's one irony in what Jon says to me at the school. For all that he wants to draw his kids away from their phones, and up into the wide world of joined-up writing, he's more than happy to use modern gizmos with the team.

"I'll do anything I can to strengthen the spirit of the squad. I've set up this WhatsApp group which only the team can access – look." and here Jon opens up the page and scrolls down some posts.[60] "They can say and share what they like. It's all positive and fun, but what I want them to know is that even if they only see their team mates three times a week, they can't go hiding from them."

---

59 If I had been more familiar with the working methods of Roald Dahl I might have seen where this curveball question was coming from.

60 These are mainly joshing comments about players caught in Rowena's match photos and (what was that I just glimpsed about the Skipton kebab shop last Saturday night?) other *stuff*.

Jon's school is in a leafy village outside Leeds. It's a school where teaching comes ahead of social work, and that seems to suit Jon to a tee. The kids obviously love him, and he has that nice knack of being able to get a hundred of them moving in the right direction with a dangled carrot rather than a waved stick. Somehow, I can't see Jon coaching a Premiership team: he wouldn't lack for expertise or experience, but at heart he is an educator and an encouraging motivator. I can't see how that skill set could best be used with an international player earning a small fortune, much of whose rugby education and motivation are already in place. And, frankly, Jon is probably too nice. He's got a steely edge, but I can't imagine him ever brandishing it cynically: his dad, Steve, tells me that when Jon was playing professionally, he once came home troubled about methods of clearing out a ruck area which a new coach was advocating: "Basically, Dad, he's training us to maim the opposition."

So I think Wharfedale suits Jon. But does Jon suit Wharfedale? Occasionally I hear voices in the Shed grumbling about the coach – that he's not getting us to play "in the Wharfedale way." Hidden in there is a suspicion about this man who is an *outsider*. I'd love to turn round and relay what Jon said to Steve when we were losing all those games back in January. "Well Dad, if they give me the sack at the end of the season I'll be gutted, but I'll understand. I still wouldn't want to leave the club, though. I think I'd just get my boots out and see if they'd have me in the Thirds." He's now an *insider*. I think Jon suits Wharfedale.

A minute into our next match, down at Richmond, I wonder whether Jon is still quite so devoted to his coaching post. With league safety now guaranteed, he's given Jamie Guy the Easter break off for university revision. At fly-half, then, Jimmy Harrison's grandson, Harry, gets another chance to extend the family's ninety-year run in Wharfedale's midfield. Perhaps it's as well that his Great Uncle Clarty isn't here to watch: our chairman of rugby is listed in Richmond's programme as being 'absent lambing'. Anyway, Harry's game lasts about thirty seconds. At the first ruck, on our 22, a Richmond player clears him out with a ferocious power that Harry will never see playing for the Foresters. As Richmond recycle the ball, somewhere in Harry's head is the knowledge that he must get up and back into the defensive line. Sadly, he obviously has no idea which direction that line is, and two shaky legs take him wobbling off up the field. Wrong way! Richmond's back-side jogs through the vacant space to score under the posts, and as the conversion goes over,

Jill the physio signals to the bench that Harry's badly concussed. Poor lad. He's barely been used since September, his mum has come down to London to cheer him on, and that's that. Off.

Jon must be scratching his head. Once again, with James as his foreman on the field, he's trying to fit square pegs into round holes. To be honest, the structure they quickly knock up isn't exactly sturdy, and Richmond spend the first half casually dismantling it. We go in 7–34 down. Is this *déjà vu*, or have we already been here this season? Of course we have, actually just down the road at Rosslyn Park, where we were losing 7–42 at the break. The situation then was almost identical, even to the whistling whine of planes sliding down into Heathrow. But then – *ha-ha!* – we scored three tries after the break to go home with at least a losing bonus point. Can we do the same here?

After an hour of the match, it seems that perhaps we can. By then we've scored our third try, and Richmond have retreated into their shells. We've twenty whole minutes to score a solitary try, but why chose one of the first nineteen minutes when the last one will be *much* more dramatic? Hence, in the final minute there we are: the Dale pack is rolling it's way to the line when, with a metre to go, Richmond pull it down. Now, when this happened at Rosslyn Park – and at Blaydon too, come to think of it – the referee awarded us a penalty try, and with that we clinched our precious point. And today the referee duly blows his whistle and awards a penalty tr… oh, right: just a penalty. Damn! From the next play we knock the ball on, and the match is over. Damn, damn, *damn!* We could cry into our beer, but hey, this is a league. Some decisions go for you, and some against. Decisions are value judgments. And this is a league. It may pain some of us to admit it, but the reality is that these things balance themselves out. Perhaps (I whisper it quietly) the balance is even in our favour! Let's just forget it. And let's move on…

…to Morley, a week later, and the Yorkshire Cup. It's actually the quarter-final stage, but our league status (too low to be excluded altogether, too high to be included in the early rounds) means that this is where we kick off our campaign. Our Title Defence, no less! And who should we be drawn against but the eleven-time winners, Morley.[61] Are we quaking? No. How times change.

---

61 Here's a riddle: how can Morley have won an annual event eleven times but have actually held the cup for seventeen years? Answer: they won in 1939, and until the business of war was over and play began again, Morley kept the cup in a box under the club secretary's bed.

Not many years ago Morley were so much stronger than Wharfedale that they would only offer a Second team to play our Firsts. At their height, when we were still battling up through the lower leagues, they were in the equivalent of the current Championship.

Today, again, they offer us their Seconds, but only because their Firsts are busy trying to stave off relegation to the seventh tier of the English leagues. A week ago they called the game off entirely, but Clarty has persuaded them to play it as a second team fixture. For all his Wharfedale roots, Clarty has a wider parish: he works hard for the game in Yorkshire as a whole, and he genuinely wants to encourage Morley to play. Even so, when we arrive on Saturday afternoon, I hear that as late as yesterday evening Morley were wanting to call the match off, talking about the "duty of care" they have for their players: they have been reassured that we have five teenagers in our team, and none of our regular first team will be present.

Well, they are. The first people I see at Morley are a gaggle of our Firsts. Thankfully for Morley they are on the touchline. They're not dressed for action, but I notice that each has brought a small bag.

"Hey," James says to Dan Solomi, nodding towards the little rucksack on his shoulder, "is that your boots in there?"

"Might be," he replies. Dan then points at the holdall by James's feet. "And you've brought yours, by the look of it."

"You're not wrong... and heh! – you know what Clarty said to us both on Thursday: he'd kill us if he found out that we'd played today!"

"Mind you, he's still busy lambing – he wouldn't have to know, would he?"

So they'd prefer to play than not. But failing that, they would prefer to spectate than not. Nice.

I wish I could say the same for the people of Morley, who are...where? Not here, that's for sure. The big old stand is virtually empty. Steve looks at it and shakes his head: "I played here when this stand was full," he remembers. Quite a few Dale supporters have come down, but rather than sit in the draught and shade of the stand, most of us head round the other side of the pitch to enjoy the spring sunshine. It's early April and in the air it feels as if the cricket season is about to start. On the scoreboard, it already has. At close of play we've run up a score of 104–0.

The biggest cheer of the day goes to the Morley captain when the referee approaches him after the score has reached 80–0: he's being offered the chance to have the Wharfedale dogs called off, but gamely he signals that an eighty-minute game is an eighty-minute game. Play on!

The biggest laugh of the day comes when we have a scrum on the Morley five-metre line. Their hooker is off injured, and the referee has decided on depowered scrums. What are we supposed to call out now? A river is a flowing, moving thing, and this pack is going precisely nowhere. At that moment I hear Alec's voice, further down the touchline.

"*CANALBALL!*"

But no, despite the wit, the sun and the score, it's all rather sad. Afterwards we make our way to the bar, through a cold and fusty function room under the stand. Faded glory. Steve, looking at the illustrious club shields above the bar, cryptically says that Morley were a great club themselves "before paying players became official." In those days, somehow, clubs like Morley managed to hold their own against the open professionalism of its Rugby League neighbours. If Union could manage parity then, surely it should have moved ahead of League when the two began playing on the same financial field. But somehow, it hasn't worked out that way at all. Not at Morley, not at Otley, not at Headingley, and not at scores of other clubs in the North where numbers are down and interest is dwindling.

"I can just about cope with Wharfedale being a rare species up here," Alec says, "but if we're left without any mates, we're buggered."

Still, the Cup defence is up and running. It will get harder from here on in, and as a Dale supporter, on balance I like that prospect. As a writer I'm just relieved.

My mind goes back to the start of the week, and a question I was asked at Jon's school.

"Do you ever have to change the ending of the book you're writing?" *Good question!* "Sometimes you have to – and sometimes it works out better that way."

Chapter 32

~ in which we hear a forbidden four-letter word, generously host Macclesfield, and see the glint of silver ahead ~

We're now into April, and at this time of year there's no doubting who the key players at the club are. Jill and Verity. The physios. The club has just posted an updated injury list on the website, and it makes for a sobering read. First there are names we'd almost forgotten, along with chillingly brief prognoses: Chris Howick – *awaiting op*; Philip Woodhead – *long-term injury*. Then there are the ones we might just see again this season: Harry Bullough – *returning to fitness after concussion*; Rob Baldwin – *in rehab (now senior water boy!)* Lastly, there is the rest of the squad. Their names aren't actually on the list, but we know that in one way or another most of them are hurting. Take the young prop Jake, who his dad tells me is "just about in bits" after starting every game of the season so far. Now that the pitches are firming up, the collisions lie not just ahead, but below too. Most of the players, when you see them get out of their cars, are hobbling across the tarmac like old veterans: and that's on their way *to* the changing room.

There is probably nothing exceptional about the extent of Wharfedale's injury tally this season. It's big, yes, but most clubs we visit claim the same hard-luck story. I wonder, though, whether other clubs attend to their list with the devotion Wharfedale seem to.[62] It's not that Jill and Verity each drive well over two hundred miles a week just to get here; it's not even the unpaid hours they put in arranging referrals, preparing rehab programmes, or travelling to away fixtures. No, my litmus test for the dedication underlying our physios' work comes on the field. I have seen the way our players respond when Jill is assessing an injury in the middle of a match, and it speaks volumes. A minute earlier they will have been bossing their way round the field like men, and all of a sudden they're boys. Now someone else is in charge. Jill respects what the players *want* to do: they respect what she is telling them they *can* do. Or can't. Sometimes I've seen an opposition player openly dispute the opinion of his physio, but when

---

62 Do I really have to use a word like devotion? Checking with my dictionary – 'Devotion: profound dedication; earnest attachment to a cause etc.' – I think I do.

Jill signals to the bench that a player can't continue, I've never seen one of our lads so much as shake his head in dissent. Whatever the nature of the relationship between player and physio at Wharfedale, evidently it runs deep and stands tall.

Although she looks younger than some of the players, Jill has been the Dale head physio for as long as I've known. Having first come to Wharfedale as an undergraduate, she now heads up what she calls a "fantastic" medical team here. But she's obviously a part of the team on the field too. I'm curious about that relationship: how does one female cope, sharing a life with thirty men for the two days an away fixture might take? There's an easy way to find out. Ask.

It's common knowledge in the club now that I'm writing this book, and people are getting used to me tapping them on the shoulder. Yet Jill always looks so focused on her work at matches that I'm wary of approaching her. Of course, when I do pluck up the courage and ask if I can find out a bit more, the mask drops immediately. "Great! Come up and see us before Tuesday training."

Now, training starts at 7pm, and Jill suggests that I turn up around 5pm, which is when they arrive. Hmm. Sounds to me curiously like *devotion*. Verity, who is physio for the Foresters, is already there in the car park when I turn up. Her car seat is back, and her eyes are shut: she's catching up on sleep which, when I later hear that both women typically start their working days at 7am and finish around 10pm, I can well understand. Like Jill, Verity is on the staff of a university sports and recreation department, forty miles away in Preston. Surely, I ask, they could both find clubs to work with closer to home in Lancashire?

"Of course," one of them says, "but once you get here you just don't want to leave. We both absolutely love it. Love it!" *Big* smiles.

Actually, they have both worked with more glamorous clubs, in this and other sports. But evidently something persuades them to come over the border three times a week to work in Wharfedale's draughty little physio room. The room itself may be cold, but perched up on the treatment table, Jill and Verity talk with completely unguarded warmth about the place. So come on, I ask, why Wharfedale?

"Respect," Jill answers firmly. "Respect is earned, and over the years we've worked our backsides off to gain it. It's built up by both sides, but it can easily be lost. Well, let me say that not one of the guys here has ever disrespected us, and I know that none of them ever would. I can't say that about every other club I've known. It's funny. In some ways we end up knowing the players better than they know themselves: I mean, we tend to know their babies' names before they're born!" – *big* smiles again – "but there's always a line to be drawn."

I'm wondering about the nature of this line, when I see it penned for myself. The clubhouse door clicks open, and we hear laughing voices heading towards us in the treatment room. Jill jumps down off the table, opens the door, and there are Dan Solomi and Tom Davidson. The laughter stops.

"Guys," Jill says, "you need to give us ten minutes. Can you go into the gym?"

There is nothing fierce or even curt in what Jill says. On the other hand, there is no mateyness which could ever be misinterpreted.

The players obediently head next door into the gym, and after a while the laughter starts up again. Jill comes back into the treatment room, and the smile breaks out again.

"Sorry about that," she says, "but if I don't say something they'll be straight in here and up on the treatment table." The two players she's talking about, I realise, are *not* on the official injury list – in which case it's time for me to scarper and let the repair work begin.

Only later do I realise that, of all the people I have spoken to in the club, Jill is the first to let a particularly unspeakable four-letter word escape her lips: love. In this club, love is the elephant in the room. There is nothing else – certainly not money – that draws people into a commitment to Wharfedale RUFC. In truth, the word 'devotion' doesn't overstate things: it understates them.

You know what they say about the course of true love, though. By the end of the Macclesfield game, with the home support grumbling its way back down The Avenue, our affections have certainly been put to the test. Macc, of course, are already relegated. They've only won two games all season. And we've beaten them when we played down in Cheshire. In other words, it's a game we should win casily. Before the match everyone is giving the same optimistic prediction, followed by the throwaway line – *so we'll probably lose - ha-ha!* Why are we joking? Why don't we yet realise what the club's history tells us? That of all games, this one has a large **L** inked in beside it.

We start the game well-enough, and albeit with a strong wind behind, are 7–0 up after ten minutes. Then things unravel. Jamie Guy does what the Shed has been wanting him to do since he arrived – follow the great attacking tradition of Dale fly-halfs and *run!* Well he does. He cuts through the line, too, but then goes down in a crumpled heap. Jill's diagnosis takes seconds: a hamstring pull. Off he goes, and we are left without a playmaker.

From that moment, our game gradually liquefies. The lineout is a shambles (I hear Richard Stockdale say that Dan, the hooker, has been up lambing every night this week) and without possession meaningful attacks are, well, *difficult*. Macclesfield's game, on the other hand, solidifies. And their spirit gains substance too. In the second half, with the wind and slope in their favour, they dot down almost immediately to level the scores. And at this point, let me jump ahead twenty-four hours…

…to Pocklington, and the semi-final of the Colts National Plate. The same raking gale has now blown across to the east of Yorkshire, and with that behind them in the first half, Wharfedale have turned round eight points up. Then, in as freaky a kick-off as any of us have ever seen, Pocklington begin the second half by kicking deep. Thinking that the wind is going to blow it dead, our Colts let the ball bounce. And bounce. Through the posts it goes, and is just about to go over the dead-ball line, when an air-borne Pocklington chaser leaps on it. Try! In that stunned moment, with a whole half to go and only a one point lead to defend, defeat seems an inevitability. Except that the Colts have not been brought up to understand the concept of *inevitability*. Somehow, through a combination of nous, grit and skill, they wake up and find a way to win. It may have been played out by a bunch of lads who have grown up with Harry Potter, but it is a drama which all the old-timers at the club would recognise. The plot couldn't be simpler: first find your adversity, then battle your way out of it. Sadly it is adversity – as we leap backwards twenty-four hours …

…to our match against Macclesfield – that is missing today. There is nothing at stake. The result is that Macc run in another three tries, and by the time the referee puts us out of our misery we have lost badly. 14–32. Actually, I think a few of us are quite pleased for Macclesfield. They've had an utterly miserable season, and this afternoon they've taken a win from us which, if we're honest, we could afford to do without. They get a good cheer as they go off. The Dale team leave to an awkward silence around the tunnel.

Having lost to the lowliest club in the league, I'm reminded of a lovely quip I came across in the club minutes. In the president's report to the AGM, back in 1975, 'Mr J.E. Harrison said that the club had lived with the best and died with the worst.' Nothing new here, then.

Amongst the strong tide of critical voices in the clubhouse afterwards, I'm pleased to overhear Woody, one of the injured, swimming the other way. "Go easy on the lads," he says. "All season the team's been told that the goal is survival. Well, they've done what was asked of them, and it's not easy to get yourself up again after you've reached your target." Amen. Personally, whenever I've just finished a marathon, if someone were to ask me to run another hundred yards, they might as well ask me to flap my arms and fly. In any sporting context, being told that the finishing line has been moved backwards is never easy to deal with.

And anyway, this loss just proves what we all know: that purely in terms of quality Wharfedale is no better than any of the teams below us. It is an extra desire that yields the results that sustain us. Even if the players tell you that the desire was there today, they'll probably admit that the *extra* has been absent. It's probably been on the treatment table, trying to loosen itself up for our one shot at real glory this season.

We're back on the Cup trail, albeit without a trained navigator. With Jamie injured, the cupboard is now totally bare of recognised fly-halfs. What on earth will Jon come up with for our visit to Cleckheaton in four days' time? The answer, when it is posted on the website, is not one we're expecting – but it's one we're all relieved to see. Andy Hodgson may be coming up to his fortieth birthday, and he may have played little of his rugby at 10, but no matter. If anyone in a green shirt knows how to read the map of a rugby field, it's Hodge. Nowadays Hodge is player-coach of the Foresters, but here he is, two years after his last game for the Firsts, trotting out in the gloaming of an April evening to take on Cleckheaton. The Yorkshire Cup can take us anywhere from the East Coast to the edge of the Peak District. Most often it takes us to the busy bit in the middle, and that's where we are this evening – as the drone from the M62 reminds us.[63]

Our team tonight is billed as the First XV, but at this time of year the distinction between Firsts and Seconds is blurred. In the centre we have genuine class – Cameron Hudson and Huw Morgan – and Hodge keeps putting them in space to fly through a defence that won't often have to deal with this level of attacking skill. But one of the beauties of rugby as a sport is that most individual efforts are only as good as their support. Whilst we score a couple of great tries in the first half, isolated runners also keep giving away penalties, and Cleckheaton land three of them. We go in only 14–9 up. When Cleck score first in the second half – courtesy of an ex-Dale player – we are behind. The wise heads around me keep pointing to the size of the opposition pack.

"Don't worry, they'll tire"

But I *am* worrying. No-one wants the season to end in the middle of nowhere

---

63 To the outsider, the boundaries between Cleckheaton, Heckmondwike, Liversedge, Halifax and Huddersfield are nebulous: elsewhere in the county this area is referred to as Cleckheckmondsedge or, more broadly, Cleckhud-dersfax. The most famous son of the region is (I've started this old joke, so I may as well finish it) Willy Eckerslike.

– least of all the man writing what he thinks is a rugby fairy tale. I see Chris Baker, who is looking on calmly.

"I don't suppose you're a nervous type, are you?" I ask.

Chris looks at me, thinks for a moment, and chuckles: "Not any more I'm not!" I suspect he's just humouring me: that he never was never the nervous type.

Out on the pitch, Cleckheaton are scrapping for everything. And they have a classy kicker who, every time he gets the ball, is sending probing kicks into empty space, pushing us back and back. They can sense the chance of an upset. More than that, Cleck can sniff that a place in the final, and a shot at a trophy, is only twenty minutes away. Jon must sense danger too, and sends on James Doherty. If he had played his cards differently last summer, James could have been playing under the bright lights of the Premiership right now. Will he really want to get his hands dirty down here, just off the motorway hard shoulder? Silly question. He looks like he wants nothing more. Twice, right in front of us, I see James fling himself on the loose ball, aware that he's about to be monstered by opposition forwards. And on both occasions, not only does he secure the ball, but he flicks it away into the backline. Miniscule, massive moments. Soon Cleck are starting to chase shadows. Holes appear in their defence, and Dale run through it for four more tries. Job done.

Colts, now Firsts. We're in the finals.

Chapter 33

*~ in which we explore the magic of the final minute, and
find ourselves on the savannah at Esher ~*

Spring has sprung. Up by the Wharfe the trees may still be holding their cards
close to their chests, but down here in Surrey the branches have decided
that it's now safe to play their hands. The time has come for the cricketers to
play too. On the village green at Weybridge they are already out in their whites
and striped caps. The summer game has begun, and we're almost back where
we started.

The last time we were driving to a game under a green canopy like this was
on our way to Hartpury for the first match of the season. The conditions may
be similar outside today, but the climate in our car has changed. The cloud of
apprehension we felt as the campaign kicked off, has lifted. Put simply, at Hartpury
we felt that we *needed* to win, and at Esher we *want* to win. Big difference.

In recent times, when we have needed to win it has been to stay up, but even
since we have been in National 1, there have been years when we have come to
crunch games at the end of the season expecting to go up if we win. Strange, but
true. Think about it: when Dale came into this league we had, in the course of
eight years, gone up from Level Seven to Level Three. We'd known nothing but
promotions, and who was saying that that climb had ended? Certainly not Dan
Harrison: "When we made it to this level we weren't there just to make up the
numbers. We always enjoyed the trips, but come the games we were very, very
determined. Thing is, we'd all grown up together. We were close friends. I think
that's why Hedley never left – and believe me, he could have played on any
stage. Hodge was reluctant to leave, too. With those two, Alex Howarth kicking
the points, and the rest of us backing them up, we were a threat to anyone."

Wharfedale also managed to lure – through dynastic marriages rather than
money – a couple of luminaries to the team: David Pears from Harlequins,
and Charlie Vyvyan from Sale. By and large it was Dale's attacking style that
confounded people – including those on the touchline. One dazzled reporter
wrote that 'There is something in the water up the Dale which renders normal
rugby theories redundant. Wharfedale play like they have suffered a collective

attack of ADHD. Hedley Verity was the epitome of Wharfedale's feverish, helter-skelter approach, which rendered kicking almost obsolete.' Playing this way, after a couple of years' acclimatisation to Level Three, only a loss away to Birmingham Solihull stopped Dale from claiming promotion up into Level Two.

It would be easy to get misty-eyed about the way Dale played – imagining that wherever they travelled they took with them the spirit of a South Sea Island carnival. Clarty, who was coach until 2006, will have none of it: "I'm not a win-at-*all*-costs man; I'm a win-at-*most*-costs man, and as if that means winning up-front, so be it. I know what our reputation is for style, and I'm proud of it, but if we'd always played like that we wouldn't still be in National 1." He's right. In Dale's second year in the league, they lost their first six games of the campaign before they turned up at The Rock to play a Rosslyn Park team unbeaten at home. On their way through Kings Cross on the Friday, one of the Dale team picked up a copy of the *Evening Standard*, which previewed the game with the prediction of a 'Park stroll'. Clarty says that the following day his team talk was simple: he just read out the article. What else needed to be said? In atrocious wind and rain, Dale certainly fronted up that day. Riverball was the call. And they won. 6–5.

Those of us who have only known Wharfedale in the last few years, have spent less time looking at the road up ahead, and more glancing in our rear-view mirrors at what lies back and below. That may all sound desperately negative, but that's not how it feels. Does any promoted side know the collective ecstasy we at Wharfedale know when our suspense is relieved only on the final page of yet another thriller?

I can't help thinking back two years, to our last away fixture of the season. At half time away to Cambridge, Wharfedale's relegation seemed set. We were winning, but only 3–0. Much worse, however, was the news from Cheshire, where our rivals for the drop were 29–0 up. Although Macclesfield had scored only three tries, with that level of domination they looked certain of five points. We would be lucky to get a plain win, and that would leave us needing an improbable result against Coventry in our last game. For us, tries followed after the interval, but four minutes into added time we still needed one more for a bonus point: we snaffled the ball on our own 22, and started off. Dale have always been happy running into a broken field, but even so, there was a mighty long way to go. Still, the passes and off-loads all stuck to hand, until Joe Donkin raced clear from half way. With only the full-back to beat, he suddenly pulled up and went to ground. A minute later he would be helped from the pitch with a torn hamstring, but first things first, he had to recycle the ball. He did, and Aaron Myers then added another chapter to his legend by scooping up and storming over the line. The final whistle was blown, and we had our five points.

But what of Macc? At that moment I saw Gordon, our radio reporter, marching down the touchline towards us: one hand had his mobile pressed to his ear, and the other had a thumb sticking up.

"Macc haven't added to their half-time score. They've only got four points! *WE'RE SAFE!*"

"Well quick, get onto the pitch and tell the boys," someone said, and Gordon raced over to a shattered-looking team. Cue the greatest scene of sporting euphoria I have ever been close enough to touch.

I'm afraid there'll be none of that down here at Esher. Then again, there will be none of the angst we knew in the lead-up to that Cambridge match. Driving here – even when a sumptuous cover-drive skims over the Weybridge cricket pitch, out across the main road and smacks with a great *ker-dunk!* against the underside of our car – nothing can disturb our pleasant anticipation of an afternoon in the sun.

This, I guess, is how every match must have felt in the days before leagues, money and ambition took hold of the game. There are some, I know, who vainly hope that those Corinthian days might miraculously return. You won't find many at Wharfedale who share that hope. It's true that as far as ambition goes we are non-committal; and our attitude to money is not exactly gung-ho. But about the leagues themselves, we are unequivocally positive.

How about Esher? Does the needle on their barometer swing left to the old rugby ethos, or right to the new one? Look on the Esher website, and the answer seems clear. There, blinking out below the headline *Esher Receive Planning Permission*, is an artist's impression of their proposed new grandstand: if this is an indication of the future, it points firmly right and up, towards life on a thrustingly futuristic planet rugby. It certainly points towards a different reality than the one Esher currently enjoy. Never mind the architect's minor optimistic glosses – the gleaming white roof, or the bright blue sky – look at the seats in his drawing: they're full. By my estimate, there are four times more people in that imagined stand than there are all around the ground this afternoon. Yes, it *could* happen. But what could also happen is that in a few years' time it's not so much a great white stand on Molesey Road, as a great white elephant. Esher may – perish the thought! – still be down here in National 1, playing the likes of Wharfedale. And whatever else we might be, we ain't exactly box office.

In the first half I find myself standing next to an Esher member. He's friendly, and candid about the conundrum facing his club.

"We have to decide what we want to be," he says. "You can invest in players, but they come and go: they're *temporary*. The problem is that once you build something, you've invested in something that is *permanent*. There's no going back."

But if Esher go forward, where are they heading? The Championship? Maybe. What then? A shot at the Premiership? Really? *Really?* What then? Presumably another conundrum, and an plan for another new stand.

To me, stood here in the sun, the solution seems obvious. Build nothing! Stay where you are! I say this, because of all the clubs we have visited this season, none seems happier in its own skin than Esher. And this has caught me by surprise. Surrey's stockbroker belt was the last place on our travels where, as a Dale supporter, I expected to find a rugby kinship. There are plenty of differences between our clubs, but despite the fact that they've had their worst season in years, the crowd at Esher remind me of us, in one significant way: they appear to be a community.

It helps that Esher have an MC who, if he lacks Adge's explosions of blasted brimstone, more than matches him for gentle geniality. He keeps up a lovely patter throughout the match (even a protested yellow card elicits a dry reference to the legal services offered by one of the club's sponsors) and he keeps the home crowd burbling away on a low simmer. For Esher, this is their last home game of the season. The end of term feel is underscored by the exotic scents of *carne-de-sol* from the Brazillian food stall, and the sounds of a steel band outside the clubhouse. What, I ask the man next to me, is all this about? "We're having a raffle to raise funds for the team we're sending to the Tobago Sevens. Look," and he shows me a £20 ticket. Crikey! That's more than a season's raffle tickets cost us at The Avenue![64]

What else do we find on our visit to Esher? Oh yes, a rugby match. But once we've found it, we straightaway go and lose it. For Esher, this is pay-back. Remember, it wasn't so many weeks ago that we were beating them in an old-fashioned slog at The Avenue. Someone remarked then that the pitch looked as if it had been prepared by a team of heavy horses. Today's pitch looks as if it has been prepared by (or at least for) a herd of wildebeest. The ground is parched, and sand flies up with every thud of a boot. It's a bizarre sight, seeing the players disappear upfield behind a cloud of dust, but somehow the sight matches the day's theme of sun and sand.

So, Esher's revenge on us is served hot. The previous week they had won away to Blaydon, and from the off this afternoon they are in that kind of form again.

---

64 Mind you, an all-inclusive holiday for two in the Caribbean rather trumps our £50 cash prize.

Twice in the first half Esher's centre bursts through our midfield to score under the posts. Simple. One of these days we'll field a back line that has played more than forty minutes with each other, and know where to stand.

Esher might score more, but once they get into our 22 and have to pass, they are suddenly flinging a bar of wet soap to each other. When one of their backs drops the ball within touching distance of the line, it's too much for the Esher man next to me. He bangs the railing. "*Christ!*" he says, "I haven't played for ten years, and *I* could have scored that. And if *I* could have scored, I have to ask myself what the hell we're paying *him* for."

Ah! Now there's a difference: in the Shed we might sometimes chastise our players, but I've yet to hear even the most penurious of Dales farmers accuse them of being overpaid.

Esher are winning then, but they're not entirely happy with their players. Nor are their players entirely happy with themselves. As they wait to defend a scrum, I hear one of their backs trying to organise their reception committee for our attack.

"You take the 13, and in case they kick I'll drop back – like normal," he says to his winger.

"Normal since when?" the winger answers back. "Since when have we been using that defence play? Eh?" He shrugs his shoulders and walks off reluctantly. They're slightly narky with each other, then. I wonder what their supporters make of this. Esher have bought talented players, but have they bought a team?

The other source of frustration, to my new friend from Esher, is our captain. Towards the end of the first half the scrums pack down. Not for the first time, James is gesticulating wildly at the binding of one of the Esher props. The man with the whistle duly blows in our favour.

"Who on *earth* is your number nine?" the Esher man asks, pointing. "Hell's teeth, he's an annoying man! So far he's refereed the whole bloody game."[65]

"Ah yes, James Doherty: studied law, training to be a teacher, scrum-half and captain. I think as far as he's concerned, refereeing just goes with the territory."

By contrast, although we're losing, our players seem quite happy with themselves. I hate to admit it, but we're quite happy with them too. All the players are battling. It may be in a losing cause, but they're battling. Only once in the whole match do they get a real reward. Yet what a perfect reward it is! In the middle of the second half we're attacking in the Esher 22, and the ball is passed to Andy Hodgson. It's not a good pass at all, but with a touch of class he scoops it up with his fingertips, dummies to flat-foot the defender, and is in for the try. Thirty-nine years young!

---

65 In the bar after the game I see James and pass this comment on. He smiles. As I suspected, he regards it as one of the highest compliments a scrum-half can receive.

His team mates mob him as if a new lad from the Colts has just opened his account. Some tries feel worth more than five points. In our technical area I can see two of our coaches, Hedley and Alex: they both played with Hodge in the promotion years, and they are beaming to see their old mate still doing the business on the pitch.

For us, that is it. No more tries, no win, and no bonus points. It's odd, though. For all that we've now recorded three league losses on the trot, I have a feeling that we've turned a corner. We may have at least one more hurrah left in us before the end of the season. The players look like a team again, and as far as results go, with Wharfedale you never know.

With Esher, I wonder what the future holds for them on the pitch. And what choices will they make off it? Will they stick or twist? For all that I would like them to stick, I'm not sure that they really have much option: they may have to twist – and go for the new stand. At least by Wharfedale's standards, a club on a piece of real estate like Esher's must cost a small fortune to run. Where there is competition for their financial favours, sponsors and supporters want to be associated with aspiration, not stasis. Down here in the seriously moneyed world, standing still is not an option. If Esher stop pumping their own ambitions, how long before another club around here start to blow up theirs? And if so, where will the hired guns in the Esher team head? By contenting themselves with where they are, Esher could easily find themselves sliding down the slope into oblivion. Let's remember that Corinthian Casuals, along with their commendable spirit and glorious history, currently rumble along the lower reaches of football's Isthmian Leagues.

Chapter 34

~ in which the Shed explodes, and the donkeys and pandas of Hartpury come to play ~

So this match doesn't matter to us at all, eh? We've nothing to play for in the league, and we'll be wanting to keep our powder dry for the Cup Final in five days' time, right? *Wrong!* It's the middle of the second half, and the Shed has just exploded. In reality, however damp the match's atmosphere is, the Shed is always a powder keg, ready to go off at the slightest spark. And right in front of us, the Hartpury winger has just provided an inadvertent ignition: he's knocked the ball on. Don't worry, we're not uncouth enough to flare up at that moment, but as the packs make their way over for the scrum, the spark makes its way down the taper. Dale's eight are jogging towards the set-piece, heads high, as if they can't wait. Hartpury College are trudging, heads down: the winger glances sheepishly at the Shed, suspicious of this volatile body. Reading the body language in front of us, the cheer grows as we sense what is coming. When the referee calls "*Engage!*" every larynx is detonated. Hartpury's eight is duly blown apart, the referee's arm goes up for a penalty against them, and the whole of The Avenue is now on fire. It may not lead to anything, but for now we're having fun. On down the field we march.

I admit it. When I read what I've just written, we sound like bullies. Hold on, though. Who are we supposed to be bullying? Hartpury are bigger, stronger and (let there be no mistake about this) better than us. As we enter this final round of games they stand fourth in the table, and are on a run of fourteen victories with only two defeats. In that time they have recorded *away* victories against Fylde, Coventry and Blaydon – all the more impressive since they seem to take with them virtually no supporters. They are the form team in the league, whilst our own form – three straight losses – indicates not just a Wharfedale L today, but a **L**.

Still, it's the last home game of the season, and beforehand, even if a celebration on the field seems too much to ask, I'm hoping we can at least fête ourselves off it. For the cover of the programme, rather than the usual action shot, Gordon has done a photo collage of some of the club's volunteers. For the inside, which Gordon has asked me to organise, I have decided to go down a similar route. I tell Jon that I'd like a player to contribute something about the volunteers.

"Hmm. You want a player to *write* something? Er, that narrows it down a bit…" and here Jon pauses as he runs through the possibilities "…to about three. Try Cameron. He's at Leeds University, so let's assume that he's not illiterate."

He's not. Cammie does me a brilliant piece, which make me realise that however focused the players may be when they run out onto the pitch, their peripheral vision takes in every jersey cleaner and *Twitter* feeder. But I want something more from the players than Cammie's piece. I want a season's highlight from each of them. Okay, stringing a paragraph together might be a tall order, but how about just a sentence? I email them. James fires back his highlights ten minutes later, but soon after that the responses dry up. Evidently even a sentence is too much. I tell the skipper I'm getting nowhere, and James says, "Leave it to me."

After the Esher match James handed me the results of his trawl down the team bus. Interesting. When I get home and look at them, the first thing to strike me is that none of the players mention themselves. More than that, a fair few don't mention their team mates either. The character that recurs most often in their highlights is the crowd.

JAMES TYSON
The crowd every Saturday, and the support they show! Especially on away trips, where I'm very proud to hear more Dale then home supporters.

MATT BEESLEY
Losses to Rosslyn Park and Coventry in horrendous conditions. Despite the results, the crowd was superb.

Now the cat is out of the bag! Every Saturday the team makes us feel special, but evidently it works the other way round too. Of course, all this self-basting will count for absolutely nothing if the team sign off their league season, against Hartpury, with the kind of half-baked display we had against Macclesfield. And whilst a victory is realistically too much to ask, we're all hoping for some spirit to cheer. When Ian Larkin goes over for a try after fifteen minutes, we're cheering with relief. At least we're not going to be whitewashed. And as they run back to half way I catch a whiff of belief from the team on the field. Another fifteen minutes, and another try. Now we're cheering with hope.

Despite having the slope in their favour, Hartpury's only score before the break is a single penalty. Throughout the half they look mighty frustrated. Across the pitch, I see arms waving in their technical area as the referee awards penalty after penalty against them for not releasing the ball when tackled. During the interval Steve comes up from his usual station behind the posts. He's rubbing his hands together. "At last," he says, "we've got Guy, Morgan and Hudson together in midfield. They trust each other, they trust Hodge behind them, and they're working perfectly! Hartpury can't cope!"

Well that's good to hear, but we're still not quite predicting a result. Surely after a little hair-drying at half time, Hartpury will come out and unfurl their pro-game. Not so. Again we force them back into the corner, where from a lineout Dan Solomi is driven over to put us 15–3 up. Now we're cheering with expectation. Actually, we'd be out of sight now, but in the last month Jamie Guy's kicking from the tee has gone all to pot.

With the realisation that they need to score twice, Hartpury are at last roused. For five minutes they attack the Dale line, in close and out wide, in ones and eights, looking for cracks and weak spots. No-go. The Greens are like the drystone wall right behind them: sturdier than they look.

Eventually the ball is knocked forward, and Dale clear with a great hoof downfield. The retreating winger spills the ball, and the taper is lit. Actually, we don't score in the next five minutes, and Hartpury eventually clear the ball out of touch near half way. There is a wonderful moment as Hodge picks the ball up and straight away looks round in the hope of a quick throw-in. Anyone for South Sea Island rugby?

"*NO!*" I hear the captain bark as he runs back. It's the same tone he uses when one of the teenagers is about to do something particularly rash, but here he's addressing someone who was already a senior when James first came to the Dale as a schoolboy. As he reaches Hodge, James taps him on the shoulder and gives a bit of an embarrassed laugh. Hodge smiles back, as if to say, "Don't worry, I was only bluffing – you don't think I'm *that* stupid do you?"

A moment later a ruck forms on our own ten-metre line. It's such a static, unpromising situation that by now we should recognise the scatter of bodies for what it is: a missile launcher. We don't, of course – none of us spot Dan Solomi pick up the ball and shoot out under the defensive shield until he's already at full pace. It's the same staccato patter we've been watching all season, but this time there's fully sixty metres between ruck and try-line. Surely not? As he approaches the full-back Dan half checks, looking either side to find the support. It can't keep up. Realising that it's all or nothing, Dan blasts off again, side-winding round the last defender to run in under the posts. He's saved the best until last, and now we're cheering with *ecstacy!* The noise doesn't let up, either. As the team head back to half way for the restart, someone in the Shed calls out Dan's name. Amidst all the handshakes he half raises an arm in acknowledgement. Now it's no longer a cheer. It's a roar! And what's this? There, a few yards up the touchline, banging on the hoardings for all that they're worth, are a couple of older members. They're the same characters that used to give Caroline and

Lynda frosty looks whenever they went percussive. How times change!

With the party in full swing, I notice that next to me, young Tom Burridge has come to stand with his dad. There are some nose-tappers in the Shed who think him to be an even better prospect than his elder brother Josh, but this afternoon Tom has been playing for the Seconds. To their great credit Hartpury have, at a few days' notice, brought up their reserves to play ours, and according to Tom they've given us a real lesson. Is he disheartened? Not a bit.

"It was a great game," I hear him say, "they were *really* good." Again, evidently it's not the final mark, but the learning and the test are important.

The final mark in the Firsts game, after we've scored a fifth unanswered try, is 29–3. Not just a W, then, but a **W**. For the final time in the season the team make their way off The Avenue pitch, to be greeted by a thunderous response.

As they make their way into the tunnel, a donkey and a panda make their way out, and round towards the bar. Ah yes, that will be a couple of Hartpury's Seconds about to dive into their end of season party. Alec sees this and gives me a nudge.

"We've a lot to thank the RFU's fixtures computer for this season. It gave us Hartpury away in Freshers' Week, and Hartpury at home in what looks like Rag Week."

He's right. Hartpury are a better side than us, and yet we've bagged nine points from our games with them this season. Now, take those points away, and where would we be in the final reckoning? See for yourself…

26 April 2015

1	Ealing Trailfinders	30	136
2	Rosslyn Park	30	127
3	Coventry	30	112
4	Fylde	30	90
5	Hartpury College	30	89
6	Blackheath	30	86
7	Richmond	30	80
8	Blaydon	30	73
9	Darlington Mowden Park	30	69
10	Esher	30	68
11	**Wharfedale**	**30**	**65**
12	Loughborough Students	30	63
13	Cinderford	30	59
14	Old Albanian	30	58
15	Tynedale	30	44
16	Macclesfield	30	21

Instead of Old Albanian, it would be us joining Tynedale and Macclesfield in the league below. A sobering thought.

As it is, Hartpury can look back on their season with good cause to party, and we can look back on this match in much the same way. When I see James I can't help voicing a word of caution.

"There's one more match James – don't forget."

"We won't. Don't get me wrong," he says, "we're going to enjoy tonight. But I promise we'll have our heads right for Thursday."

The Cup Final, and the ending of the fairy tale, looms.

Chapter 35

*~ in which we come full circle to another Yorkshire Cup
Final, where we find a giant standing in our way ~*

Is it really a year since we were last doing this – making our way into a neutral ground to take on local rivals for the small matter of a cup and preening rights? A lot of water has flown under bridges since then, to say nothing of cars and coaches under motorway flyovers. It could all seem a bit futile, to have travelled so far and spent so much energy, just to arrive back in the same spot. But a season is a cycle, and as the wheel comes round full circle, we can look up and realise that we are just a little further along our road of choice: we're still jousting with great clubs the length and breadth of the country, and we're still the envy of teams around us in the county. Nothing that happens in tonight's match with Harrogate will change any of that. But sports people are insecure at heart – and we wouldn't mind a little confirmation of where we stand.

The auguries are good. Don't ask me how, but even though the injury list only seems to have grown, Jon has somehow been able to name his strongest side of the season for the final. I ask Alec if he has any worries, and he says, "I have. It's a cup match – anything can happen: and another thing – can we kick straight?" Good point. In the last few weeks our goal kicking has been woeful. Still, even with that impediment we've just beaten a side well above us, and Harrogate are in a league below. Speaking of whom, what do we know about our opposition? Someone says that their 10 is classy, and that their big second-row, Sam Brady, "means business" – but other than that we're in the dark.

We begin where we left off against Hartpury. The opposition isn't in the same class, but no matter, we can only play what is in front of us. When Harrogate kick deep, Wharfedale immediately spin the ball wide. Intent. At Bramhope's West Park ground the slope is against us, but with backs flying and forwards bullocking, we soon find ourselves fifteen metres out from the Harrogate line. We have the ball at the back of a ruck and – any idea what comes next? – that's right, Dan Solomi zips through to score by the posts. Easy as you like! Two minutes gone, and we're 7–0 up. Ah yes, wasn't this *exactly* where we were in last year's final against Otley? And what transpired then? Well we won, but it wasn't easy.

Within ten minutes we realise that this isn't going to be easy either. It isn't that Harrogate score — at least not on the board. Where they do score is that they take out our captain. The incident occurs over on the far side, behind the referee. But the touch judge has seen it, and indicates foul play. A Harrogate forward has driven James head-first into the ground. He isn't moving.

Silence.

Eventually James sits up, but his legs won't take him any further. Jill is there for ages going through the usual protocols, but it looks bad. When James is helped to his feet, he obviously has no idea where he is. He's off. Still, at least we will only be playing fourteen men for the rest of the match. The referee duly gets out his card and — what's this? It's yellow. *Yellow!* On the touchline we're incredulous.

The real punishment, then, is meted out to us, not Harrogate. All season long, by fair means or foul, opposition teams have targeted James as the vital cog in the Green Machine, and all season long we've wondered what happens if they succeed. With Woody, our other scrum-half, still on the injury list, we've no-one on the field or bench who has played there. Hodge puts his hand up, but it soon becomes obvious that he doesn't know the position. He doesn't even know where to stand — at the first defensive lineout the referee has to tell him the rule about which side of the five-metre line he has to be. It's like a minis match, with a helpful father as referee, and on another day it would be hilarious. Not today. And there's worse.

Whatever Hodge's other skills these days, a bulleting pass isn't one of them — and no scrum-half is better than the speed of his pass. So whenever the ball reaches Jamie Guy at fly-half, the Harrogate backs are already up on him, and his options are limited. He can't pass wide for fear of an intercept, with a recent hamstring pull he's reluctant to run, and so as a last resort he kicks. He kicks deep — and straight into the hands of the defence. He dummies and drops for goal — and misses. And his confidence visibly starts to wane. First one penalty, then a second goes wide. Brady comes back on to cheers from some of the Harrogate supporters. They, at least, are feeling a bit better. When our dominant forwards win us yet another penalty, but back in our half, a couple of Harrogate wags behind me yell out to Jamie, "Go for goal!"

And this, I'm afraid, is where it is so different to last year's game against Otley. The atmosphere around us is plain ugly. Lynda can only stand so much before she turns round and suggests that they stick to cheering for their side, and not against ours. But they're big lads, pints in hands, and they're not going to heed that kind of advice. The jeering goes on.

Back on the field, Harrogate are chipping away at our lead. Their fly-half is on good form. Kick, kick, kick, and by half time we are 7–9 down. Still, we have the slope in our favour for the second half. More than that, we have a pack that is embarrassing Harrogate at every scrum, and a set of backs just waiting for their chance.

Trouble is, between those two sets of match-winners we now have a loose connection. More than that, without James on the field, we lack an obvious leader. Our last three captains are either on the bench or injured, so it's Josh Burridge who takes over. Now, Josh is already a leader – he's captaining Yorkshire Under-20s at Twickenham in three days' time – but this situation requires an experienced strategist. Josh may be that one day, but right now he's a leader from the front. He high-tackles a Harrogate player, goes to the bin for ten minutes, and whilst he's there we concede a try. 7–16.

But we're Wharfedale. Adversity is what we feed on, isn't it? Josh comes back on, powers over from five metres out, and although Jamie misses with the conversion, we've at least narrowed the difference to less than a try. If only we can buy our backs an inch of space! Yet time is running out, and Harrogate are doing most of the pressing. Then, with the clock deep into added time, at last the ball finds its way into Taylor Prell's hands. And he's gone. From his own 22 he slices his way up past half way. Will he try the little chip over the full-back that won us glory against Richmond? No, he takes the percentage choice, plays it safe, and takes the ball into contact. Dan Solomi is first there, picks the ball up, and charges on. But he's snagged. The next man in picks up, drives on, and, and…spills the ball. Forwards.

That's it.

Game over.

We've lost.

We've lost. We're all genuinely speechless. Half-formed thoughts about muggings and injustices are floating around, but not much is said. It's not as if we're unused to losing, but I can't remember a Dale loss that has ever tasted half as bitter as this. We all stay to applaud Harrogate as they accept the Cup, but bearing in mind what they've done to our captain, it's not easy. Eventually Dale's team huddle breaks up, and they head off the field. I hear James, with a worried-looking dad beside him, burbling a bit incoherently about what has happened: "Yellow… I can't believe it… just yellow? I mean what…yellow?" Only four days ago James was assuring me that his head would be right for this match, and here he is, away in la-la land. Then the coach comes past. I grab Jon's hand and offer a word of commiseration, but he just looks at me, shrugs his shoulders, and walks on down the tunnel. Fair enough – I've nothing much to say either. The one person I do want to say something to is Jamie Guy. His head is down, and he's trying to avoid eye-contact with anyone. I grab his hand and pull him back.

"Hey Jamie, listen: thanks for your kicking against Darlington and Fylde. We won't forget that – and you shouldn't either."

When he realises what I'm saying he half laughs, but shakes his head and walks on. It's true, though. Without a functioning Jamie at 10, and James at 9, it's difficult to see how we would have survived in the league this season. Well they were, and we did. But tonight they weren't, and we didn't.

I know what you're thinking. *I thought this was supposed to be a fairy tale!* Well yes it is, and you shouldn't give up on the prospect of a genuinely happy ending. You never know, perhaps a *very* happy ending. But before we have a chance of happily resolving our tale, it has to take another sorry twist. The morning after the final I get an email from Josh Burridge's dad. John says that in the changing room after the match Jon Feeley announced that he was having to step down as head coach. Apparently the players were visibly upset.

Straightaway I check on the Wharfedale website, but nothing has been announced, so I fire off an email to Jon, just suggesting that he takes his time before deciding. During his lunch break at school, I get a reply:

> Hi Simon,
> I desperately don't want to stand down as head coach, but I can't find a way to commit the time during the week that it demands, and that's not fair on the players. Telling them last night was one of the hardest things I have ever done. I genuinely care for them. Hopefully I'll win the lottery in the next couple of weeks and I can ask for the job back!
> Regards,
> Jon

Understood. Jon has been trying to do two full-time jobs in one life and has had to accept the reality that two into one just won't go. It's the one that pays the mortgage that has to stay. Money! Most of the time we're quietly proud of knowing that we are a poor club: of knowing that whatever we achieve it is because of who we are, and not what we have. But at times like this we wouldn't mind the fairy with the magic wand to make an appearance.

That's the coach. What of the skipper? After the match James was taken to hospital. Severe concussion. A few days later I'm told that James has again checked in with the medics. He's still feeling terrible – nausea and splitting headaches – and wonders if this is normal. He's wary, and so are the medics. The rest of us are just worried.[66]

And what of me? I'll admit it, I'm feeling a bit sick too. I began this book with high-minded thoughts that I was just writing about a club I had feeling for. Of course there were people involved, but I wouldn't need to get involved with them as individuals, would I? I certainly wouldn't have to *feel* for them. And here I am, at the end of the season, feeling sick not for the club but for the people. How daft could I have been, not to realise the most basic truth of all: that the club is nothing but the people.

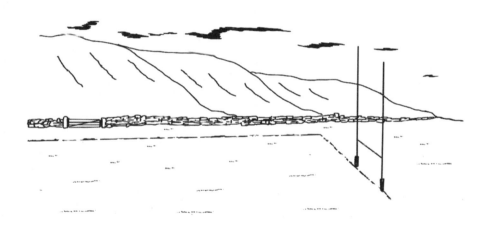

---

66 The happy part of this footnote is that within a fortnight James had recovered. The unhappy part is that Sam Brady expressed no regret about the incident. For the first time in Wharfedale's history, the club felt it necessary to cite a player. Confronted by the video evidence, Sam Brady was effectively banned from all rugby for six months.

Chapter 36

~ in which we go in search of a happy ending ~

So if this is all a fairy tale, which one could it mirror? I think we can safely bypass the romance of Rapunzel: the only character we have with hair like that is our second-row Adam Howard, and I can't see Prince Charming climbing up his locks. We can also forget tales of Circe and her magic wand: truth is, however much we might sometimes wish for it, if someone came and sprinkled their millions in our direction, we know that the fairy tale would instantly lose its lustre. No, I think the tale which best fits with Wharfedale is Tom Thumb. Remember – the little fellow who goes off on various capers, gets into any number of tight scrapes, but happily survives to tell the tale?[67]

As we drove away from Bramhope and the Cup Final, we passed by Jon's school, and I was reminded of one of the children's questions – *do you ever have to change the ending of the book you're writing?* I've changed it once, when it became clear that our final league match was not going to be any kind of Judgement Day, and leaving the Final without silverware I realised I would have to change it again. Actually, perhaps this change is not such a big deal, because for a few weeks now another possible ending has been coming into view. We have one final adventure left, and for the club it's potentially the most exciting of all.

Our Under-19 team have made it through to the final of the National Colts Plate. With recent winners including Gloucester and Bristol, the Plate has a roll of honour we'd be more than proud to grace. This will not decide who is the best of the best – that is the Cup – but best of the rest. Well, that is exactly what we aspire to be as a club, and at least as far as the future of Wharfedale is concerned, here is our chance to achieve it.

With league and cup matches coming thick and fast, the season has been hotting up as we approach its end. At Bedford Blues' ground, on May Bank Holiday Monday, the temperature is really starting to climb. Soaking up the festival atmosphere are a good number of neutrals, enjoying the sun and

---

67 Including, of course, being monstered by a giant. No prizes for guessing which opposition player central casting have in mind for this role.

refreshments, ready to cheer just about anything that moves. There's also is plenty of hollering support for both teams.

If we're ready, then, let's take a deep breath and roll the cup dice again!

The two teams run out, and now that I'm getting familiar with them, I'm struck again by just how closely our Colts seem to mirror our Firsts. Facing us across the half-way line, Havant look like a team of prize specimens. We, on the other hand, look not quite right. I mean, our lad with the 2 on his back – he's slighter than their scrum-half! And our 11 doesn't look much older than the number on his shirt! More than that, as a team we look a bit *raggledy*: as if it's not a national final we're about to play in, but a mid-week run-around.

Nor do the early exchanges remove the suspicion that we've come all the way down here for a wincing mincing. Havant power through our midfield for a first try, convert it, add a penalty, and within ten minutes we're 0–10 down. Another team would let their heads drop at this moment, but thankfully a significant chromosome in Dale's DNA has been passed down to these youngsters: resolve. From their huddle behind the posts they race back into position. They will see if they can find a way. One thing is clear. Not for the first time since 1923, a Wharfedale side will have to rely on its wile more than its weight if they are to get a result.

And now I'm reminded of something that Len Tiffany told me. Tiff was there at the start of junior rugby at The Avenue, and he told me how, back in the seventies, he prepared his lads for what they would meet against other teams: "I'd say to them, 'You're going to come up against bigger lads all the time,' and I'd get them to tackle me. I was a bit past it as a centre by then, but even so, it got them ready for whatever came their way." Juniors tackling seniors is, of course, a strict no-no in today's protocols. But even so, I've noticed that from young Oli in the Under-10s, to Woody in National League 1, the tiniest homegrown Dale players think nothing of whumping down players twice their size. For some of them, I imagine that if they have grown up bossing fickle cattle across the skittery floor of a milking shed, even the most outsize lock-forward will hold few terrors.

So the first thing our Colts do to check Havant's march is to get in amongst them and stop them in their tracks. When Havant next approach the Dale line, our harrying defence is right in their faces. We force them into a rushed inside pass. It goes to ground, we pick it up, and are away into a broken field. At the heart of our sniping attack is a small scrum-half we've already seen playing for the senior teams – James Otulakowski. He gets the ball just inside his own half, runs at the full-back, chips over his head – and is first to reach the ball over the try line. Through a combination of nuggettyness and nous, we're in business.

And it soon gets better. By half time we're even five points ahead, and thinking that we've somehow found a way.

But here, duly delivered, comes the revelation that this Colts team also carry with them another vital part of the Wharfedale DNA. In true Tom Thumb style, they decide that the whole adventure will be a poor show unless they carry the drama to the final page. They duly let Havant score — not once, but twice — and with quarter of an hour to go we are back behind by three points.

I can't believe it. We're back where we were in the dying minutes against Harrogate, trying to wrest the initiative back from a tenacious opponent and a ticking clock. And I'm sorry, but after a whole season of these white-knuckle rides, I really think I've had enough. The sun is high in the sky, telling me that it is time to be up with the curlews on Threshfield Moor, or down watching the trout rise on the Wharfe — anywhere *please* but watching another adrenalin-fuelled turf war. Or at least trying to watch. Briefly I shut my eyes, wishing I was somewhere else. In just a few minutes the season will be over, and the summer will be mine, but right now every drop of tension I've experienced over the last ten months seems distilled into this moment. Like it or not, I have to open my eyes and, with the rest of the Dale support, open my mouth one more time.

At least Dale are still up and running. Havant are wilting in the heat, and during a break in play a good number of them sink to the ground. Surely, *surely* we can finish them off now! But after countless approaches to the opposition try-line, somehow Havant get their hands on the ball at a ruck, and win a penalty. How long can be left? The touch judge tells us that there are still three minutes on the clock. On the touchline our nerves are shredded. I close my eyes as Havant clear the ball out of play past half way. That's it. I've resigned myself to another loss, and the reality that this *is* reality — not any kind of fairy tale.

Hold on though. Their big prop fumbles the ball at the lineout, and we have another life. Again, we press up into Havant's half, and eventually we win a penalty just outside their 22. The clock is now dead. This penalty will be it. Three points will draw us level, but what happens then? Who gets the spoils if a draw is the final result? The referee consults with the blazers on the touchline. Eventually the deliberation is over — we have scored one try fewer than Havant, so we will have lost. No silverware. No happy ending. With no other option we tap and go. We thrust and dart and batter, but although the Havant players are out on their feet, somehow their line holds: as far as spirit goes, we have definitely met our match here. But eventually the scrum-half Otu receives the ball and runs across field, luring in defenders, before spinning a pass out wide to full-back Joe Gill. Joe has a straight ten metre run to the corner, arrives there a hair's width ahead of the despairing tackler, and with the last action of the game, bangs the ball down for the winning score. A sparkling try, a glowing victory, and a glinting prize. Now *that's* how a rugby fairy tale should end!

Almost. As we all know, any self-respecting fairy tale should end with the words 'and they all lived happily ever after', and I'm sorry, but no yarn on Planet Earth can be woven quite that far. Wharfedale's story might seem to be cast under a magic charm, but for all the club's dreamy aspirations, the characters in the tale are real people doing real things. Over time the characters will change, and with them the course of the plot. For now, what we can say as we reach the end of another season, is that we're living as happily as ever.

Through the Colts, the club's juniors have just given us the best, happiest send-off into the future we could have hoped for. Next year those Colts will no longer be juniors, but rapping on the door for selection into the senior teams. They'll have to knock loud, because the day before they won glory at Bedford, five Wharfedale lads were running out at Twickenham for Yorkshire to win the Counties Under-20s title. Three of them have been lynchpins in a Foresters side which, yet again, has won the Yorkshire league for second teams. So they are happy. The Foresters have also topped the one league which a Wharfedale side always win: the Cath Harrison Trophy, awarded to the senior side in the club with the best winning record.

The Firsts never win that league these days, any more than they are likely to win National League 1. In both they rumble around closer to bottom than top, with more losses than victories. Are they failures? The statisticians might say so, yet as far as we are concerned they are mystifyingly successful. In a couple of months, when the wounds have been licked, they will begin a record twentieth season in the third tier of English rugby. They're happy.

Oh, and Mick Greenwood's Fourths (the social ones) have ended with a season's record of W20 L7. They're happy too.

That leaves us with one team to account for. On midweek evenings over the last few weeks I have been enjoying a little tryst at the back of the Shed. When I roll up to watch our Thirds progress through their quarter and semi-finals of the Aire-Wharfe Plate, The Avenue is not exactly full. There are perhaps fifty spectators over by the clubhouse, and at the back of the Shed only one. After his tea, Tom Slater has walked out through his garden gate to see what is going on. He sits on one of three old wooden bar stools at the back of the Shed.

Occasionally his old mate Chris Baker will wander over to see Tom. Together, they might occasionally reminisce – about that Boxing Day when they both played for Wharfedale at home in the morning, drove over to watch North Ribb in the afternoon and were drafted into playing – but they are much more intent on the game being played out in the here and now. *That scrum-half – isn't he the young lad from the Colts? Eh, he's got something about him!* Standing here with them, in the gleam and balm of a Dales spring evening, I can't think of a more privileged seat in any sporting house. The games are hard but free-flowing – older players passing on what they know, and youngsters showing what they've learnt. The Dale side win both matches, and after each, Chris goes back over to the clubhouse to help Clarty and the others turn out the lights and put the club to bed. Tom wanders back home. We're *all* happy.

Yes, it's a fairy tale alright, but the Tom at its heart is not an octogenarian Tom Slater. It's a Tom Slater who's just celebrated his tenth birthday. His granddad tells me he's doing fine. The prognosis is good.

Thanks

With the broadest brush I can wield, I want to thank the global rugby community as a whole. We may all shout for different sides, but we stand together, and deep down we're shouting for one and the same daft thing: it's that shared sense of silliness I want to raise my hat to. Although I know I'm biased, within that global body, England's National 1 seems a unique community – large enough to cover a whole country, small enough that once a match is over we can shoe-horn ourselves into each others' clubhouses and be the best of friends. However odd this will sound to non-rugby people, I particularly want to thank the Dale's regular adversaries for what we share.

As for the Wharfedale club itself, I want to record my thanks to everyone I spoke to. Not one person pulled up the drawbridge when they saw me coming. Quite the opposite – they seemed to welcome me and my microphone into their homes. For most of my life I have been walking, cycling and driving past these Dales farmhouses, and to experience the warmth inside was a privilege. I would also like to thank the people at the club that I didn't speak to, but whose voices are recorded in this book every time you read the call of *River!* What I have written here is the club's story as it revealed itself to me, but I am aware that I could have written a similar book with an entirely different cast-list. Well, almost entirely different: the players are the players, and in this book there could be no substitutes for them. I'm not singling people out, because that's not how things are done at the club, but if you wear green come Saturday – jersey, scarf or blazer – consider yourself sincerely thanked.

I do need to identify some people outside the club, though. For reading what I've written, and commenting on it acutely and honestly, I would like to thank my old friends Julian Spicer, Andrew Green and Tom Bearpark. Vision Sports have been the perfect publisher: as the old-timers at Wharfedale would say, they *got* it. So thanks to Jim, Toby, Paul and Ulrika for their enthusiasm and expertise.

I've told my story with words, but the pictures in the book provide a wonderful extra dimension. I've been comparing notes with Sally Brodermann since we were in neighbouring prams, so it should be no surprise that she intuited and executed my ideal design for the book's cover. As for the photographs themselves, few teams can be spied on by a lens more perceptive and sympathetic than that of Rowena Burridge. Ro's photographs (and occasionally her husband John's) have been a true gift — as has been their company on touchlines up and down the country.

Then, finally, there's the lass who drew the sheep. Yes, it's my wife Caroline. Her contribution went way beyond that, though: she shared every touchline and scrutinised every textline. It may be my name on the cover, but be under no illusions: this story of a team is by a team.

Simon Ravens, Ilkley, 2015

CHARACTERS RECURRING IN THE TALE

On the pitch

Jake Armstrong	prop
Rob 'Badger' Baldwin	back-row forward
Jack Barnard	back-row forward
Matt Beesley	prop
Harry Bullough	fly-half
Josh Burridge	no. 8
Tom Davidson	centre
James Doherty	scrum-half, captain
Matt Freeman	prop
Jamie Guy	fly-half
Andy Hodgson	fly-half / centre
Adam Howard	prop / second-row forward
Chris Howick	back-row forward
Cameron Hudson	centre
Scott Jordan	wing
Jim Mason	back-row forward
Huw Morgan	centre
Aaron Myers	back-row forward
James Otulakowski	scrum-half
Taylor Prell	wing / full-back
Richard Rhodes	second-row forward
Dan Solomi	back-row forward
Chris Steel	prop
Dan Stockdale	hooker
Matt ven Sertima	wing
Philip Woodhead	scrum-half

In the dug-out

Jon Feeley	Head Coach
Alex Howarth	Coach
Hedley Verity	Coach
Jill Alexander	Physio

In the clubhouse

David Baker	Chairman
Gordon Brown	Programme Editor
Ian 'Adge' Douglass	voice
Michael 'Clarty' Harrison	Chairman of Rugby
John Spencer	President
Ed Williams	Press Officer

On the sideline

Chris Baker	ex player and Chairman
Lynda Feeley	coach's mum
Steve Feeley	coach's dad
Alec Geist	typical Dale supporter
Daniel Harrison	ex player
Tom Slater snr	ex Secretary
Len Tiffany	ex player and Colts coach